ice cream

and iced desserts

ice cream

and iced desserts

Over 150 irresistible

ice cream treats—from

classic vanilla to elegant

bombes and terrines

**Joanna Farrow and
Sara Lewis**

Photography by Gus Filgate

LORENZ BOOKS

First published in 2000 by Lorenz Books

© 2000 Anness Publishing Limited

Lorenz Books is an imprint of
Anness Publishing Inc.
27 West 20th Street
New York, NY 10011

PUBLISHER: Joanna Lorenz
EXECUTIVE EDITOR: Linda Fraser
EDITORS: Margaret Malone
Finny Fox-Davies
DESIGNER: Luise Roberts
PHOTOGRAPHY: Gus Filgate (recipes),
Craig Robertson (equipment and
techniques, steps and still lifes)
FOOD FOR PHOTOGRAPHY: Joanna Farrow (recipes),
Annabel Ford (equipment and
techniques, and steps)
STYLING: Penny Markham
COPY EDITOR: Jenni Fleetwood
PRODUCTION CONTROLLER: Ann Childers

10 9 8 7 6 5 4 3 2 1

contents

The world of ice cream

Ice cream must be one of the few foods in the world that is loved by virtually everyone, from the young to the young at heart, the full-fledget gourmet searching for the ultimate flavor combination to the devotee with more traditional tastes and a preference for timeless and classic favorites.

AN ADAPTABLE TREAT

With ice cream, there really is something for everyone. At one end of the spectrum is the simple ice cream cone—irresistible on a hot summer's day—while at the other is the elaborate layered molded dessert, perfect for entertaining. In between come the lighter ices, including refreshing fruit sorbets and snow-like granitas, ideal for serving between courses to cleanse the palate, after an elegant supper or relaxed *al fresco* meal.

Within this comprehensive guide are the very best ice creams, ices, sorbets and granitas, from the stunningly simple to the impressively elaborate. You'll find all the classics, plus more adventurous mixtures that prove just how exciting ice creams can be. Some of the desserts are highly indulgent, but there are also low-fat treats for those on special diets, or trying to control their calorie intake.

We explore the history of this fascinating food, take you on a cook's tour of specialties from all around the world, and unravel the differences between sherbet and ices, sorbet and semi-freddo, gelato and granita. We guide you through the maze of ingredients, flavorings and techniques, and show you detailed, easy-to-follow photographs, so that even the most inexperienced cook will feel confident about attempting every recipe, however complicated, and will be rewarded with perfect results every time.

PROFESSIONAL TIPS

There are lots of helpful tips for successful ice creams with or without an ice cream maker, and advice on the best way to store frozen desserts after you have made them. Throughout the book, detailed serving instructions give guidance on transforming simple scoops of ice cream or sorbet into desserts that would not look out of place in the most stylish restaurant.

For those who want to impress their friends with their culinary skill, there are elaborate molded desserts and terrines, extravagant bombes and mousses and a wide selection of sophisticated and elegant desserts. These

ABOVE: *Made with simple ingredients, sorbet is a light and delicious dessert.*

ice creams look sensational, and most of the effects are surprisingly easy to achieve. Frozen gateaux, for instance, come in all sorts of shapes and guises. Fruit and nuts, cookies and meringue—the combinations are endless and the results outstanding. Strawberry ice cream and lemon curd or rich chocolate ice cream and brownies complement each other perfectly. The more unusual frozen brûlées, roulades and tortes look and taste superb, while ice cream sundaes get a modern makeover when layered in elegant glasses with fruit and liqueur sauces. For an element of surprise, there is even a chapter on hot ice cream desserts that are deliciously surprising.

AN INTERNATIONAL FLAVOR

The range of recipes includes ice creams and ices from the Mediterranean, Eastern Europe, India, the British Isles and the Americas. Many of these are standard mixtures, but some are sweetened with honey or maple syrup instead of sugar, while others are based on yogurt or boiled milk, rather than cream. Some of the more unusual flavorings include flower extracts, herbs (such as lavender and bay), nuts and even spices.

In this modern age, when electrical equipment is readily available, it is easy to forget that there was ever a time without the domestic freezer. Yet three hundred years ago, when ice cream was becoming popular in Europe as the ultimate dessert for the very rich, the only way to freeze it in summer was by using ice that was cut from frozen lakes in winter and stored in deep underground pits. Imagine the dazzling spectacle it must have made when served to large gatherings at a dinner or a ball.

Ice cream is no longer a symbol of wealth, but is one of life's affordable luxuries. Universally acknowledged as one of the best loved comfort foods, it gives you a lift when you need it, and many problems have been solved—or friendships forged—over a container of chocolate ripple or rocky road. Of course, ice cream can be mass produced, with cheaper ingredients than any you'll find in this book, but there is really no substitute for the real thing in all its calorie-laden glory.

The New Yorker cover — July 16, 1990, Price $1.75

ABOVE: *Although ice cream-making started off slowly in Italy, it soon spread and Italian ice creams have enjoyed worldwide popularity ever since.*

ABOVE: *A welcome refresher from the heat, ice cream is sold at an ice cream parlor near Broken Hill in New South Wales, Australia.*

ABOVE: *Despite the wintery weather, a young child enjoys ice cream near Winnipeg, Manitoba.*

EARLY HISTORY OF ICE

It is known that ice houses were built around four thousand years ago at Mari, beside the river Euphrates, in Mesopotamia. These were apparently used for cooling wine, and it is likely that chilled wines and fruit juices were the precursors of our modern-day ice cream.

By the beginning of the 1st century A.D., there is some evidence that snow and ice were being appreciated for themselves, and not just as a means for cooling other ingredients. The Roman emperor Nero Claudius Caesar is reputed to have sent his slaves into the mountains to gather fresh snow, which was dressed with honey and fruits, for a special feast.

Such uses for snow and ice appear to have been rare, however. By the 5th century, there is evidence that snow was sold at the markets of Athens, but this would undoubtedly have been far too dirty and full of debris to have been used for more than cooling drinks and possibly for short term preservation of food.

The Mameluke kings of Egypt had snow shipped from Lebanon to Cairo in the 13th and 14th centuries, while in Spain there is evidence that snow pits were used from 1387 onward. These early European ice houses were simple unlined pits. Although primitive in construction, they worked quite well, because the constant temperature maintained below ground is such a good insulator. There is record of an Italian ice trade that began on a small scale in the 15th century and developed into a system of hauling ice by horse-drawn wagon to the major cities of northern Italy. At this stage, ice was still used largely as a coolant; it was ideal for chilling drinks and food but ineffective when it came to actually freezing liquids.

THE FIRST FROZEN DESSERTS

No one knows for certain who produced the world's first ice cream, although it is probable that it was the Chinese who first developed the art of making frozen desserts. They are known to have chilled fruit juices and tea, which led to their making primitive fruit-flavored ices some two thousand years ago. When Marco Polo returned from the East in the 13th century, he told of a frozen drink that consisted of a sweetened flower extract, paste or powder, which was diluted with water, then chilled with ice or snow. The drink was called "chorbet" in Turkish and "charab" in Persian and although it was never actually frozen, it evolved to become sorbet, the frozen dessert we know today.

A SCIENTIFIC ADVANCE

In 1620 scientists and chemists working with nitre (potassium nitrate and sodium nitrate) discovered that it was possible to use it to liquefy ice and snow, and in so doing to reduce the temperature below the freezing point. This endothermic effect could also be achieved using common salt (sodium chloride), and when a mixture of ice and salt was packed around a container of water, the water turned to ice. This had many implications including the potential for making frozen desserts.

the world of ice cream   7

Ices for the elite

During the seventeenth and eighteenth centuries, fashionable society throughout Europe enjoyed elegance and opulence in all things. The style of clothes, interiors and entertaining was rich and sumptuous, and spectacular frozen desserts became an essential addition to the menu on any grand occasion.

EARLY ICES

As more efficient ways of freezing were developed, the technique of making ices rapidly developed into an art form and a status symbol for the very rich. As scientists and scholars across Europe continued to study the laws behind freezing water, given further impetus by the invention of the thermometer in the 18th century, others turned this knowledge into creating objects of beauty.

There is evidence that ices were made in Italy in the 1550s, and when Marie de Medici married Henry IV of France in the late 16th century, she introduced the French court to "sorbetti." Banquet tables were soon glittering with beautiful ice pyramids. These sorbetti—or sorbets—were quite different from the ones served today. Made with an alcoholic base, they were eaten between savory main courses, and also substituted for liqueurs at grand banquets. Making them was highly skilled work, which was carried out by a "liqueriste." The most renowned of these were L. Audiger, a professional confectioner and distiller of liqueurs and aromatic waters to the young Louis XIV in the 1660s, and Massialot, who featured recipes for chocolate ice and custard ice in his cookbook, which was published in 1692. It is interesting to note that these early ice creams were sometimes referred to as "cheeses," possibly because they were usually made in the dairy.

Fruit flavors predominated in these early sorbets, but flower waters, such as jasmine, violet, tuberose, orange blossom and jonquil, were also used, as were infusions of green fennel, burnet and chervil.

ABOVE: *A colored engraving showing fashionable ladies choosing ice cream, "An Embarrassment of Choices," from "Le Bon Genre," Paris 1827.*

MASSIALOT'S FROMAGE A L'ANGLOISE

"Take 16 ounces of sweet cream and the same of milk, 1/2 pound powdered sugar, stir in 3 egg yolks and boil it until it becomes a thin pap. Take it from the fire and pour it into your ice mould and put it on ice for 3 hours. When it is firm, withdraw the mould and warm it a little in order more easily to turn out your cheese, or else dip your mould for a moment in hot water, then serve in a compotier."

This recipe from Massialot's book The Court and Country Cook *was reprinted in Elizabeth David's book,* Harvest of the Cold Months, *Michael Joseph, 1994.*

RIGHT: *A Sevres dessert service was only for the very wealthy. It includes a* plat de ménage, *dish, cup and saucer and large ice cream bowl. From the Blue Cameo Service, Sevres, 1778–9. Part of a collection belonging to the Hermitage, St. Petersburg, Russia.*

Britain was slow to follow this new European fashion. Ice houses were not introduced until the beginning of the 17th century, and it was not until 1675 that we have the first recorded instance of ice cream being served, when King Charles ll dug into strawberries and ice cream at a grand banquet. Interest in frozen desserts grew during the reign of William and Mary, and by the time Queen Anne ascended the throne in 1702, they were extremely popular.

In Regency Britain, elegance and extravagance were all-important, and London society was the heart of the British Empire. During the reign of George lll and later the Prince Regent, ice creams became extremely fashionable. Frozen desserts were spectacular scented and molded creations, set in complicated hinged molds and served at grand balls, or brought to elaborate summer picnics by teams of servants bearing small portable "ice caves" or cabinets. Although very grand in appearance, it must be remembered that these frozen desserts were not beaten during freezing, so would have been very icy to eat.

EARLY RECIPES

Mary Eales, Confectioner to the Queen, recorded some of these early recipes, which were first published in her book, *Mrs Eales's Receipts,* in 1718, some years after she supplied ice creams to the royal court. The recipes call for very large amounts of ice to freeze these simple ice creams, as

much as 20 pounds of ice mixed with 1 pound salt, and it is also interesting to note that there are no eggs in many of the recipes. The ice cream is frozen without the use of a churn, so would have tasted quite different from our modern ice creams. It wasn't until later in the 18th century that the French introduced eggs and cream cheeses to ice creams, making them much richer.

A few years after Mary Eales published her book, Mary Smith, in 1722, included ten frozen desserts in her publication *The Complete House-Keeper and Professed Cook.* These included Brown Bread Ice Cream, which is often thought of as a modern invention. Also on the list were Italian Ice Cream, Raspberry Cream, Orange Cream, Peach Cream and Apricot Cream. Some were cream-based and others were ices, but as at this stage ice creams did not include eggs they were, literally, frozen creams.

IMPROVEMENTS IN TASTE AND TEXTURE

During the 18th century, it was recognized that a superior ice cream could be made if the mixture was churned until it was thick and semi-frozen, then spooned into a mold for a second freezing. Ice cream made by this method had a creamier, smoother texture than that of earlier ice cream desserts, and the ice crystals were much finer.

Flavorings become much more adventurous, too, and varied from exotic fruits such as bananas and pineapples to fresh berries, preserves, chestnuts, cinnamon and white coffee cream. Other flavorings included Italian cream with cinnamon, lemon, brandy and the nut liqueur, noyau. One of the more bizarre offerings included lightly poached cucumber, ginger, brandy, coffee and cream. By 1885, modern cooks were publishing books on making ice cream, cooking schools included the art of making frozen desserts and hand-cranked ice cream makers became available.

From ice houses to refrigerators

No discussion on ice cream would be complete without mention of the ice houses that were needed to produce a ready supply of ice in summer as well as winter. Ice houses were first introduced in the 17th century, and rapidly became status symbols in Europe.

DESIGN FEATURES

Not all ice houses proved successful. Early ice houses were simple structures covered with thatched roofs and covered with earth and shrubs for added insulation, so that only the entrances were visible. Some were badly drained, and others were built below the water table, so the mud-lined structures simply filled with water. By the mid 19th century, ice house construction had greatly improved and became enduring structures with caulted brick roofs. Those built outside were usually entered through a north-facing door, which led down to a narrow passage divided by two or more doors, sometimes edged with leather or sheepskin for extra insulation. The passage led to a deep chamber, usually built with brick and between 8 feet and 33 feet wide. Some of the larger chambers had circular walkways; some even had brick steps down into the pit to allow easier access, although ladders were generally used to get down to the ice. Most brick-built ice houses had a chute in the roof to make it

easier to fill them with ice, which was cut from frozen lakes or ponds in the winter and transported as quickly as possible. Most large estates would have had at least one ice house. These were often quite elaborate, especially if the landowner was particularly proud of his acquisition. Some of the more ostentatious owners added decorative stone arches and columns to the entrances of their ice houses. Although most ice houses were round, square ones were also built, and some of the very elaborate ones even had dovecotes in the roofs. In some cases, the ice house was combined with the game store or linked to the banqueting house. Some of the larger town houses also had ice stores, which were built in their basements.

HARVESTING THE ICE

For ease of harvesting, ice houses were usually constructed near a lake or river, or by the side of a man-made pond known as the "freezing pond."

A team of estate workers would cut the ice with the help of long spiked poles, or by bouncing a long stretch of heavy chain across it until it broke. The ice would then be broken up, loaded into a cart and taken to the ice house, where it would be packed in tight layers in the pit. The method of packing varied from estate to estate. In some cases, the ice was packed alternately with straw; in others it was packed with a little salt and additional water. The top layer was then covered with a thick layer of straw or sawdust. Great care was taken to keep the ice as clean as possible, although it must still have been flecked with twigs and leaves.

ABOVE: *Illustration of two common ice houses. The one on the left has a thatched roof, whereas the one on the right has a vaulted roof that is made of brick.*

ABOVE: *Cutting out ice that has been stored in the ice house. Workers used long spiked poles for breaking up the ice and removing it from its straw packing.*

STORING THE ICE

Food was never stored in ice houses. They were used solely for the ice itself, which was transported to the house by the wheelbarrow load, where it was washed and used in the cellars or ice storage cabinets. If the ice had been made from pure water, it could be used for desserts and drinks. If not, it would have been crushed and mixed with ammonium chloride, sodium chloride (common salt) or potassium nitrate to reduce the freezing point before being spooned into decorated china ice pails or two-tiered dishes for the serving of ice cream. The lower or outer dish would hold the ice mixture, while the ice cream would be placed in an inner dish or on the top tier.

A NEW AGE

Ice houses were very popular on large estates in Britain, but it was in America that it was refined and developed. The exclusivity that was so much a part of its history in Europe did not survive long in the United States, especially after the invention of small, cheaply built ice houses that could be built above ground. This invention made its way to Britain, and, with the lifting of printing restrictions in the 1840s, printed plans of ice houses became freely available. Ice houses were now within the reach of the suburban middle classes as well as their wealthier contemporaries.

The transport revolution meant that ice could be shipped from America and Norway to Europe. In 1894, 400,000 tons of ice was exported from America to the United Kingdom despite the considerable cost per ton. The ever increasing railway network throughout Europe made it possible for ice to be supplied from large urban depots to country houses.

Domestic ice storage containers were also introduced, enabling ice to be kept in the house for several days. These basic ice cupboards, known as ice safes or ice preservers, were the forerunners of our modern refrigerators and freezers. These wooden cupboards were generally zinc or

ABOVE: *With the introduction of mechanized ice churners, such as these wooden pails with metal canisters inside, ice cream could be produced and sold on a large scale by enterprising street sellers.*

aluminum-lined with a reservoir for water and ice and would be used for keeping butter, milk and other foods cold. Ice was generally bought from the ice man, who ran a home delivery service, usually once a week, and the ice would keep foods cold for several days if mixed with salt. Ice cream would need to be made on the day of the ice delivery, as the storage container was little more than the modern insulated cool box.

The Americans took ice to India by ship in the 1830s, and although storage in India proved a problem at first, by the 1870s the ice trade was well established. Ice was stored in domestic mahogany or teak chests lined with zinc or slate. The wealthy British soon took to this kitchen aid, and the ice chest became an indispensable household item.

THE FIRST ICE CREAM MACHINES

Very early ice cream makers consisted of small earthenware or metal pots filled with milk or cream mixtures, and placed inside deep urns or cabinets lined with either wood or lead, and surrounded with ice, ice and straw or ice and salt.

By the middle of the 19th century mechanized ice cream makers were introduced. These looked like wooden pails, with a small metal canister inside for the ice cream. The pail was filled with an ice and salt mixture and the ice cream was churned with a hand-stirrer.

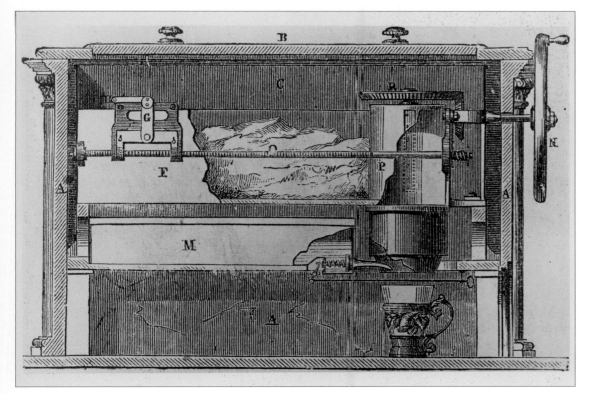

LEFT: *Illustration of an early ice cream machine using a hand-cranking device for churning the ice cream*

Early American ice cream machines worked by packing the ice cream mixture into a small pot that was shaken up and down in a wooden pail packed with ice and salt. The most famous hand-cranked ice cream maker was invented in 1843, by Nancy Johnson, a naval officer's wife in America. Later that century, in England, Agnes Marshall also developed a hand-cranked ice cream machine.

THE ITALIAN CONNECTION

Italy had always been famous for its superior ice creams, but it was not until the late 19th century that Britain and America discovered the joy of Italian ice cream. This came about when political upheaval in Italy led to a huge exodus of young Italians, many of whom set up as ice cream makers in the countries that gave them refuge, often in makeshift premises on the dockside.

In the early days, ice cream street sellers were a cross between a wandering musician and street hawker. Their organ music first attracted customers to their barrows, which could be quite simple affairs or highly decorated and colorful carts. Early carts were reported to have been made in the shape of a gondola. As ice cream grew in popularity, so the numbers of street sellers increased, and by the turn of the century, 900 ice cream barrows were registered in Clerkenwell, London, alone.

With the growth in the number of street sellers, fighting broke out as sellers vied for the best spots. Much of the ice cream produced was manufactured in slum conditions in domestic kitchens. Milk was boiled the previous night, then frozen with ice the next day. The dishes used to serve the ice cream, known as penny licks, were simply reused and never washed. The inevitable outcome was the spread of bacterial infections, and the transfer of disease, particularly tuberculosis,

became widespread. As a result of a lobby to ban the sale of ice cream, manufacturing moved to hygienic business premises, and barrows were licensed to sell ice cream at specific points. This resolved the hygiene problem and restored peaceful trading. Finally, with the introduction of the edible ice cream cone in 1905, ice cream sellers became respectable once again.

Many more Italian immigrants came to Britain and America after war ended in Europe in the 1940's, in a bid to rebuild shattered lives and homes. Family-run cafés, ice cream parlors and factories were quickly set up by the new immigrants, and Italian bakers lost no time in switching from cookie making to making ice cream cones and wafers to meet the demands of the growing popularity of ice cream.

CENTER: *As ice cream vendors prospered, some stalls became very elaborate, permanent structures.*

ABOVE AND LEFT: *Many early hand carts were replaced by horsedrawn carts and these, in time, became the ice cream trucks familiar today.*

LARGE-SCALE PRODUCTION

The world's first ice cream plant opened in America in 1851. It was founded by Jacob Fussell, a Baltimore milk dealer, who wanted to find a new market for cream during the summer months when the supply of cream peaked. As a milk dealer, he had an advantage over his rivals, and by undercutting their prices his ice cream soon became so successful that by 1864 he had opened ice cream factories in Washington, Boston and New York.

In November 1909 the American trade journal *"Ice and Refrigeration"* featured a piece from a report written by the United States Consul in Canton, China, describing the crowds that gathered around the city's street vendors. Rather than taking out ready-frozen ice cream, the vendors were making it *in situ* with ingenious ice cream machines. Although the use of ice wasn't new to the Chinese, the style of ice cream was very different. By the 1930s, China's first American-style ice cream factory opened, and Peking sales soon reached a staggering 1,000 tons a year.

ABOVE: *Ice cream factory in Holstich, Germany, 1895*

In Russia, the first ice cream factory was built in the 1920s by Anastas Mikoyan, and the people of the former Soviet Union enjoyed ice cream at any opportunity. To Western tastes, it may seem odd to eat ice cream in extreme winter temperatures, but this was one of the few permitted luxuries and as such was greatly enjoyed whatever the weather.

By the 1920s England was also producing ice cream on a large scale, first by the famous Wall's company and a year later by the Lyons group best known for its triple flavored Neapolitan ice cream and the Lyons Corner Houses in London. Originally known for his meat pies, Thomas Wall first introduced ice cream manufacture into the business as a way of improving summer profits. At first ice cream production was small and used sophisticated American production techniques. The ice cream was shaped and frozen in small briquettes, each one hand-wrapped in paper and sold by street sellers riding tricycles featuring a "stop me and buy one" sign. As popularity and production grew, so the company expanded from just one ice cream factory in Acton with seven street sellers in the 1920s to 136 depots and 8,500 tricycles by 1939.

With the outbreak of the Second World War, Wall's ice cream production stopped, as food rationing was introduced. Many European factories also closed, and soon the American armed forces became the biggest manufacturers of ice cream in the world.

Americans still have perhaps the greatest love of ice cream of all countries and consume 37 pints per person per year, compared to just 14 pints per person in England.

ELECTRIC DEEP FREEZERS

Early mechanical refrigerators didn't appear until the beginning of the 20th century and followed the development of the steam driven motor and later the electric motor. The very first electric refrigerator was a Domelre, made in America in 1913. A later version, the Kelvinator model, made in Detroit in 1914, soon came on the market, but both were noisy and extremely expensive. Not surprisingly most Americans preferred the cheaper wooden insulated cabinets or chests, which they cooled with regular ice supplies.

In 1922 Baltzar von Platen and Carl Munters, two young engineering students in Stockholm, developed a cooling machine that could convert heat to cold by absorption. It could be driven by electricity, gas or kerosene. Initially called the D refrigerator, it was marketed by

MAKING ICE CREAM AT HOME

With the increased availability of affordable ingredients and improvements to ice cream makers, middle class housewives sought the advice of highly skilled cooks, such as Mrs. Agnes B. Marshall and Mrs. Beeton. In 1885 Agnes Marshall published her first book, in which she included detailed advice on making a range of ice creams, such as "cheap," "ordinary" and "common" ice cream. Her "cheap ice cream" was made using 2½ cups of cream, 8 egg yolks and ½ cup of sugar. Next came her "ordinary ice cream," in which the cream was replaced with milk. Her "common ice cream" was made with the same quantity of milk and sugar, but only two whisked eggs, while the "cheap ice cream" dispensed with eggs altogether, and thickened the sweetened milk with 2 tablespoons of arrowroot.

ABOVE: *An ice cream mold*

RIGHT: *An early hand-cranked ice cream machine*

RIGHT: *Illustration from* Süsse Speisen und Eisbomben, *published in Germany in 1907, showing a variety of frozen confections.*

Electrolux in 1925. As technology advanced, prices came down, and by 1935 the early air-cooled refrigerators were within the reach of many households. Although gaining in popularity and availability in America, the British were more cautious. Frigidaire first tried marketing refrigerators in Britain in 1924, but they remained a luxury item for the very rich until after the Second World War. It must also be remembered that supplies of electricity were unreliable and expensive and usually only available in the homes of the wealthy; working people had to rely on gas.

The chilled and frozen food industry originated in America when Clarence Birdseye revolutionized shopping and the preparation of food for the American and British housewives by going into partnership with the English ice cream manufacturer, Thomas Wall. By 1960, many had domestic refrigerators, and by the 1970's, many homes owned a deep freezer, making the storage of bought and homemade ice cream possible.

A surfeit of choice

Ice cream has come a long way since the first ice cream parlor opened in 1776. Swirled, layered and mixed, in almost every conceivable flavor, ice cream is now available to suit every occasion, taste and preference, from low-fat sorbets to rich dairy premium ice cream, and sold in any amount from a single cone to a half-gallon carton.

THE ICE CREAM CONE

It was a young Italian immigrant to America, Italo Marchiony, who first came up with the idea of an edible container for ice cream. When he started selling his ice creams and sorbets on Wall Street in New York, he spooned them into glasses. These were cumbersome and wasteful, so he started making shaped cups from waffle batter. The cups proved very popular, and he patented them in 1902. Two years later, he patented an ice cream cone, although the credit for this innovation is often given to a Syrian, Ernest A. Hamwi. According to the story, Mr. Hamwi was selling waffles at the World's Trade Fair in St. Louis in 1904 when a neighboring ice cream seller sold out of dishes. He persuaded Mr. Hamwi to roll one of his waffles into a cone, let it cool and filled it with his ice cream.

Made with a mixture of flour, milk and sugar, the ice cream cone quickly became popular. To help prevent breakages and spillages, a ring of non-crushable cookie was also molded to the top of the cone, making it ideal for small children, as it caught any drips of melting ice cream.

The British traders of the 1920s were reluctant to sell these large imported cones, as they were more costly and needed a greater amount of ice cream to fill them. They preferred to sell ice cream briquettes sandwiched between much cheaper rectangular wafer cookies. In the 1930s a box of 1,200 wafers was very cheap to produce, making it possible to sell ice creams for 1 penny. However, by 1935 waffles for ice cream were introduced to supersede wafers, with the rather unusual advertising line of "Have a waffle in the cinema." Sales of wafers continued until the 1950s, until soft ice cream and the famous "99" ice cream was introduced, complete with its much loved chocolate flake bar.

ABOVE: *With the rise in the number of street sellers, ice cream became a more available treat for all. No longer sold in unhygienic glass dishes, but in small hand-wrapped briquettes, they were sold in Britain from the famous "stop me and buy one" Wall's tricycle.*

THE ICE CREAM SUNDAE

In late 19th century America, drug stores sold seltzer throughout the country. Flavored with fruit syrups and whipped cream, these drinks were popular with young and old. In 1874, Robert Green of Philadelphia ran out of cream when making sodas for the 50th anniversary of the Franklin Institute. He substituted ice cream, much to the delight of the guests.

The ice cream soda soon became very popular, but you couldn't buy one on a Sunday. This was because many people believed seltzer to be alcoholic, even though it was nothing of the kind, and drinking it was regarded as improper, particularly on Sundays. An ingenious drugstore concessionaire got around the ban by serving the ice cream and syrup without the seltzer. He called it Ice Cream Sunday. The name was later changed to Sundae, which was judged more seemly.

LEFT: *Ice cream cornets, now called cones, are given free to children in London, to celebrate Coronation Day in 1937.*

ICE CREAM PARLORS

The first ice cream parlor is reputed to have opened in New York City in 1776, but the business really boomed during the prohibition years. Bar owners had always served ice cream in the summer months, and when prohibition came in 1920, the more enterprising among them saw that swapping ice cream for hard liquor was one way of staying in business. By 1930, ice cream parlors were very much a part of the American scene. To stay competitive, manufacturers developed new flavors and shapes of ice cream. Eskimo pie and popsicles became popular.

MODERN DEVELOPMENTS

The majority of homes in America and Europe now have a refrigerator and a freezer, and many of us add a container of ice cream to our weekly shopping cart as a regular item. Not only is ice cream available in a wide range of flavors, with prices varying from the budget family-sized container up to the most expensive and decadent chocolate combinations, but it is also easier now than ever before to make ice cream at home with electrical labor-saving gadgets that make tasks such as beating frozen ice cream quite effortless.

ABOVE: *An ice cream parlor, popular in the United States since prohibition, when enterprising brewers converted their liquor bars to ice cream parlors and served chilled ice cream sodas and thick creamy milk shakes instead.*

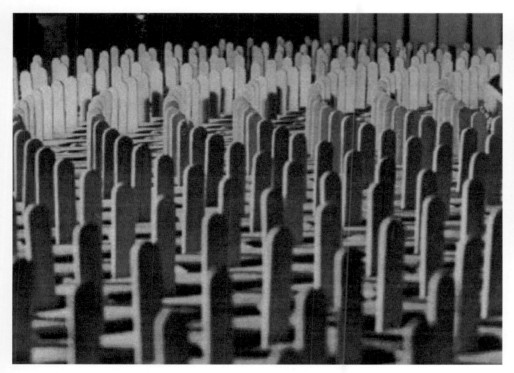

ABOVE: *The 1 penny wafer of the 1930s, and later the larger American ice cream cones, quickly grew in popularity for the young and the "young at heart."*

LEFT: *Popsicle sticks at a factory in Lyon, France, 1963.*

Ice cream is loved all over the world, and although it will always remain a warm weather treat, it is now also seen as an everyday luxury. Consumed in the greatest amounts by Americans, it is also enjoyed across Europe and India; even in Russia during winter they enjoy ice cream bought at street kiosks when there is snow on the ground!

Ways of serving ice cream have also changed dramatically over the centuries. While there is still a place for refreshing and fruity sorbets and ices, rich creamy ice creams still remain at the top of all opinion polls. Meanwhile, food trends have moved away from the multi-colored, pile it high, glorious ice cream sundae of the 1950s and the 60s' banana split, and contemporary tastes now favor simpler, softly scooped ice creams with more imaginative but subtle flavors.

From such elitist beginnings it would have been hard to imagine that by the beginning of the 21st century there would be 500 commercially prepared ice creams available, ranging from the classic vanilla, chocolate and fruit flavors to the more exotic and eccentric, such as peanut butter, lobster and bubble gum.

Dedicated ice cream cafés, parlors and franchized stores now flourish in all the world's major cities. Ice cream is swirled, rippled, layered and mixed; you can buy low-fat ice cream, kosher ice cream, frozen yogurt and a wide range of sorbets in every shape and size, from tiny individual cartons, to half-gallon containers.

Efficient ice cream makers are now affordable, so more and more people are discovering the delights of making their own ice cream at home. This book aims to teach you to do just that, and also offers suggestions for incorporating both homemade and bought ice cream into a wide range of exciting and delicious desserts.

Ice cream, however simple or elaborate, should be full of natural taste and body. If you make it with the very best ingredients, you will always enjoy the most delicious homemade ice cream.

making
ice cream

Making ice cream at home is surprisingly simple, needs little equipment and is enormously satisfying to prepare as well as to eat. Covering every aspect of making ice creams in all their variety, as well as sauces, cones, baskets and decorations, this chapter provides all the skills and techniques for even the most ambitious and elaborate frozen desserts.

Essential equipment

You will probably already have most of the equipment you need to make successful ice cream and sorbet. Ice cream made by hand can simply be frozen in a plastic container, although ice cream enthusiasts may want to invest in a free-standing electric machine.

BASIC EQUIPMENT

Making ice cream by hand is the simplest method of all, and is known as "still freezing." All that you need are glass bowls and a fork, a manual or electric hand-held beater for beating and a freezerproof container with a lid. You will also need a heavy saucepan for making the custard and sugar syrups and cooking fruit, plus a sieve for puréeing and a lemon squeezer and fine grater for citrus fruit.

A food processor is a useful aid for breaking down the ice crystals; this labor saving method does produces a similar texture to ice cream made in an electric ice cream maker.

For storage

You will need a selection of freezerproof containers in varying sizes, with tight-fitting lids to eliminate the transfer of strong smells and flavors and prevent the surface of the ice cream from drying out. Use containers a little larger than the amount of ice cream, to allow for beating during freezing and increased volume when frozen. A headspace of ¾-inch is adequate. Granita is the exception to this, as it requires as shallow a container as possible to reduce freezing time. Only use stainless steel or aluminum while making ice cream or sorbet, as other metals can impart a metallic taste.

The freezer

An upright or chest-style domestic freezer is the essential item. For making ice cream the temperature should be -66°F. A freezer thermometer is a very useful tool. The colder the freezer the more quickly the ice will freeze, making smaller ice crystals and smoother ice cream. If the freezer is badly packed the motor will have to work harder to maintain temperature.

Adding volume

1 Using a fork requires more effort, but is an effective way of increasing volume by introducing air into sorbet and granitas.

2 For making large batches of ice cream, a hand-held electric beater saves time and adds even more volume to the mixture.

For making parfait

You will need all the items for making ice cream, plus a good candy thermometer; they can be expensive but do ensure perfect results. Choose one with a clip to hold it in place on the pan.

For making molded frozen desserts

Specialty equipment is available, but you can usually improvise with bowls and containers from your kitchen.

ICE CREAM MAKERS

These labor-saving electric machines vary greatly in price. The two basic types are those with a built-in freezing unit and those with a detachable double-skinned bowl that has to be pre-frozen before use. There are also ice cream machines that can be run inside a standard freezer. These have very poor motors and similar, if not better, results can be obtained by making ice cream by hand.

The most efficient—and most expensive—models are those with an integral freezing unit. Motors vary, depending on the make of the machine. If you are investing in an ice cream maker, choose the one with the most powerful motor and, if possible, see it in operation, as noise levels vary considerably. As this type of ice cream maker tends to be larger than a food processor, working and storage space are prime considerations. These machines come with two bowls, a stainless-steel bowl built into the unit and a separate aluminum bucket that can be slotted into the larger bowl. Most machines of this type have a see-through lid for easy viewing, plus a vent for pouring in additional ingredients. This plastic top simply slides off for easy washing.

RIGHT: *Ice cream maker with integral motor and freezing unit*

Pre-freezing ice cream maker

For a slightly cheaper option, look for a model with a detachable bowl filled with freezing liquid. This type of machine will need to be frozen for at least 18 hours before use. When you are ready to use the ice cream maker, you simply fit the motor and paddle to the frozen bowl, switch on the power, and fill the bowl with the ice cream or sorbet mixture. It usually takes 25–40 minutes for the ice cream to churn.

If the freezer is large enough, the bowl can be stored there, giving the option to make homemade ice cream at any time. For larger batches, it is very useful to have a second detachable bowl on standby and make two batches of ice cream.

When possible, eat the ice cream soon after it is made to fully enjoy the wonderful texture of machine-made ice cream.

ABOVE: *Simple ice cream maker with motorized paddles*

FOR THE BEST RESULTS

- Pre-cool the machine or bowl following the instructions given in the manufacturer's handbook.

- Chill all ice cream or sorbet mixtures thoroughly before freezing; never add them to the machine while still warm.

- Do not overfill the ice cream maker.

- Allow plenty of room for ventilation while the machine is running.

Useful extras

Scoops

There are plenty of ice cream scoops on the market. Choose from half-moon-shaped stainless-steel scoops with sleek steel handles, simple spoon-shaped scoops with metal handles, easy-grip molded plastic handles or brightly colored plastic scoops with quick release levers. To be really impressive, use silver scoops.

ABOVE: *Ice cream scoops are available in many different shapes, materials and colors.*

Cone molds

For a really professional finish, use wooden molds. These are available only by mail order, but you can improvise by making your own cone molds from aluminum foil-covered cardboard.

ABOVE: *This wooden cone mold is a very simple but useful tool for making professional-looking cones.*

Melon ballers

Ice cream looks very attractive when scooped with a melon baller. Available at good cookware in stores varying sizes, from pea to grape size, the larger size is best for ice cream. To make a ball, press the upturned cup into slightly softened ice cream, then rotate it. Arrange in a glass dish or on a plate, with fresh fruits.

ABOVE: *Use melon ballers to make miniature scoops of ice cream and sorbet, and pile them up on a plate.*

Kulfi molds

Freeze Indian-style ice creams in these traditional kulfi molds available at some large Indian supermarkets. You can also use popsicle molds, dariole molds or plastic cups.

ABOVE: *Unmolding kulfi is easy with a specially designed all-in-one kulfi mold.*

Basic ingredients

Nothing beats the cool, creamy smoothness of the ultimate indulgence, homemade ice cream. The choice of flavors and flavor combinations is limited only by your own imagination, so begin with our basic formulas and adapt or develop them to incorporate all the tastes you love. You will rapidly build a repertoire of wonderful frozen desserts, all completely additive-free and made with only the ingredients that you choose.

Ice cream

Cream

You just couldn't make true ice cream without cream. Surprisingly, whipping cream, with its natural creamy taste, makes the best ice cream, especially when mixed with strong rich flavors such as coffee, toffee or chocolate. Heavy cream is, however, a must for vanilla or brown bread ice cream. Crème fraîche, the thick, rich lightly sour French-style cream, make delicious additions to fruit, honey and spice ice creams. Do be careful when using heavy cream as its high butter-fat content can give ice cream a buttery flavor and texture, especially if it is overchurned.

Milk

There is a wide variety of milks in most supermarkets, from skim, low-fat, and whole milk to the now more readily available goat's milk, and soy and rice milk. Skim milk is best avoided when making ice cream at home, due to its low fat content and "thin" taste, but it is difficult to distinguish between low-fat or whole milk, especially when they are mixed with cream. Whole, low-fat and goat's milk all make delicious ice cream.

Yogurt

The use of yogurt is highly personal: it seems people either love frozen yogurt or absolutely hate it! If you are not sure how your family will react, start with mild plain yogurt, with its creamy smoothness and, if that is successful, work up to stronger, sharper sheep and goat's milk yogurts.

ABOVE: *Fresh eggs and heavy or whipping cream give homemade ice cream luxurious richness.*

Cheeses

Light, virtually fat-free fromage frais can be added to fruit or vanilla ice creams and is ideal for those who adore ice cream but have to watch their fat intake. Ricotta, an Italian whey cheese, has a white, creamy, soft texture. It is much like a cross between cottage and cream cheese and can be used successfully in certain ice creams. For the richest results of all, try mascarpone, another Italian cheese. It has a deep-buttery yellow color and a texture similar to that of cream cheese. For the best of both worlds, mix mascarpone with fromage frais for a rich tasting, reduced fat dessert.

Nondairy products

Look for soy and rice milk, either unsweetened or sweetened, in longlife cartons, and canned coconut milk—both ideal for vegans or those on a milk-free diet. Coconut milk is also a great standby for a dinner party ice cream when mixed with lime or lemon.

Eggs

Whenever possible use fresh, organic eggs for the best color and flavor. They cost little more than ordinary eggs but do make such a difference to the finished result of homemade ice cream.

Sweeteners

Granulated sugar has been used in the majority of the recipes, as it dissolves quickly in the custard, maintaining a smooth, silky texture. Light brown and dark brown sugar can also be used as sweeteners in some recipes, where the darker color and stronger flavor is used to great effect. Honey and maple syrup also make delicious additions, either on their own or mixed with granulated sugar. They are particularly good in ice cream flavored with nuts.

Cornstarch

Many purists will throw their hands up in horror at the idea of cornstarch being used in custard for an ice cream. They might well argue that it is much better to make the custard in a double boiler or a large heatproof bowl set over simmering water. It is certainly true that cornstarch is not a standard ingredient in a classic custard, but it does help to stabilize the custard and reduces the risk of curdling. Custard that contains a little cornstarch is easier to handle, so can be gently cooked in a heavy pan. It will thicken in 4–5 minutes, as opposed to 15 minutes or more in a double boiler, greatly reducing the cooking time.

COOK'S TIP *Put leftover egg whites in a small plastic box. Cover with a tight-fitting lid and label the box clearly. Freeze up to 6 months and thaw at room temperature for 4 hours. Use to make pavlovas, meringues and meringue-based ice creams.*

Ices

Sugar syrup

A simple sugar syrup is made by heating a mixture of granulated sugar and water in a medium saucepan, stirring until the sugar has dissolved. It is no longer thought essential to boil the syrup, just to heat it for long enough to dissolve the sugar. Granulated sugar has been used for syrups in the recipe section of this book because it dissolves very rapidly, but light brown sugar or honey can also be used. Once made and cooled, the syrup can be stored in the refrigerator for several days.

Flavorings

Choose from a wide range of fresh fruit purées, such as strawberry, raspberry, peach or pineapple, or mix with tropical fruits, such as passion fruit, mango and lime. Dried fruits are sometimes steeped in apple or grape juice or in water and brandy or a liqueur mixture before being puréed. Citrus zests (orange, lemon or lime) can be infused in the hot syrup for extra flavor and then fresh juice added to heighten and strengthen the flavor. Spice infusions or mixtures of spices and fruits also work very well and create unusual ice creams that are particularly successful with those who prefer a light dessert that is not too sweet.

ABOVE: *Honey can be used on its own or with sugar.*

Egg whites

The purpose of adding egg whites to a semi-frozen sorbet is twofold. Firstly, it helps to stabilize the mixture, which is important for those sorbets that melt quickly, and secondly, it can be used to lighten very dense or fibrous sorbets, such as those made from black currants or blackberries. The egg whites require only a minimal beating with a fork to loosen them and need not be beaten until frothy or standing in peaks, as used to be suggested.

HOW TO SEPARATE AN EGG

Crack the egg on the side of a bowl. Gently ease the halves apart, keeping the yolk in one half and letting the white fall into the bowl below. Separate any remaining egg white from the yolk by transferring the yolk from one shell half to the other. Do this several times if necessary, until all the egg white has fallen into the bowl and what remains is the pure egg yolk. If you do drop any egg yolk into the bowl below, scoop it out with one of the eggshell halves; the jagged edges will trap the yolk and prevent it from sliding back into the bowl.

Making ice cream

Many classic ice creams are based on a custard made from eggs and milk. It is not difficult to make, but as it is used so frequently, it is worth perfecting by following these very simple guidelines.

How to make a classic ice cream

Making the custard-base

INGREDIENTS

FLAVORING to INFUSE (optional)

1¼ cups LOW-FAT MILK

4 medium EGG YOLKS

6 tablespoons SUGAR

1 teaspoon CORNSTARCH

1 Prepare any flavorings. Split vanilla beans with a sharp knife; crack coffee beans with a mallet. Cinnamon sticks, whole cloves, fresh rosemary and lavender sprigs or bay leaves can be used as they are.

2 Pour the milk into a saucepan. Bring it to a boil, then remove the pan from heat, add the chosen flavoring and let infuse for 30 minutes or until cool.

3 If you have used a vanilla bean, lift it out of the pan, and scrape the seeds back into the milk to enrich the flavor. Whisk the egg yolks, sugar and cornstarch in a bowl until thick and foamy. Bring the plain or infused milk to a boil, then gradually whisk it into the yolk mixture. Pour the combined mixture back into the saucepan.

4 Cook the mixture over low heat, stirring it continuously until it approaches the boiling point and thickens to the point where the custard will coat the back of a wooden spoon. Do not let the custard overheat or it may curdle. Take the pan off the heat and continue stirring, making sure to take the spoon around the bottom edges of the pan.

5 Pour the custard into a bowl and cover the surface with plastic wrap to prevent the formation of a skin, or cover the surface with a light sprinkling of sugar. Let cool, then chill in the refrigerator until needed. If you are making the ice cream in a machine, ensure that the custard is chilled before starting.

COOK'S TIP *Reduce the temperature of custard by pouring it into a cool bowl. Stand this in a larger bowl of cold or ice water and change the water as it warms.*

Using flavorings

If you haven't infused the milk, you may want to flavor the custard. To make chocolate custard, break white, dark or milk chocolate into pieces and stir these into the hot custard in the saucepan, off the heat. Stir occasionally for 5 minutes, until the chocolate has melted completely, then pour the flavored custard into a bowl, cover and cool. Chill in the refrigerator.

Other flavorings that can be added include strong coffee (either regular or instant dissolved in boiling water), flower waters such as orange flower water or rose water and sweeteners that also add flavor, such as maple syrup or honey. Vanilla, peppermint or almond extracts are popular flavorings. These should be added to the custard after it has cooled.

Adding cream

If you are making ice cream in an ice cream maker, follow the preliminary instructions for your specific machine, pre-cooling the machine or chilling the bowl in the freezer. Stir whipping cream, whipped heavy cream or any soft cream cheeses into the chilled plain or flavored custard and churn until firm.

Creams with a high fat proportion—heavy cream or crème fraîche—should only be added to ice creams that are partially frozen, as they have a tendency to become buttery if churned for too long. Heavy cream is sometimes added at the start, but only for small amounts and minimal churning times.

Make the ice cream by hand in a freezerproof container, by folding soft whipped cream into the chilled plain or flavored custard and pouring the mixture into the container. Allow enough space for beating the ice cream during freezing. Crème fraîche and cream cheeses can also be added at this stage.

Parfaits

Making a basic parfait

Made correctly, a parfait is a light, cream-based confection with a softer, smoother texture than ice cream. Unlike ice cream, it does not need beating during freezing, so is ideal for anyone who does not have an electric ice cream maker.

Parfaits are traditionally set in molds, tall glasses, china or, more recently, in edible chocolate cups. The secret of a good parfait lies in the sugar syrup. Dissolve the sugar gently without stirring so that it does not crystallize, then boil it rapidly until it registers 239°F on a candy thermometer, which is known as the soft ball stage.

Quickly whisk the syrup into the whisked eggs. Cook over hot water until very thick. Cool, then mix with flavorings, alcohol and whipped cream. Freeze until solid and serve straight from the freezer.

SERVES FOUR

INGREDIENTS

generous ½ cup SUGAR

½ cup WATER

4 medium EGG YOLKS

FLAVORINGS

1¼ cups HEAVY CREAM

1 Mix the sugar and water in a saucepan. Heat gently, without stirring, until the sugar has dissolved completely. Meanwhile, half-fill a medium saucepan with water and bring it to the simmering point.

2 Bring the sugar syrup to a boil and boil it rapidly for 4–5 minutes, until it starts to thicken. It will be ready to use when it registers 239°F on a candy thermometer, or will form a soft ball when dropped into water.

3 Put the eggs in a heatproof bowl and whisk until frothy. Place over the simmering water and gradually whisk in the hot sugar syrup. Whisk steadily until creamy. Take off the heat and continue whisking until cool and the whisk leaves a trail across the surface when lifted.

4 Fold in the chosen flavorings, such as melted chocolate and brandy, ground cinnamon and coffee, whiskey and chopped ginger, kirsch and raspberry purée or kir and strawberry purée. In a separate bowl, whip the cream lightly until it just holds its shape. Fold it into the mixture.

FLAVORINGS

Traditionally flavored with coffee or chocolate and a dash of brandy or whiskey, parfaits are also delicious made with ground spices such as cinnamon with apple or ginger with banana. Heavy cream adds just the right degree of richness, although crème fraîche or whipping cream can also be used with very good results. Another traditional combination is fruit purées mixed with liqueurs such as kirsch, Cointreau or Grand Marnier; these make a sophisticated frozen dessert at a dinner party.

5 Pour the parfait mixture into molds, dishes or chocolate-lined shells. Freeze for at least 4 hours or until firm. Decorate, if desired, with whipped cream, spoonfuls of crème fraîche, caramel shapes or chocolate-dipped fruits. Serve immediately.

COOK'S TIP *Heavy cream adds just the right degree of richness to parfaits, although crème fraîche or whipping cream can also be used with good results.*

Boiling sugar successfully

1 If you don't have a candy thermometer, check whether the boiling sugar syrup has cooked to the right consistency, the soft ball stage, by lowering a spoon into it and then lifting it up. If the syrup falls steadily from the spoon, it is not yet ready to use, and if you were to add it to the eggs at this stage, the frozen parfait would set hard. Cook it for a little longer and check again with the spoon.

2 The syrup is ready to test for the soft ball stage when it looks tacky, and forms pliable strands when two spoons are dipped in it, back to back, and then pulled apart.

Take the pan off the heat and then test the boiling syrup by dropping a little of it into a bowl of ice water. The syrup should form a ball. Wait a few seconds until it cools, then lift the ball of solidified syrup out. You should be able to mold it with your fingertips.

3 Once the syrup has reached the soft ball stage prevent it from overcooking by plunging the bottom of the pan into cold water, either in a sink or in a shallow container. If the syrup is allowed to overcook it will crystallize in the pan and form brittle glass-like strands that snap. Adding over-cooked syrup to the eggs will cause the mixture to solidify into a rock-solid mass that would be impossible to mix.

Freezing ice cream

Beating or churning

Freezing is obviously a crucial stage in the making of homemade ice cream, and there are two basic methods. Freezing without a machine is also known as "still freezing," while the action in an ice cream maker is "stir freezing." We are so used to electrical machines that it is hard to imagine how labor-intensive it must have been for the cooks of one hundred or more years ago

beating ice cream by hand in churns standing in packed ice hewn from frozen rivers. Making ice cream by hand today requires freezing it in a container and beating it several times during the freezing process. It is this beating or churning process that is done automatically in an ice cream maker.

The secret of a really good ice cream is the formation of minute ice crystals. The finished

ice cream should be light and taste cold, not icy. If the ice crystals are large, the ice cream will have a grainy, coarse texture, which will detract from the creamy, smooth taste you are aiming to achieve. Beating the ice cream, either by hand or with an ice cream maker, breaks down the crystals. The more it is beaten while it is freezing, the finer and silkier the finished texture will be.

Freezing with an ice cream maker

1 Having prepared your ice cream maker according to the manufacturer's instructions, pour the chilled custard and whipping cream into the bowl, attach the paddle, attach the lid and begin churning.

2 After 10–15 minutes of churning, the ice cream will have begun to freeze. The mixture will thicken and will start to look slushy. Continue to churn the mixture in the same way.

3 After 20–25 minutes, the ice cream will be considerably thicker. It will still be too soft to scoop, but this is the ideal stage to mix in your chosen additional flavorings, such as praline or browned bread crumbs.

Making ices

Sorbets, like ices, are made with a light sugar syrup flavored with fruit juice, fruit purée, wine, liqueur, tea or herbs. They should not contain milk or cream, and are best made in an ice cream maker, as the constant churning ensures that the ice crystals are as tiny as possible.

Sorbet

Making a basic sorbet

SERVES SIX

INGREDIENTS

¼–1 cup SUGAR

¾–1¼ cups WATER

FLAVORING

1 EGG WHITE, lightly beaten

FRUIT PURÉES

As an approximate guide, 5 cups of berries will produce about a scant 2 cups of purèe. Mix this with a generous ½–¾ cup sugar (depending on the natural acidity of the fruit), which has been dissolved in 1¼ cups boiling water and then made up to 4 cups with extra cold water, lemon or lime juice.

1 Put the sugar and water in a medium saucepan and heat the mixture, stirring, until the sugar has just dissolved.

2 Add pared citrus zests, herbs or spices, depending on your chosen flavoring. Let infuse. Strain and cool, then chill well in the refrigerator. Mix with additional flavorings, such as fruit juices, sieved puréed fruits, herbs or tea.

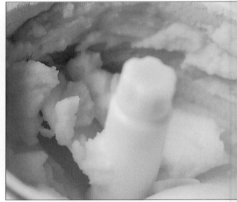

3 USING AN ICE CREAM MAKER: Pour the syrup mixture into the machine and churn until it is thick but still too soft to scoop.

4 USING AN ICE CREAM MAKER: Lightly beat the egg white with a fork and pour it into the ice cream maker, either adding it through the top vent or removing the lid and stirring it in, depending on the method recommended by the manufacturer of your machine. Continue churning the sorbet until it is firm enough to scoop with a spoon.

5 BY HAND: Pour the mixture into a plastic or freezerproof container. It should not be more than 1½ inches deep. Cover and freeze in the coldest part of the freezer for 4 hours or until it has partially frozen and ice crystals have begun to form. Beat until smooth with a fork, or hand-held electric beater. Alternatively, process in a food processor until smooth.

6 BY HAND: Lightly beat the egg white and stir it into the sorbet. Freeze the sorbet for another 4 hours or until firm enough to scoop.

COOK'S TIP *If making by hand, ensure that the freezer temperature is as low as possible to speed up the freezing process, and beat at regular intervals.*

Granitas

Making a citrus granita

This wonderfully refreshing, simple Italian-style ice has the fine texture of snow and is most often served piled into pretty glass dishes. You don't need fancy or expensive equipment, just a medium saucepan, a sieve or blender for puréeing the fruit, a fork and room in the freezer for a large plastic container.

INGREDIENTS

There are no hard-and-fast rules when it comes to the proportions of sugar to water, nor is there a standard amount of flavoring that must be added. Unlike sorbets, granitas consist largely of water, with just enough sugar to sweeten them and prevent them from freezing too hard. A total of 4 cups of flavored sugar syrup will provide six generous portions of granita.

1 Squeeze the juice from six lemons, oranges or four ruby grapefruit. Add a generous ½–1 cup sugar; the precise amount will depend on the natural acidity of the fruit. Dissolve the sugar in 1¼ cups boiling water, then mix it with the citrus juice and zest. Top up to 4 cups with extra water or water and alcohol. Add enough alcohol to taste, but don't be over generous or the granita will not freeze.

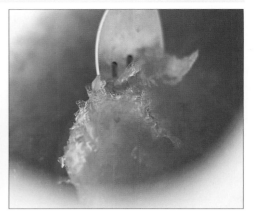

2 Pour the chilled mixture into a large plastic or freezerproof container. It should not be more than ¼–1 inch deep. Freeze it in the coldest part of the freezer for 2 hours, until it is mushy around the edges.

Take the container out of the freezer and beat the granita well with a fork to break up the ice crystals. Return the granita to the freezer. Beat it at 30 minute intervals for the next 2 hours, until it has the texture of snow.

Making a hot infusion

Some of the most delicious granitas are based on hot mixtures. Coffee is just one example. Pour hot, strong filtered coffee into a bowl or saucepan and stir in sugar to taste. For a ginger granita, infuse finely chopped fresh ginger root in boiling water, then sweeten it. Chocolate granita is made by mixing cocoa powder into a smooth paste with a little boiling water and sweetening to taste. All hot infusions must be cooled, then chilled in the refrigerator before being frozen.

Making a fruit-flavored granita

To make a fruit-flavored granita, purée berry fruits such as raspberries or strawberries, then sieve the purée to remove the seeds. Alternatively, purée ripe peaches, then sieve to remove the skins. To make a melon granita, scoop the seeds out of orange- or green-fleshed melons, then purée the flesh. Peeled and seeded watermelon can be puréed in the same way, or the flesh can be puréed along with the seeds and then sieved afterwards.

SERVING AND STORING GRANITAS

Coffee granita is classically served in a tumbler with a spoonful of whipped cream on top. Other types of granita look pretty spooned into tall glasses and decorated with fresh fruits or herb leaves and flowers. Because of its soft, snow-like texture, a granita is best served as soon as it is made. If this is not possible, you can leave it for a couple of hours in the freezer, beating it once or twice more if convenient. If you must freeze a granita overnight or for even longer, let it thaw slightly and beat it really well with a fork before serving. The ice crystals will become smaller, but the taste will be the same. As a granita does not contain dairy products, there are fewer concerns with food contamination or deterioration.

COOK'S TIP *Before you make the granita, make sure that the container you choose will fit in your freezer. A new stainless steel roasting pan can be used to freeze the granita mixture. As this metal is such a good conductor, the granita will freeze much faster than it would in a plastic container. Do not use aluminum, as the metal could react with the fruit acids to give a metallic taste to the finished granita.*

Serving ice creams and sorbets

Impress your friends at your next supper or dinner party by trying one of the following serving suggestions. They are not difficult to achieve, but look stunningly professional.

Oval shapes

These quenelle shapes are very easy to make and look attractive, especially when three different flavors of ice cream or sorbet are used. Arrange them on a plate flooded with chocolate sauce or Melba sauce and complete the picture with a sprig of red currants, a few whole fruits, a mint leaf or a few pieces of chocolate caraque.

1 You need two teaspoons. Take a scoop of ice cream with one spoon. Slide the second spoon underneath the ice cream, transferring the oval, then repeat the process.

2 Gently ease the ice cream oval onto a plate, then draw the edge of the spoon along the top of the ice cream to create a decorative line.

Shavings

Pare off long shavings of ice cream or sorbet by pressing a teaspoon into the surface and dragging it at an angle of 45°. Mixtures that are soft-set can be scooped right from the freezer, but in most cases ice cream or sorbet should be allowed to soften slightly before being scooped.

Using a melon baller

1 Press a medium or large melon baller into the frozen sorbet, rotate it, then put the ball in a dessert glass or serving dish.

2 Add more balls in the same way, piling them up attractively. Decorate with wafer cookies or mint leaves dusted with confectioners' sugar.

3 Another very effective presentation is to arrange balls of grape juice or apple sorbet on a flat plate to look like a bunch of grapes, adding a grape, strawberry or mint leaf to the top.

4 Balls of raspberry sorbet arranged in a circle on a plate flooded with apricot sauce look wonderful, especially when the center is filled with fresh raspberries.

Using an ice cream scoop

Dip the scoop into warm water, press it into the ice cream and run the scoop along the surface, pressing it against the side of the ice cream container until a well rounded scoop has been formed. Put this on a serving dish. Rinse the ice cream scoop and continue.

Piping shapes

Whirls of sorbet can be piped right onto serving plates or into fruit shells or chocolate molds from a large piping bag fitted with a fluted cream tube. The ice cream or sorbet must be soft enough to pipe, so choose a variety that will not melt too quickly. If you are using sorbet, you may need to set it slightly with a little gelatin before piping and freezing it.

Creating a bed of ice

On very hot summer days, keep ice cream and sorbets cold by scooping them into dishes set over a plate or shallow dish filled with crushed ice. To crush the ice, wrap ice cubes in a clean dish towel and break them up by hitting them with a rolling pin. Keep the chunks of ice fairly large so that they will not melt too quickly.

Using citrus shells

1 Colorful fruit shells look very pretty filled with sorbet. Cut the top off a lemon, lime or orange, loosen the edges of the flesh with a small, sharp knife, then scoop out all the flesh with a teaspoon, taking care to keep the shell intact. Having prepared more shells in the same way, rinse them all with cold water and drain them well. Use the flesh in another dessert.

COOK'S TIP *Do not be tempted to repeatedly thaw ice cream until it is soft enough to scoop and then refreeze the leftovers. The rich dairy content and fluctuating temperature will make this the perfect breeding ground for bacteria.*

2 Pipe or spoon the prepared sorbet into the hollowed fruit shells, wrap them in plastic wrap and freeze them until they are needed. Serve each sorbet garnished with a tiny sprig of fresh mint. Freeze with the "lids" replaced, if desired.

3 If you have a cannelle knife, you can cut decorative grooves in the skin of the fruit before cutting a slice off the top, hollowing out the centers and filling them with sorbet.

SERVING TEMPERATURE

We have all been faced at some time with ice cream that is just too hard to serve. The majority of homemade ice creams will freeze very hard, so it is worth taking the ice cream out of the freezer and transferring it to the refrigerator for 20 minutes or so before serving, and while you eat your main course. This allows the ice cream to soften slightly and also to "ripen," so that the full flavor of the ice cream can be enjoyed. Alternatively, it can be thawed slightly in a microwave for 2–3 minutes on the defrost setting or for 1 minute on full power and then left at room temperature for 10 minutes. If you forget, serve the ice cream by dipping the scoop into a bowl of hot water each time you form a ball of ice cream.

Flavorings for ice creams

Visit a modern ice cream parlor and you'll be dazzled by the number of flavors available. Yet this is no comparison to the endless possibilities you can create at home. Spices, herbs, fruits of every kind, flower waters, chocolate, coffee and nuts can all be used—singly or in combination. Experiment to find the tastes you and your family like best, remembering that freezing dulls some flavors, so you can often afford to be bold.

Herbs and flowers

Edible flowers

A sprinkling of just a few petals or tiny flower heads from the garden can turn even a few simple scoops of homemade strawberry or vanilla ice cream into a dinner party dessert. A few vibrant pansies or tiny violas mixed with primrose petals or even a few dainty violets would be perfect for a springtime party, while pastel-colored rose petals, borage flowers or sprigs of lavender would make a fine decoration in summer, as would a misty haze of elderflowers or sweet cicely flowers. For something bolder, use yellow or orange marigold petals (but not French marigolds) or nasturtiums. If selecting other flowers, please be aware that not all flowers are edible. Avoid plants that grow from bulbs or are otherwise inedible.

Flower waters

Orange flower or orange blossom water and rose water add a delicate fragrance to ground almond or berry ice creams and sorbets. Add a few drops and seal the bottle well to prevent evaporation.

Herbs

Rosemary, bay, mint and lavender make wonderful additions to creamy ice creams, sherbets or sorbets. For best results infuse a few sprigs of rosemary or lavender, two to three whole bay leaves or a small bunch of fresh mint in cream or sugar syrup that has just come to a boil. Leave in the liquid until cool, then sieve. You can also add a little fresh chopped mint or other extra herbs to the finished ice cream or sorbet.

RIGHT: *Sprigs of flowers or flower water give a delicate flavor to ice creams and sorbets.*

Spices

Ginger

TYPES/FORMS: The rhizome of an elegant tropical plant, ginger appears in many guises. The root is widely available fresh and is also preserved in sugar syrup as stem ginger. Chopped candied ginger and crystallized ginger are other forms of this delicious spice.

USES: Ginger makes a wonderful ice cream ingredient just on its own but it gives a glorious lift to fruit ices, especially with fruit such as rhubarb or pears, and it is a natural partner for tropical fruit. Preserved ginger, ginger syrup and ginger wine make delicious ice cream sauces.

PREPARATION: Peel ginger root, then slice or chop it thinly. Alternatively, grate it with the fine-tooth surface of a grater. Slice or chop preserved stem ginger; finely chop candied or crystallized ginger if pieces are large.

Using ginger

1 Peel off the skin on the ginger root, using a swivel-blade vegetable peeler or a small, sharp knife. Take care when peeling to remove only the thin outer skin.

2 Grate the ginger on the fine section of a regular grater or a nutmeg grater. This is easiest to do if the ginger is frozen. It will thaw instantly on being grated.

Vanilla

TYPES/FORMS: Beans of the climbing vanilla orchid plant are sold singly or in pairs. The spice is also finely ground, mixed with sugar and sold in envelopes labeled vanilla sugar. It is best known, however, as vanilla extract.

The beans are picked while still unripe. On drying, their yellow color deepens to a dark brown, and they acquire a natural coating of vanillin crystals, which are the source of the characteristic spicy aroma. The word "vanilla" comes from the Spanish "*vainilla*," meaning "little sheath." Although always associated with sweet dishes, the vanilla bean is not itself sweet.

Beware of cheap vanilla flavorings, as their harsh, almost bitter, flavor can be overpowering and could spoil the delicate flavor of some ice creams. Real vanilla extract is always labeled "natural vanilla extract."

USES: Vanilla is delicious in ice cream, whipped cream and custard and is used extensively when making patissiere cream and confectionery.

PREPARATION: Slit the whole vanilla bean, add it to cream or milk that has just come to a boil, then let cool and infuse. Lift up the bean, and holding it over the liquid, scrape the tiny black seeds with a small knife so that they fall into the liquid. The flavored cream or milk makes excellent ice cream. Don't throw beans away after use. Rinse under cold water, pat dry with paper towels and store two or three in a jar of sugar to make your own vanilla sugar. Vanilla extract is highly concentrated and you only need ½–1 teaspoon for ice cream.

Cinnamon

TYPES/FORMS: Cinnamon is obtained from the bark of the cinnamon tree, which is native to India. The bark is rolled into sticks or quills and dried. Cinnamon is also sold finely ground. The ground spice is seldom used in ice creams, except as a decoration, although it is widely used in baking. Cassia is a related spice. It resembles cinnamon in terms of aroma and flavor but is coarser and more pungent. Cassia is usually cheaper than cinnamon.

USES: Ice cream may not be the obvious use for cinnamon, a spice better known as an ingredient in cakes, cookies and savory dishes, but it adds a delicious flavor, especially with fruits such as peaches or nectarines.

PREPARATION: Infuse halved cinnamon sticks in milk or cream that has just come to a boil. When it has imparted its flavor, strain the milk or cream and use it to make custard as the basis for ice cream. Cinnamon sticks can also be used to flavor fruit purées or compotes by infusing in the liquid in the same way.

Using vanilla

Using a sharp knife, slit a whole vanilla bean. Add it to milk or cream that has just come to a boil. For maximum flavor, scrape out the tiny black seeds from the bean and let them fall into the milk or cream.

Nutmeg

TYPES/FORMS: Sold whole, nutmegs are the dried seeds of the fruit of the nutmeg tree, which is native to the tropics. Blades of mace, the pretty orange outer coating, are also sold separately, and both are sold ground.

USES: Nutmeg's wonderfully aromatic and slightly bitter flavor complements both sweet and savory dishes. It is delicious in milk-based desserts such as ice cream.

PREPARATION: For the best flavor, grate a little off a whole nutmeg as and when you need it, using a fine-toothed surface of a grater or, better still, a small nutmeg grater. Ready ground nutmeg rapidly loses its pungency when stored.

Star anise

These pretty star-shaped pods are a favorite of Chinese cooks, but are becoming popular in the West. Use them whole for sauces and compotes or infuse them in sugar syrups or custards for ices with a lovely aniseed flavor.

Using cardamom

Traditionally used in Indian, Arabian and North African cooking, cardamom also adds a wonderful delicate aromatic fragrance to sorbets, ice creams and fruit compotes. If the recipe calls for cardamom seeds, crush the beans with the back of a cook's knife until they split. If necessary, use the tip of the knife to remove any remaining seeds from the beans. Use both the bean and the seeds for maximum flavor.

Cloves

TYPES/FORMS: The unopened flower buds of a tree related to the myrtle, cloves look like tiny nails. They are available whole and ground.

USES: Although cloves are most commonly used in savory dishes, they are also widely used in desserts, particularly with apples and other fruits. Their pungent flavor means that they are a somewhat unlikely ingredient in ice cream, but if used sparingly, they add an intriguing flavor.

PREPARATION: Infuse whole cloves in milk or cream. This is especially appropriate when making a custard to form the basis of a fruit ice cream. Don't overdo this flavoring—the taste should be subtle and not strident.

Lemongrass

Mainly known for the delicate lemon fragrance it contributes to Thai and Vietnamese cooking, lemongrass is now widely available. Most supermarkets stock the fresh stalks, which are pale green and tipped with white; it is also available as dried whole stems or ground lemongrass and sold in jars. To extract the delicate flavor the dried stalks must be soaked in warm water for at least two hours before use. Fresh lemongrass can be finely sliced or crushed and infused in the milk to be used for custard-based ice cream or infused in the sugar syrup for a granita or sorbet.

Chocolate

CHOOSING THE BEST

A chocolate with a good, strong flavor is vital when making ice cream, as the flavor of the chocolate is dulled when it is mixed with custard and cream. For the best and strongest flavor choose a good quality dark or bitter chocolate with a high proportion of cocoa solids. Confectioners and good food stores will have a selection of superior chocolates, but many of the larger supermarkets now stock several different types of good quality cooking chocolate. Choose one with "luxury" or "Belgian" on the label, as it will almost certainly have at least 75% cocoa solids and good flavor and taste will be guaranteed.

Chocolate Menier can also be used. It has a stronger flavor and is less sweet than some other types of chocolate, but is well suited to ice cream making. Semi-sweet chocolate contains between 30 and 60% cocoa solids. Check the side of the pack for details—the more cocoa solids, the stronger the chocolate flavor will be, so avoid using any chocolate with less than 45% cocoa solids if possible.

In general, commercial chocolate bar should be avoided, as this has a mild, less chocolatey taste. With its added vegetable fat, it is more suited to making chocolate curls or caraque. What you can do, however, is to mix this chocolate with an equal amount of luxury dark chocolate. This way, you get the easy melting and molding qualities of the former, coupled with the superior taste of the latter.

Couverture

This pure chocolate contains no fats other than cocoa butter. It is used mainly by professionals and is only available at specialty suppliers. It generally requires "tempering" before use to distribute the cocoa fat evenly. This is quite a lengthy process that involves warming and working the chocolate until it reaches 90°F. Couverture is usually used for molding or decorating because of its glossy finish. It is available as white, milk and dark chocolate chips or in a block.

White chocolate

As when buying dark chocolate, choose "luxury" white chocolate or "Swiss" white chocolate for the best flavor. White chocolate is made from cocoa butter extracted during the production of cocoa solids. Although it includes about 2% cocoa solids, many purists would argue that this is not enough to make it a true chocolate, especially as the cocoa butter is then mixed with milk solids, sugar and flavorings.

As a result of these additional ingredients, white chocolate does require extra care when being melted: it quickly hardens if overheated. Do check the package before buying, and choose a brand with a minimum of 25% cocoa butter, as any chocolate with less than this will be difficult to melt. The more cocoa butter there is, the creamier and softer the chocolate will be. Some brands may even include vegetable fat or oils, so always check the ingredients list.

Melting chocolate in a microwave

Break dark or milk chocolate into squares, and place them in a bowl that can be safely used in a microwave. Heat it on Full Power, allowing 2 minutes for 4 ounces chocolate; 3 minutes for 7 ounces. The chocolate will retain its shape until you stir it. Don't be tempted to heat if for longer or you may spoil the chocolate. White chocolate melts easily and is best microwaved on Medium Power or in a bowl placed over a saucepan of "just boiled" water.

How to melt chocolate

1 Pour water into a saucepan until it is about one third full. Bring to a boil, turn the heat off, then fit a heatproof bowl over the pan, making sure that the water does not touch the bottom of the bowl. Break the chocolate into pieces and put it in the bowl.

2 Leave the chocolate pieces for 4–5 minutes, without stirring, until the chocolate has melted; the chocolate pieces will hold their shape. Stir the chocolate briefly before folding it into ice cream, or using it as the basis of a sauce.

Cocoa

This rich, strong, dark powder is made by extracting some of the cocoa butter during chocolate production. What remains is a block containing around 20% cocoa butter, but this varies with each manufacturer. The cocoa is then ground and mixed with sugar and starch. The addition of starch means that cocoa needs to be cooked briefly to remove the raw, floury taste. This can be done by mixing it into a paste with a little boiling water, which is the usual technique when flavoring ice cream. If the cocoa is to be used in a sauce, it will probably be mixed with hot milk.

The very best cocoa is produced in Holland. It is alkalized, a process that removes the acidity and produces a cocoa with a mellow, well-rounded flavor. The technique was devised by the manufacturer, Van Houten, some 150 years ago, and this is still the very best cocoa available. Although it is more expensive than some other brands, it is definitely worth using for ice cream and chocolate sauces.

Milk chocolate

Mild and creamy, milk chocolate is made with up to 40% milk or milk products and contains fewer cocoa solids than dark chocolate. Because it has a mild flavor, you will need to add more than when using dark chocolate. You can use a combination of melted milk chocolate and chopped milk chocolate. As with white chocolate, the addition of milk products means that it requires more careful heating than dark chocolate.

Carob

Although not a true chocolate, carob is viewed by many as an acceptable alternative. It is the ground seedpod of the carob or locust tree and can be used as a chocolate substitute. Usually available at health food stores and sold in bars or in a powdered form as a flour.
If you are using a bar, be cautious, as it is highly concentrated. The flour can be used in a similar way to cocoa.

STORING CHOCOLATE

Wrap opened packages of chocolate well or pack them in a plastic box. Store in a cool, dry place away from foods with very strong flavors, such as spices, which may taint the chocolate. Avoid very cold places, or the chocolate may develop a dull whitish bloom. Chocolate has a long shelf life, but check use-by dates before cooking.

Fruits

Berries

TYPES/FORMS: Berries make delicious ice creams and sorbets. You can choose from standard raspberries, bright red strawberries, blueberries and blackberries. Look for golden raspberries, too. These tend to be grown in small amounts by avid gardeners and are often difficult to find, but they are well worth trying when available.

USES: Delicious in ice creams, sorbets and sherbets, berries can easily be transformed into superb sauces. Melba sauce is an obvious example, but there are plenty more to choose from. A delectable frozen summer dessert that teams sliced strawberries with strawberry ice cream and berry sorbet makes perfect use of summer fruits. Blueberries and red berries look most attractive sprinkled on ice cream sundaes or crushed and added to just setting ice cream for added texture and color. Expensive alpine strawberries should be used for decoration only.

PREPARATION: Purée ripe berries, press them through a fine sieve to remove the seeds, then use the purée in ice creams, sherbets or sorbets. Berry purées are also delicious spooned over ice cream or mixed with a sugar syrup and lemon juice for a refreshing ice cream sauce.

RIGHT: *Red currants*

MAKING A PUREE

Purée berries in a food processor or blender until smooth, then press the purée through a sieve into a large bowl, using the back of a large spoon or ladle.

Cane fruits

TYPES/FORMS: This category includes black, red and white currants, green gooseberries and the more unusual red gooseberries. As their short midsummer season is soon over, enjoy them while they are available fresh and bursting with rich flavor .

USES: All cane fruits make good ice creams, sherbets and sorbets. They can also be used to make coulis and sauces. Currants look beautiful and are often used for decoration.

PREPARATION: Gently remove currants from their stems, using the tines of a fork. As black currants have such a sharp flavor, it is wise to poach them first with sugar and a little water until just tender. Red and white currants can be eaten raw or lightly poached.
Gooseberries should be trimmed with scissors before being cooked. Purée and sieve currants or cooked gooseberries if adding to ice cream, sorbet or sherbet. Gooseberry and ice cream made with cream is a wonderful summertime treat.

Orchard fruits

TYPES/FORMS: Choose from apples, pears, plums, damsons, cherries, apricots, peaches and nectarines.

USES: Orchard fruits, particularly peaches and nectarines, make irresistible ice creams. Use them in sorbets and similar desserts, with a little liqueur, if desired.

PREPARATION: Apples and pears should be peeled and cored; plums, peaches and apricots should be halved and pitted. The fruit should then be poached in a little water and sugar until tender before being processed into a smooth purée. Ripe peaches, nectarines and apricots can be puréed raw, then sieved to remove the skins. Damsons are small and difficult to prepare, so poach, then scoop out the pits. Alternatively, press the cooked fruit through a sieve to remove the pits. Use pitted cherries whole or roughly chopped. Larger fruits can be used for decoration, provided they are ripe. Slice or chop them if necessary, and toss apples and pears in a little lemon juice to prevent discoloration.

How to pit and string cherries

1 Remove cherry pits easily with this handy gadget that pushes the pits out of the fruit. Usually available at good kitchenware stores.

2 Cherries threaded on a skewer or toothpick make an attractive decoration, especially for a frozen drink.

Citrus fruits

TYPES/FORMS: Choose from lemons, limes, oranges, tangerines, clementines, kumquats and grapefruit.

USES: All citrus fruit can be used to make sorbets, granitas and sherbets. In addition, oranges make a very good ice cream. Citrus fruit can also be used to make sauces, and the zest is frequently used as a decoration.

PREPARATION: Grate the zest or pare it thinly, taking care to remove only the colored skin, leaving the bitter white pith behind. Cut the fruit in half and squeeze it, then strain the juice to remove any seeds. Mix it with cream and custard for ice cream or with sugar syrup for sorbets, sherbets and granitas. Kumquats can be poached whole or in slices and used to accompany frozen desserts.

RIGHT: *Halved lemons and limes*

Rhubarb

TYPES/FORMS: Strictly speaking, these pretty pink stalks are not a fruit at all but a vegetable. For making frozen desserts, choose the early forced rhubarb with its delicate flavor and baby-pink stalks. Maincrop rhubarb has thicker, darker stalks and a coarser texture.

USES: Puréed cooked rhubarb makes an excellent sorbet and granita, or flavor it with ginger for an old-fashioned ice cream. Lightly poached rhubarb can be served as an accompaniment to vanilla, cinnamon or goat's milk ice cream.

PREPARATION: Both early forced and maincrop rhubarb need to be cooked with sugar and just a tablespoon or two of water.

Melons

TYPES/FORMS: Choose from Cantaloupe, Charantais, Galia and Ogen melons. Test them for ripeness by pressing the stem area of the skin. The melon should smell quite perfumed.

USES: With their delicate perfume, melons make the most wonderfully refreshing sorbets and granitas. The shells make excellent and attractive containers for serving melon ices.

PREPARATION: Cut them in half, scoop out the seeds, then purée the flesh before use. Watermelons can also be used, but as the seeds are speckled throughout the flesh it is often easier to leave them in when processing the fruit. Sieving the purée will remove them. As watermelons have rather a bland flavor, mix the purée with grated lime zest and juice.

How to segment an orange or grapefruit

1 Using a sharp knife, start by cutting a slice off the top and bottom of the orange or grapefruit.

2 Using a small serrated knife, slice off the skin and pith cleanly. Work your way from the top down to the bottom of the fruit.

3 Holding the fruit over a bowl to catch the juices, carefully cut between the membranes to remove the whole fruit segments.

Tropical fruits

TYPES/FORMS: Choose from bananas, pineapples, mangoes, passion fruit, grapes and kiwi fruit. These fruits are available year-round and are a welcome alternative to seasonal fruits.

USES: Mash peeled bananas or purée them with a little lemon or lime zest to prevent discoloration and make them into smooth ice creams with honey, ginger, chocolate or cinnamon. Puréed or chopped pineapple flesh makes wonderful ice cream, especially when pieces of crushed meringue or a few tablespoons of rum are added. Pineapple can also be puréed and made into sorbets. Look for the extra sweet varieties, with their bright yellow flesh. Mix puréed mango with ginger, lime or coconut for a sorbet with a Caribbean flavor. Grapes and kiwi fruit are best served as a colorful accompaniment to frozen desserts, although both can be made into sorbet.

PREPARATION: Sliced or diced tropical fruits can be used as a decoration or sautéed in a little butter and sugar and then flamed in a little brandy, rum or orange liqueur for an easy ice cream accompaniment.

PREPARING PASSION FRUIT AND PINEAPPLES

Passion fruit are easy to prepare. Just slice them in half and scoop out the fragrant seeds with a teaspoon. If necessary, press the pulp through a sieve.

To prepare pineapples, slice the top off the pineapple, then cut it into slices of the desired width. Cut off the rind with a small sharp knife. Cut off any remaining eyes from the edges of the pineapple slices.

Remove the central core of each slice with an apple corer, pastry cutter or knife.

Preparing a mango

1 Place the mango, narrow-side down, on a board. Cut a thick, lengthwise slice off the sides, keeping the knife blade as close to the central pit as possible. Turn the mango around and repeat on the other side.

2 Make criss-cross cuts in the mango flesh, cutting down only as far as the skin, then turn the large slices of mango inside out so that the diced flesh stands proud. Scoop it into a bowl.

3 Cut all the remaining fruit off of the pit, remove the skin and dice the flesh.

Dried fruits

TYPES/FORMS: Golden raisins, raisins, prunes, apricots, peaches, dates and figs are all suitable, as are dried apples and pears, although these are seldom used for making ice creams and sorbets. Several types of dried fruit are sold in vacuum packages and these do not need soaking before use, although they are sometimes macerated in wine or liqueur for extra flavor. More unusual dried fruit includes mango, cranberries and blueberries.

USES: Using dried fruits in ice creams is nothing new—rum and raisin is a classic combination. Drying fruits such as peaches and apricots intensifies their flavor, so they make excellent purées. These can either be incorporated in ice creams or sorbets, or used as sauces for any ice cream dessert.

PREPARATION: Use the smaller varieties of dried fruit whole or chopped, and steep them in fruit juice, wine, spirits or liqueur, if desired. Larger fruits, such as apricots and peaches, need to be soaked and puréed before being added to ice cream, although chopped fruit can be added when the ice cream is partially frozen to give extra texture and color.

Candied fruits and citrus peel

These vibrant, jewel-like treats make a pretty addition to partially frozen ice cream, and are the traditional flavoring in the classic Italian Tutti Frutti Ice Cream. They can also be used to decorate elaborate ice cream sundaes. Most fruits can be candied, and a wide selection is available at supermarkets. Choose from candied cherries of various colors, candied pineapple and candied citrus peels. Large whole or sliced candied fruits tend to be expensive, but are great for special occasion desserts. Sugar is a natural preservative, and candied fruits will keep well in an airtight container, but they are best used as soon as possible and purchased fresh as needed.

Using candied fruits

Use a small, sharp knife to finely chop the candied fruits, then fold into just setting vanilla ice cream for a classic Tutti Frutti.

Nuts

Nuts

TYPES/FORMS: Choose from a wide range of whole nuts such as almonds, hazelnuts, pistachios, walnuts and pecans, plus macadamias, Brazil nuts and unsalted peanuts.

USES: Nuts are most popular in cream-based ice creams and are seldom added to ices. Add chopped toasted nuts or praline for extra crunch in ice creams, or sprinkle them on elaborate ice cream sundaes. Roughly chopped sugared almonds with pastel-colored coatings look good and make an easy decoration. Ground nuts infused in milk or cream give a delicate flavor to ice creams that are inspired by recipes from the Middle East.

PREPARATION: Toast the nuts, chop them roughly and fold them into partially frozen ice cream. Alternatively, use them to make praline, which can be broken up and folded into ice cream that is on the verge of setting. Finely ground almonds or cashews can be added to just boiled milk or cream, then left to cool. The flavored milk can be strained or used as is to make a custard-based ice cream.

BELOW: *Pistachios are an attractive addition to ice cream.*

Blanched nuts

1 Put nuts such as pistachios or almonds in a bowl and pour on just enough boiling water to cover. Let stand for a minute or two, until the skins expand and soften.

COOK'S TIP *Canned coconut milk combines convenience and full flavor for an ice cream that tastes good and is very easy to make.*

2 Drain the nuts. To pop nuts such as almonds out of their skins, simply pinch them. Skin pistachios by putting them in a dish towel and rubbing them together.

Toasted nuts

For maximum flavor, toast whole or roughly chopped nuts in a dry frying pan on the stove, in a shallow cake pan under the broiler or on a baking sheet in a medium oven until golden and lightly roasted. There is no need to add oil, as they have such a high natural oil content. Dry, shredded coconut can also be toasted in this way but because it is so finely processed you will need to keep a very close eye on it. It browns in a matter of seconds.

Spread out whole, sliced or roughly chopped nuts on a baking sheet. Broil for 3–4 minutes, shaking the sheet frequently so that the nuts brown evenly.

Making praline

1 Put sugar, whole nuts and a little water into a heavy frying pan. Heat gently, without stirring. Do not use superfine sugar, and do not stir as this would cause the sugar to crystallize, making it solidify and become opaque. Continue to heat the sugar, but don't be tempted to stir the mixture with a spoon. Tilt the pan gently, if necessary, to mix any sugar that has not dissolved completely.

2 Keep a watchful eye over the nuts as the sugar and nuts begin to turn golden. Remember to keep the heat low.

3 Quickly, pour the praline onto an oiled baking sheet. Let cool and harden.

4 Cover the cooled praline with plastic wrap or put it in a strong plastic bag. Break it into rough pieces by tapping with a rolling pin.

5 If finely ground praline is needed, crush it in a food processor or coffee grinder.

Other flavorings

Coffee

Frozen desserts can be made successfully with freshly-made coffee or good instant coffee. Strong espresso is preferable for coffee granita, while coffee ice cream can be made with cracked coffee beans. Bring milk or cream to a boil, add the beans and infuse them, then strain the mixture and use the flavored milk as the basis for the custard in the ice cream. Another way to make coffee ice cream is by blending cold, strong coffee or instant coffee dissolved in a very small amount of water with thick custard and cream. While cracked coffee beans give perhaps the best flavor and a pretty speckled finish (after straining), it can be difficult to judge amounts, so this method is more demanding. If too many beans are used or the custard is overcooked, the finished ice cream can be bitter.

Spirits and liqueurs

The addition of a favorite spirit such as brandy, Calvados or whiskey to ice cream, gin or vodka to sorbet, or an orange-flavored liqueur to a fruity granita can lift a simple frozen dessert into the realm of gourmet dining. While it is important to add enough alcohol to flavor the mixture (bearing in mind that freezing will dull the flavor), it is also vital to note that too much alcohol can prevent the ice cream or sorbet from freezing hard.

Purists or professional ice cream makers test the density and balance of an ice cream before freezing, using a saccharometer, but a beer-making hydrometer may also be used. This enables the level of sugar to liquid to be checked, ensuring satisfactory freezing. The home cook is unlikely to go to these lengths, and the best guide when adapting or making up recipes is to taste the mixture before freezing. If it is bland, don't add extra spirits, but pour a little on the ice cream just before serving.

> ### FLAVORING DURING FREEZING
>
> To add additional flavor and texture, praline, sugared bread crumbs, crumbled cookies, diced chocolate, diced candied fruits or brandy-soaked dried fruits can be folded into semi-frozen ice cream. If you are using an ice cream maker, transfer the ice cream to a plastic or similar freezerproof container when it is thick, but still soft, before folding in the chosen flavoring. If you are making the ice cream by hand, fold in the flavoring after the second beating.

ABOVE: *Spirits and liqueurs can be used in small quantities to add flavor to ice creams.*

Honey

For a single pot of honey, bees have to visit more than two million flowers. The type of flowers and the time of harvest determine the flavor, color and texture of the finished honey. You can choose from clover, lavender or heather honey, and cheaper blends are also available that include honey from more than one country. Heather honey has the best flavor for making ice cream and tastes especially delicious mixed with goat's milk.

ABOVE: *Alcohol is an excellent flavoring for all frozen desserts.*

Using molds

There is no need to buy specialty equipment unless you plan to make molded ice creams on a regular basis or you have a particular favorite. Look through your kitchen cupboards and you may be surprised to find that an item you use regularly or had forgotten about is just the shape you need. Any item not specifically designed to be used for making ice cream should be lined with plastic wrap. Use a generous amount, so that there is enough overlap to cover the exposed surface of the ice cream to keep it from drying out in the freezer.

TRANSFORMING EVERYDAY EQUIPMENT

- For rectangular ice cream bombes or terrines, metal loaf pans can be used. Both the 1-pound and the 2-pound sizes are suitable, or you can experiment with the larger, hinged metal pâté pans. Unless pans have a nonstick finish, line them with plastic wrap. If all your loaf pans have sloping sides, don't despair. Simply cut a piece of cardboard the length and height of the pan and use it to make the shape rectangular. Line this with plastic wrap, pushing it carefully into the corners.

- For bombes or cassatas you may have a plastic pudding mold with a lid left over from last year's bought Christmas pudding, or you may have bought such a mold for refrigerator storage. These make ideal molds, as the thin plastic conducts the cold well in the freezer and the plastic can be flexed to aid turning out.

- For kulfi, use conical-shaped popsicle molds without their lids or sticks. New disposable plastic cups also work well.

- For individual molds, old china cups can be lined with plastic wrap. If you can lay your hands on them, the tiny plastic pots with lids used for freezing baby food are ideal.

- New disposable plastic cups or small, well-washed cream cartons also make good containers. Metal dariole molds or individual metal steamed pudding molds can also be used if they are first lined with plastic wrap.

- If you don't have an ice cream cone mold, make a cardboard cone from an empty cereal box and cover it with aluminum foil. Alternatively, stuff cone shapes made from crumpled aluminum foil into cream horn pans so that they become one-third longer.

LEFT: *Specialized bombe, dariole and ring molds will ensure a professional finish, but they can be an expensive piece of kitchen equipment.*

BELOW: *Individual metal steamed-pudding molds can be used if lined with plastic wrap.*

- If you have used an ordinary glass or china mold, do not dip it in hot water or the mold may break. Simply insert a knife between the plastic wrap and the side of the mold to release the vacuum. Invert the mold on a serving plate, then warm the outside by covering it with a hot dish cloth. Count to 20 and then lift the basin off. Glass and china are poor conductors of heat, so will require longer and more gradual warming than metal. When dipping molds, use hot tap water rather than boiling water from the kettle, which would cause the outside of the ice cream to melt instantly and run over the plate when turned out.

Improvising shaped molds

Individual ice cream molds can also be shaped from 1–1½-inch strips of flexible cardboard that have been wrapped in a layer of aluminum foil. These covered strips are folded or curved and then stapled into the desired shape. You might try making hearts, circles or ovals, or fold the edges of the cardboard and make into squares or triangles.

1 Wrap a sheet of aluminum foil around a strip of cardboard cut to the desired height.

2 Bend the cardboard into a heart shape, then staple the two ends together.

3 Support the shape on a baking sheet, fill with ice cream that is on the point of setting, then level the surface with a knife and freeze until completely firm.

4 Cut the foil-covered cardboard with scissors and peel it off. Slide a spatula under the shaped ice cream, lift it onto a serving plate and decorate with fruit or chocolate curls.

ADDING INTEREST TO LAYERS

Ice cream layers in a molded dessert don't have to be restricted to traditional horizontal lines but can be set at angles by propping up the mold as it freezes. The ice cream can be frozen in one layer to form a triangle or frozen as three layers, each set at opposing angles for a zigzag effect. Terrine or loaf-shaped pans, and square shapes are ideal. Make sure that there is room in the freezer before you begin, as the angled mold and its supports take up quite a lot of space. Bags of frozen vegetables or small boxes of frozen fruit are ideal for wedging the pan at a 45° angle. When the first layer is frozen, add the next on the opposite side of the mold and wedge in position.

Unmolding a frozen dessert

1 Dip the filled metal or plastic mold into hot water and set it aside for a couple of seconds. Lift it out and blot the excess water. If the mold is lined with plastic wrap, carefully insert a knife between the plastic wrap and the mold to loosen the ice cream.

2 Invert the dessert on a serving plate, lift off the mold and peel off the plastic wrap. If you have difficulty turning out the dessert, try dipping the mold into the hot water for a few seconds more and repeat the process as before.

3 Another way to ease a frozen dessert from its mold is to invert it on the serving plate and cover the mold with a clean dish towel that has been dipped in boiling water, and then wrung out. Leave the dish towel in place for a few seconds, and lift off the mold.

Layering and rippling

For a professional look and a dramatic effect, create different layers of harmonizing ice creams in large or small, rectangular or round molds. There are plenty of possibilities—just let your imagination take over.

How to layer ices

Simple three-tier ice cream

Checkerboard

1 When the first flavor has thickened and is semi-frozen, pour it into a 10 x 3 x 3-inch terrine or loaf pan that has been lined with plastic wrap. Spread it in an even layer and freeze it in the coldest part of the freezer for 1 hour or until firm.

2 Pour in the second layer of semi-frozen ice cream and spread it out evenly. Freeze until firm, then add the final ice cream layer and freeze for 4–5 hours, until hard. When ready to serve, turn out the ice cream from the mold, peel off the plastic wrap and cut the terrine into slices, using a warm knife.

1 Make a two-tier terrine, using two of your favorite ice creams layered in a terrine or straight sided 2-pound loaf pan. Turn out the two-tier terrine onto a board and cut it in half lengthwise, using a hot knife.

2 Turn one of the halves over to reverse the color sequence. Wrap tightly in plastic wrap. Refreeze to harden. To serve, peel off the plastic wrap and slice with a hot knife.

Frozen roulade

1 Prepare two batches of semi-frozen ice cream in flavors that complement each other well. Line a 12 x 9-inch baking sheet with plastic wrap or waxed paper. Spread one batch of thick, semi-frozen, flavored ice cream. Freeze for 20 minutes.

2 Spoon the second batch of semi-frozen ice cream onto a second piece of plastic wrap or waxed paper to make a rectangle a little smaller than the first. Freeze for 20 minutes. Carefully place this sheet of ice cream over the first layer, then peel off the plastic wrap or waxed paper.

3 Roll the layered ice cream, as if making a jelly roll, starting from the longest edge and using the plastic wrap or paper to roll it. Pat the ice cream into a neat cylinder, then wrap it in more plastic wrap. Freeze for several hours, overnight if time permits, until the roll is hard.

4 Peel off the plastic wrap or paper and put the roll on a board. Cut it into thick slices, using a warmed knife.

Classic cassata

This classic Italian frozen dessert is traditionally made in a rounded metal mold with a lid. Some think that it is modeled on the dome of the Brunelleschi cathedral in Florence; others believe that the famous dessert was the result of a culinary accident, when cream and wine were accidentally spilled into a soldier's metal helmet which was being stored in a chilly cave. Whatever its true origins, cassata is traditionally served in Italy at weddings and Easter celebrations and is made of two or three layers of ice cream, depending on the size of the mold in which it is made. If you don't have a metal mold, a plastic or thick glass pudding mold can be used instead.

1 Line a 5-cup pudding mold with plastic wrap. Line it with a ¼-inch thick layer of semi-frozen strawberry ice cream, using the back of a metal spoon to press the ice cream against the sides and bottom of the mold. Cover and freeze for 1–2 hours or until the ice cream lining is firm.

2 Again using the back of a metal spoon, press chocolate ice cream onto the strawberry ice cream in the mold to make a second ¼-inch thick layer of chocolate ice cream against the frozen strawberry layer. Leave a space in the center. Cover and freeze for 1–2 more hours or until the chocolate ice cream is firm.

3 Pack the center of the mold with tutti frutti ice cream and smooth the top. Cover and freeze the dessert overnight until firm. Dip the mold in hot water for 10 seconds, insert a knife between the plastic wrap and the mold to loosen the cassata, then invert it onto a serving plate. Lift off the mold and peel off the plastic wrap before decorating the dessert with candied fruits or chocolate caraque. Serve in wedges.

Individual bombes

1 Line four individual metal molds with plastic wrap, then press a ½-inch layer of dark chocolate ice cream on the bottom and sides of each mold, smoothing the ice cream with the back of a teaspoon. Cover and freeze for 30 minutes or until the ice cream is firm.

2 Add a scoop of vanilla ice cream to the center of each lined mold and insert a brandy-soaked prune or cherry into the middle. Smooth the surface, cover and freeze for 4 hours, until firm.

3 Dip the filled molds into a roasting pan filled with hot water for 2 seconds. Invert the molds onto serving plates and quickly remove the pans and plastic wrap.

4 Decorate the top and sides of each individual bombe with long sweeping lines of piped white chocolate. Serve immediately.

How to ripple ices

This dramatic and eye-catching effect is surprisingly easy to achieve, using ice creams and sauces in contrasting colors, which are lightly swirled together while the ice cream is semi-frozen.

Flavored ice cream
Choose softly set ice cream that is too soft to scoop but thick enough to hold its shape. The colors should be markedly different for the most dramatic effect.

Sauces
Marble a chocolate, caramel or fruit sauce through ice cream that is on the verge of setting. Be careful with caramel sauces, as they can dissolve into the ice cream, so losing the effect.

Raspberry ripple ice cream

Fruit purée
Puréed and sieved fruit purées can be used unsweetened but can taste rather icy. It is better to mix them with a thick sugar syrup before swirling them with semi-frozen ice cream.

Jam
For the easiest rippled ice cream of all, use softly set fruit jam straight from the jar. You can use firmer jams, but they will need to be mixed with a little boiling water to soften before being used. Make sure the jam is cold when you use it, or it will melt the ice cream. Any fruit jam can be used but the contrast of berries looks the most attractive.

LEFT: *Use softly set jam for ice creams.*

1 Make the vanilla ice cream by hand or churn it in an ice cream maker until it is thick but too soft to scoop.

2 Mix 6 tablespoons sugar with ¼ cup water in a pan. Heat until the sugar has dissolved, then boil for 3 minutes, until syrupy, but not colored. Cool slightly. Purée 1½ cups fresh raspberries in a food processor or blender, then press through a sieve over a bowl. Stir in the syrup and chill well.

3 Add alternate spoonfuls of the soft, partially frozen vanilla ice cream and the chilled raspberry syrup to a 4-cup plastic or other freezerproof container. Don't be alarmed if the contrasting layers look a little messy to begin with.

4 Stir through the syrup and ice cream two or three times to create a rippled effect. Freeze.

CLASSIC COMBINATIONS

Ripple one of the basic recipes in this book with one of your own favorite flavors. Use the same basic technique as for raspberry ripple.

Mixed berry swirl—strawberry ice cream with raspberry syrup.

Coffee caramel swirl—dark classic coffee ice cream swirled with a rich caramel sauce.

Double chocolate—smooth dark chocolate ice cream rippled with smooth white chocolate ice cream.

Apricot and orange ripple—orange and yogurt ice rippled with apricot sauce.

Creamy caramel ripple—rich caramel sauce rippled through creamy vanilla ice cream.

Raspberry ripple—try the homemade version made with the very best of ingredients for a truly timeless classic.

Marbling ice cream

Although very similar to the technique used when making a rippled ice cream, marbling creates softer, less defined swirls. The same combinations of ice cream and syrup, sauce or purée can be used as for making rippled ice creams, but the softer effect is achieved by combining more thoroughly.

1 To achieve this effect, spoon alternate layers of partially frozen ice cream into a plastic or other freezerproof container. Drizzle colored liquid flavoring or syrup, onto each layer, using a spoon.

2 Pass the handle of a wooden spoon through the ice cream and liquid flavoring five or six times to produce a lightly marbled effect. Freeze the ice cream for 4–5 hours or overnight, until firm.

COOK'S TIP *Soft marbled ice cream need only be lightly swirled with the end of a spoon to create the desired effect. Choose a colored liquid flavoring that complements the base ice cream in color and taste.*

ABOVE: *A single scoop of marbled ice cream*

SECRETS OF SUCCESS

- Line the mold with plastic wrap so that it is easy to remove the frozen dessert.

- Choose flavors that contrast or complement each other, such as dark chocolate with pistachio, or vanilla and strawberry.

- Freeze ice cream after each layer has been added so that soft mixtures do not merge together. That way, the finished dessert will have well-defined layers.

- Make sure that the colors of the ice cream are in harmony, but are strong enough to be visible.

- Freeze the mold thoroughly after layering, preferably overnight, so that the layers will not separate when the ice cream is sliced.

- Dip the mold in hot water for 10–15 seconds so that the dessert will turn out easily. Peel off the plastic wrap and use a knife dipped into warm water for slicing.

Ice cream bars and popsicles

Everyone loves an easy ice cream bar, especially children, and these are particularly delicious. Making your own is also a good idea because you know exactly what ingredients they contain.

SINGLE FLAVORS

Milk maid
The simplest ice cream bar of all. Made with whole milk poured into molds and frozen until firm. Ideal as a first ice cream bar for small children.

Orange refresher
An easy popsicle, made by simply filling molds with freshly squeezed orange juice or juice from a carton. The flavors can be varied, try tropical fruit juices, apple, cranberry juice or mixed juices.

Strawberry yogurt
Mix a ⅔ cup carton of strawberry yogurt with the same amount of whole milk. Stir in 2 teaspoons strawberry milkshake powder, pour into popsicle molds and add extra milk if needed.

Banana custard
Mash two small ripe bananas with 1 teaspoon lemon juice, then mix with a small carton of ready-made custard. Add enough whole milk to fill the molds.

ABOVE: *Popsicle molds have handles.*

MULTICOLORED POPSICLES

Traffic light popsicles
Fill each popsicle mold one-third full with sieved strawberry purée, then freeze until hard. Add a second layer, the same width as the first, of lemonade. Freeze that until hard, then fill with orange juice tinted with a little blue food coloring so that it turns green. Freeze until hard.

Rainbow popsicles
Experiment with color combinations. Fruit purées, sieved and sweetened with a little sugar if very sharp, work very well. Try mango, kiwi fruit, strawberry and blackberry, for example. Alternatively, create layers of different colors by tinting orange juice with drops of edible food coloring. A few drops of green will turn orange juice blue; a little blue will change it to green; red will intensify the orange color. A combination of fruit purées and tinted juice also works well, and for creamy variations you can use different flavors of sorbet or ice cream. Let your imagination run wild, but always use sorbet or ice cream that is partially frozen and do make sure to freeze each colored layer until it is hard before adding the next layer or the colors will bleed into each other.

TWO TONE AND DOUBLE DECKER POPSICLES

Summer sunset

Pour a layer of sieved strawberry or raspberry purée into popsicle molds, and freeze. Fill up with orange juice and freeze until solid. Add a little vodka or tequila for an adult version.

In the pink

Slide a slice of strawberry down the side of each mold, then half-fill with partially frozen homemade strawberry ice cream. Freeze until firm, then top with homemade strawberry sorbet, and freeze.

SWIRLED AND RIPPLED POPSICLES

Night and day

Add alternate spoonfuls of semi-frozen white and dark chocolate ice cream to popsicle molds. Lightly mix them together with a fine metal skewer for a swirled effect and freeze until solid.

Banana and raspberry ripple

Fill the popsicle molds with alternate spoonfuls of semi-frozen banana ice cream and raspberry syrup. Lightly stir them with a fine metal skewer and freeze until solid.

COATED AND DIPPED POPSICLES

Double chocolate
Fill molds with partially frozen homemade chocolate ice cream, freeze until hard, then remove from the molds and coat the top half of each bar with finely grated dark chocolate.

Strawberry sprinkle
Fill molds with partially frozen homemade strawberry ice cream, freeze until hard, then remove from the molds. Drizzle melted white chocolate on the top portion of each bar, then sprinkle this with pastel-colored sugar crystals. For a simpler version, press the sugar crystals right onto the ice cream.

FREEZING POPSICLES
Popsicle molds come in various sizes; some enable you to make six small popsicles; others have space for four large ones. Pour in the mixture to come almost to the top, then press in the popsicle handles. Freeze for at least 6 hours or overnight until hard.

COOK'S TIP *If you don't have any popsicle molds or want to make lots of popsicles for a children's party, use small disposable plastic cups or a deep ice cube tray. Empty mini containers that originally contained yogurt can also be used, provided they are thoroughly washed. Popsicle sticks can be saved and recycled, or you can improvise with a length of doweling bought from your local hardware store. Cut it into suitable lengths, sand it well so that the wood is completely smooth, and wash the sticks thoroughly before use.*

Turning popsicles out

Hold the rounded ends of the molds under running hot water or stand the molds in a bowl of hot water. This should not be so deep that the water comes up to the handles—two-thirds of the way up is ideal. Count to 15, then flex the handles and lift out the popsicles.

Ice cream petits fours

1 Arrange a toasted almond, hazelnut or brandy-soaked cherry in each of the sections of an ice cube tray. Cover with thick ice cream that is partially frozen. Level the top of each cube with a knife and freeze until solid.

2 Pour just-boiled water from a tea kettle over the upturned ice cube tray, drain, then flex the tray to release the ice cream cubes. Arrange these on a small fine-meshed cooling rack set over a plate or baking sheet.

3 Spoon melted chocolate over the cubes, covering the tops and sides, and let it set. Turn each cube over and coat the underside and any gaps. Return to the freezer for a minute or two, then arrange on the inverted lid of a plastic container. Decorate with any remaining chocolate. Put on the bottom of the container and freeze until needed. Let soften for a few minutes before serving.

Ice cream kebabs

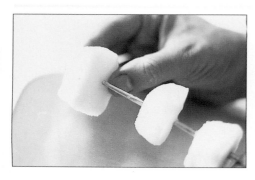

1 Pour a little of your favorite fruit ice cream into each section of an ice cube tray, freeze until solid, then turn out and thread onto hot metal skewers, leaving a little space between the ice cream cubes. Quickly put the kebabs in the freezer so that the ice cream stays hard.

2 When you are ready to serve, arrange two skewers on each serving plate. Decorate each ice cream cube with a slice of strawberry or kiwi fruit and serve with Melba sauce.

COOK'S TIP *Vanilla or chocolate ice creams are perhaps the best choice for these dainty petits fours, but cashew and orange, pistachio, coconut or orange and yogurt are also delicious. Cover the ice cream cubes in batches of five or seven and work quickly so they don't melt before they are completely covered with chocolate. Using a plastic box for storage in the freezer protects them from any knocks, and makes it easy to transfer them to plates for serving.*
Warm the skewers by dipping them in water that has recently boiled, or by holding them in an oven mitt and warming them over the flame on a burner so that they pierce the hard ice cream easily. Kebabs can also be made from a solid block of ice cream that has been cut into cubes.

Baskets, cookies and cones

Not only beautiful to look at, these sensational edible containers are easy to make and bound to impress your guests. They are the ultimate stylish and professional presentation.

How to make baskets

Spun sugar baskets

These impressive baskets look stunning filled with ice cream or upturned and placed over a single scoop of ice cream to form a cage and arranged in the center of a large white dinner plate. Use an oiled soup ladle instead of oranges for slightly flatter baskets, and loosen with the tip of a small knife before removing. Add rich color by decorating the plate with tiny clusters of blueberries, a few raspberries and a sprig or two of red currants or any combination of berries. Dust lightly with confectioners' sugar for the final effect.

MAKES SIX

INGREDIENTS

3 ORANGES, to serve as molds

a little OIL for greasing

generous 1 cup SUGAR

5 tablespoons WATER

VANILLA ICE CREAM and
FRESH BERRIES, to serve

1 Smooth squares of aluminum foil over three oranges and brush lightly with oil. Put the sugar and water in a saucepan and heat gently, without stirring, until the sugar has completely dissolved. Increase the heat and boil the syrup until it turns golden and starts to caramelize.

2 Take the pan off the heat and plunge the bottom of it into a bowl of cold water to prevent the caramel from overbrowning. Let the caramel cool for 15–30 seconds, stirring it gently until it starts to thicken, then lift the pan out of the water.

3 Hold a foil-wrapped orange over the pan and quickly drizzle caramel from a teaspoon onto half the orange, making squiggly lines and gradually building up layers to make the basket shape. Let the caramel set and make a second and third basket in the same way. Warm the caramel when it gets too stiff to drizzle.

4 Ease the foil off the first orange. Carefully peel off the foil and put the finished sugar basket on a lightly oiled baking sheet. Repeat with the remaining baskets, then make three more in the same way, reheating the caramel as needed and adding a little boiling water if it gets too thick to drizzle.

5 Use the baskets on the day you make them, filling them with vanilla ice cream and berries and adding a dusting of sifted confectioners' sugar. The baskets are extremely fragile, so scoop the ice cream onto a plate or baking sheet first and lower it carefully into each basket with the aid of two forks.

Chocolate tulips

These easy-to-make tulip baskets take only minutes to prepare and can then be set aside to harden. Fill with one large scoop of ice cream and decorate with blueberries and halved strawberries, or fill with tiny scoops of ice cream shaped with a melon baller and decorate with tiny chocolate shapes.

VARIATIONS *Any of the chocolate basket ideas suggested here is a perfect way of setting off your favorite chocolate, coffee or vanilla ice cream. You do not have to use dark chocolate to make the baskets—Belgian white or milk chocolate work just as well.*

1 Using the back of a teaspoon, spread 6 ounces melted dark chocolate over six 5-inch circles of nonstick baking parchment, taking it almost, but not completely, to the edge, and giving it a swirly, wave-like edge.

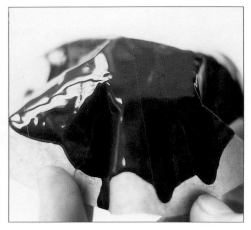

2 Drape each paper circle, chocolate-side outward, over an upturned glass tumbler set on a baking sheet. Ease the paper into soft pleats and place the baskets in a cool place to set. When ready to serve, lift the baskets off the glasses and carefully peel off the paper.

A large chocolate bowl

1 Smooth a double thickness of aluminum foil into a suitably sized mixing bowl or basin, so that it takes on the shape of the container. Carefully lift the foil out of the bowl.

2 Spoon melted chocolate into the bottom of the foil bowl. Spread it to an even, fairly thick layer, taking it over the bottom and sides with the back of a spoon or a pastry brush.

3 Chill well until set, then carefully peel off the foil and place the bowl on a plate. Store in the refrigerator until ready to fill with ice cream.

COOK'S TIP *This bowl can be made in any size. Small ones are perfect for individual portions, while larger bowls can serve up to four. Make it thicker than the other bowls and don't fill it too full or the weight of the ice cream might cause the chocolate to crack.*

Individual chocolate cups

1 Cut six 12 x 6-inch strips of nonstick baking parchment. Fold each strip in half lengthwise, roll into a circle and fit it inside a 3-inch plain cookie cutter to make a collar. Secure with tape. Ease the cookie cutter off and make five more collars, leaving the last collar inside the cutter. Place on a baking sheet.

2 Melt 9 ounces dark chocolate in a heatproof bowl over a pan of hot water. Brush chocolate evenly on the bottom and sides of the paper collar, supported by the cookie cutter, and make the top edge jagged. Carefully lift off the cookie cutter and slide over the next paper collar. Make six cups and let set.

3 Fill each of the set chocolate cups with parfait. Chill again in the freezer, then carefully peel off the paper on each cup. Using a spatula to transfer each filled cup to a plate, decorate them with a light dusting of sifted cocoa and serve.

COOK'S TIP *When melting chocolate, it is important that the chocolate isn't overheated or allowed to come in contact with steam or small amounts of moisture, as these will cause it to stiffen or "seize." Make sure that the base of the bowl doesn't touch the water and don't allow the water to boil.*

How to make cookies

Tuile cookies

These classic French cookies are named after the similarly shaped roof tiles found on many old French homes. Made with ground and crushed almonds, these cookies are shaped by being draped over a rolling pin as they cool, but cigar-shaped rolls or cones are also made.

SERVES SIX

INGREDIENTS

little OIL, for greasing

¼ cup UNSALTED BUTTER

¼ cup SLICED ALMONDS

2 MEDIUM EGG WHITES

6 tablespoons SUGAR

½ cup ALL-PURPOSE FLOUR, sifted

ZEST of ½ ORANGE, finely grated
plus 2 teaspoons JUICE

SIFTED CONFECTIONERS' SUGAR, to decorate

1 Preheat the oven to 400°F. Lightly brush a wooden rolling pin with oil, and line two baking sheets with nonstick baking parchment. Melt the butter in a saucepan and set it aside. Preheat the broiler. Spread out the sliced almonds on a baking sheet and lightly brown under the broiler. Let cool, then finely grind half; crush the remainder roughly with your fingertips.

2 Put the egg whites and sugar in a bowl and lightly fork them together. Sift in the flour, stir gently to mix, then fold in the melted butter, then the orange zest and juice. Fold in the finely ground nuts.

Cigarettes russes

These cookies are smaller and rolled more tightly than tuiles, but can be made using the same recipe. Omit the nuts, orange zest and juice and add 1 teaspoon vanilla extract. Make 2–3 cookies at a time, each time using 2 teaspoons of the mixture spread into a thin circle. The mixture makes 15 cigarettes russes.

3 Drop six teaspoons of the mixture onto one of the lined baking sheets, spacing them well apart. Spread the cookies into thin circles and sprinkle lightly with the crushed nuts. Bake for 5 minutes, until lightly browned around the edges.

4 Loosen one of the cookies with a spatula and drape it over the rolling pin. Shape the remaining cookies in the same way. Let sit for 5 minutes while baking a second sheet of cookies. Continue baking and shaping cookies until all the mixture has been used. Dust with confectioners' sugar and serve with ice cream.

COOK'S TIP *It is important to transfer the cookies to the rolling pin as quickly as possible. As the cookies cool they will set and become crisp and it will not be possible to shape them.*

Bake the cookies until they are golden around the edges, then turn them over and wrap them around lightly oiled wooden spoon handles.

Brandy snaps

Traditionally rolled into fat cigar shapes, these crisp, lacy cookies can also be made into tiny petits fours or even baskets—all perfect accompaniments to homemade ice cream.

MAKES 32

INGREDIENTS

a little OIL, for greasing

½ cup UNSALTED BUTTER

generous ½ cup SUGAR

½ cup LIGHT CORN SYRUP

1 cup ALL-PURPOSE FLOUR

1 teaspoon GROUND GINGER

1 tablespoon LEMON JUICE

1 tablespoon BRANDY

COOK'S TIP *Brandy snaps can be made the day before being served. Store them covered with waxed paper in a cool, dry place. They can also be frozen. Pack in layers in a rigid plastic box, interleaved with waxed paper.*

1 Preheat the oven to 375°F. Lightly oil the handles of two or three wooden spoons (or more if you have them). Line two baking sheets with nonstick baking parchment. Put the butter, sugar and syrup into a medium saucepan and heat gently, stirring occasionally, until the butter has melted.

2 Take the pan off the heat and sift in the flour and ginger. Mix well until smooth, then stir in the lemon juice and brandy.

4 Quickly roll each brandy snap around the handle of an oiled wooden spoon and put seam-side down on a wire rack to cool. Let set for 1 minute, then remove the spoon from the first cookie and shape the others on the tray in the same way, by which time the second batch of cookies will probably be ready.

3 Drop four teaspoons of the mixture onto the lined baking sheets, spacing them well apart. Cook for 5–6 minutes, until they are pale brown, bubbling and the edges are just darkening. Take the sheet of cookies out of the oven, let them stand for 15–30 seconds to set slightly, then loosen the cookies with a spatula.

CHOCOLATE SNAPS

For chocolate-flavored brandy snaps substitute 2 tablespoons of sifted unsweetened cocoa powder for 2 tablespoons of the flour. Do not use hot-chocolate powder, as this has added sugar and dried milk powder.

Mini cookies for petits fours

1 Spoon half teaspoons of the basic brandy snap batter onto lined baking sheets. Bake until golden brown, then shape around oiled wooden saté sticks or metal kebab skewers. Work quickly, as the small cookies will cool rapidly.

2 For mini cornets, shape the cookies by wrapping them around the ends of oiled cream horn pans or large piping tubes. Remove the pans or piping tubes and dip the ends of the cookies into melted white or dark chocolate, if desired.

Brandy snap cookies

1 Drop 1 tablespoon of the basic brandy snap batter onto a lined baking sheet, spread it into a circle and cook for 6–7 minutes. Cool for a few seconds, until firm enough to remove. Quickly lift the cookie and drape it, textured side outward, over an orange that has been lightly brushed with oil.

2 Flute the edges by easing the cookie into folds with your fingertips. Let cool. As soon as it has set, lift it off the orange.

COOK'S TIP *These baskets are best made one at a time. They cook quickly and are shaped in a couple of minutes.*

How to make cones

Chocolate cones

1 Line the inside of as many cream horn pans as you need with nonstick baking parchment so that it sticks out of the ends of the pans slightly and the ends overlap inside.

2 Brush the inside of each paper cone with melted chocolate, chill for 15 minutes, then brush on a second layer of chocolate. Chill well, then fill with softly set ice cream. Stand the filled cream horn pans in mugs to keep them upright or wedge them in a plastic container, using crumpled paper towels or aluminum foil to keep them upright. Freeze until firm.

3 Carefully pull the chocolate cones out of the pans, holding them by the paper, then gently peel off the paper. Lay the filled cones on individual plates and decorate with chocolate curls. Dust each plate with sifted cocoa.

Tuile ice cream cones

1 Use the basic recipe for tuiles to make ten lacy ice cream cones on wooden molds. They are extremely fragile, so fill with care. These cones are best eaten on the day they are made. Make two cones at a time, using 1 tablespoon of mixture per cone. Spread thinly into 4-inch circles, sprinkle with nuts and bake at 350°F for 5 minutes, until golden around the edges.

Mini cones

1 Using about 2 teaspoons of cookie batter each time, make two well-spaced mounds on a lined baking sheet. Don't bother to spread them flat. Bake for 4 minutes, until the cookies are starting to brown around the edges.

Transforming bought cones

1 Liven up ready-made cones by dipping the tops in a little melted dark, white or milk chocolate and then sprinkling with chopped toasted hazelnuts, toasted sliced almonds or roughly chopped pistachios.

2 Have ready an oiled, wooden ice cream cone mold. Loosen a cookie, using a spatula, turn it over and put it on a clean, folded dish towel supported on the palm of your left hand. Lay the cone mold on top and wrap the cookie around it to form the cone shape. Repeat with the second cookie, then repeat with the remaining mixture.

2 Let the cookies cool slightly, then loosen them with a spatula, turn them over and carefully roll them around cream horn pans (see Cook's Tip).

COOK'S TIP *If desired, you can make cream horn pans bigger by stuffing them with crumpled aluminum foil until they are about one third longer. Brush them lightly with oil before using them as molds. Wooden ice cream cone molds are available at some specialty stores or by mail order.*

2 Coat the rims of cones in melted white chocolate and sprinkle with grated dark chocolate or curls.

3 For children's parties, stud cones with jewel-like arrangements of candy flowers, sticking them on with dots of melted white chocolate. Or dip the rim of each cone into melted white chocolate, then into pastel-colored sugar sprinkles.

Making ice bowls

These impressive ice bowls make a wonderful dinner party centerpiece. They are incredibly easy to make and need no specialty equipment—but make sure you have enough room in your freezer!

A decorated ice bowl

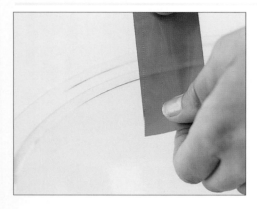

1 You will need two pyrex or plastic bowls that will fit one inside the other leaving a gap of about ¼–1 inch. Tape the bowls together, using packing tape and making sure that the gap between them is constant all the way around.

2 Put the double bowl on a plate to catch any drips. Carefully fill the gap between the bowls with cooled boiled water. It should come almost to the top. For a more frosted look, use cold water straight from the tap.

3 Slide slices of citrus fruits, small flowers, herbs or spices into the water between the bowls, using a skewer to tease them into place if necessary. Freeze overnight until hard.

4 To unmold the ice bowl, peel off the tape. Place the bowls in a bowl half filled with hot water and pour a little hot water into the smaller bowl. Count to 30, then lift the bowls out of the water, pour the water out of the smaller bowl and loosen the ice bowl with a thin, round-bladed knife.

5 Lift out the inner bowl, turn out the ice bowl and put it on a large plate. Decorate the plate with a few extra flowers or leaves and fill the bowl with ice cream. If you are serving it as part of a buffet you could unmold it ahead of time, fill it with ice cream and return it to the freezer until ready to serve. Decorate the serving plate just before taking to the table.

BEAUTIFUL BOWLS

• In summer there are many edible garden flowers and herbs that can be used to decorate ice bowls. Try pansies and chives with rosemary and sweet cicely, or strawberries, flowers and leaves for a very pretty effect. Fill the bowl with berry sorbet, or vanilla and strawberry ice cream.

• For a fresh citrus look, use orange, lemon and lime slices to make the ice bowl, adding a few sliced kumquats, if available. Decorate the serving plate with nasturtiums or calendula marigold flowers and fill with scoops of ice cream or sorbet in complementary colors.

• Celebrate the festive season with an ice bowl decorated with an arrangement of bay leaves and cranberries made to look like sprigs of holly. Add cinnamon sticks, whole star anise and a few orange slices too. Fill with a rich ice cream, rum raisin or tutti-frutti.

Classic ice cream sauces

No ice cream sundae would be complete without one of these popular sauces. For convenience, they can all be made in advance and stored in the refrigerator until needed, and can be served hot or cold, as preferred.

How to make sauces

Chocolate sauce

Rich, dark and irresistible. Pour the warm or cold sauce over vanilla or milk chocolate ice cream or serve with an ice cream sundae made with your favorite flavors.

MAKES 1⅔ cups

INGREDIENTS

2 tablespoons BUTTER

2 tablespoons SUGAR

2 tablespoons LIGHT CORN SYRUP

7 ounces LUXURY SEMI-SWEET COOKING CHOCOLATE

⅔ cup LOW-FAT MILK

3 tablespoons HEAVY CREAM

1 Mix the butter, sugar and syrup in a saucepan. Break the chocolate into pieces and add it to the mixture. Heat very gently, stirring occasionally, until the chocolate has melted.

2 Gradually stir in the milk and cream and bring just to a boil, stirring constantly, until smooth. Serve hot or cool, refrigerate and reheat when needed.

Butterscotch sauce

Smooth and glossy, this creamy sauce is extremely rich. It is delicious with vanilla or coffee ice creams. Once made, it can be stored in the refrigerator for up to 4 days.

MAKES 2 cups

INGREDIENTS

1 cup SUGAR

3 tablespoons each
COLD WATER and
BOILING WATER

6 tablespoons BUTTER

⅔ cup HEAVY CREAM

COOK'S TIP *Don't be tempted to stir the sugar syrup when it is boiling or you may find that the sugar will crystallize and solidify. If this happens, the mixture cannot be retrieved. You will have to throw it away and begin again.*

1 Put the sugar and 3 tablespoons cold water in a saucepan and heat very gently, without stirring, until all the sugar has dissolved.

2 Bring the mixture to a boil and boil until the sugar starts to turn golden. Quickly take the pan off the heat and immediately plunge the bottom of the pan into cold water to prevent the sugar from overbrowning.

3 Standing as far back as possible, and protecting your hand with an oven mitt, add the 3 tablespoons of boiling water to the caramel mixture, which will splutter and spit. Add the butter and tilt the pan to combine the ingredients. Let cool for 5 minutes.

4 Gradually stir in the cream and mix well. Pour into a pitcher and serve warm or cool.

Melba sauce

Of all the classic ice cream sauces, this is perhaps the best known. It is very easy, requires no cooking and is delicious served with scoops of vanilla ice cream and sliced ripe peaches. Some versions of this sauce are cooked and thickened with cornstarch, but this simple version is by far the best.

MAKES scant 1 cup

INGREDIENTS

1⅓ cups fresh or thawed FROZEN RASPBERRIES

2 tablespoons CONFECTIONERS' SUGAR

1 Purée the raspberries in a food processor or blender until smooth.

2 Pour the purée into a sieve set over a bowl. Press the fruit through the sieve and discard the seeds that remain behind in the sieve. Sift in the confectioners' sugar, mix well and chill until needed.

USING RIPE FRUIT

This is a wonderful way of using up very soft ripe raspberries. If they are particularly soft, don't purée them first; check them over, then simply press through a sieve with the aid of a wooden spoon.

Apricot Sauce

Delicious with vanilla ice cream, this fruity sauce is a good way of persuading children to eat fruit without realizing what they are doing.

MAKES 1½ cups

INGREDIENTS

scant 1 cup DRIED APRICOTS

scant 2 cups WATER

2 tablespoons SUGAR

VARIATION *The apricots can also be poached in apple juice or a mixture of half apple juice and half water.*

1 Put the apricots in a saucepan and add the water and sugar. Cover and let simmer for 10 minutes, until the apricots are tender and plump. Let cool.

2 Transfer the mixture to a blender or food processor and process into a smooth purée. Scrape into a bowl and chill until ready to serve.

Combining sauces

Spoon a little Melba sauce onto half a serving plate, then spoon apricot sauce over the other half. Tilt the plate very gently, first in one direction, then the other, to swirl the edges of the sauce together. Add the ice cream and decorate with sprigs of mint.

INSTANT DESSERTS

Serving plain ice cream with a combination of sauces is a very quick and easy way to produce an exciting dessert. Sauces that contrast in color or texture are very attractive when used together, but avoid using flavors that are not complementary.

COOK'S TIP *Sauces that contrast with each other can be rippled or swirled in exactly the same way as rippling ice cream. Ice cream is then placed on the top.*

Toppings and decorations

Complete the simplest dish of beautifully scooped ice cream or a party-style sundae with one of these professional looking decorations and you will be sure to impress your dinner guests.

How to make decorations

Chocolate caraque

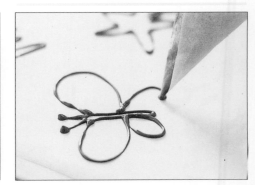

1 Using a rounded knife or the back of a spoon, spread melted dark chocolate onto a marble slab or cheese board, or a piece of kitchen countertop, to a depth of about ¼ inch. Put in a cool place to set.

2 Draw a long, fine-bladed cook's knife across the chocolate at a 45° angle, using a see-saw action to pare away long curls. If the chocolate is too soft, put it in the refrigerator for 5 minutes or in a cold place for 15 minutes. Do not overchill.

Piped chocolate shapes

Spoon a little melted dark chocolate into a paper piping bag and snip off the tip. Pipe squiggly shapes, stars, hearts, butterflies, musical notes or even initials onto a lined baking sheet. Peel off when cool and chill until needed.

Two-tone caraque

1 Spoon alternate lines of melted white and dark chocolate onto a marble slab or cheese board, or a piece of countertop and spread lightly so that all the chocolate is the same height. Let cool and harden.

2 Pare off long, thin curls of chocolate with a fine-bladed cook's knife in the same way that you do when making plain chocolate caraque.

Chocolate rose leaves

Brush melted dark chocolate, as evenly as possible, over the underside of clean, dry rose leaves. Avoid brushing over the edges. Put the leaf onto a nonstick parchment-lined baking sheet and put in a cool place to set. Carefully peel off each leaf and chill until needed.

Simple chocolate curls

Holding a bar of dark, white or milk chocolate over a plate, pare curls off the edge of the bar, using a swivel-blade vegetable peeler. Lift the pared curls carefully with a flat blade or a spatula and arrange as desired.

COOK'S TIP *If the chocolate used for decoration is not at the right temperature, the curls will either be too brittle or won't hold their shape. Set the chocolate aside at room temperature for 20 minutes before working with it.*

How to make dipped fruits

Fruit looks and tastes fabulous when half dipped in melted dark or white chocolate. Choose from tiny strawberries (still with their green hulls attached), tiny clusters of green or red grapes, cape gooseberries or cherries, with their stems. It can also look very effective if you dip half the fruits in dark chocolate and the remainder in white chocolate. Let set on a baking sheet lined with nonstick baking parchment.

Caramel-dipped fruits

For a more unusual fruit decoration for ice cream dishes, half-dip peeled cape gooseberries, whole strawberries or cherries (with the stems intact) into the warm syrup, then let cool and harden on an oiled baking sheet.

COOK'S TIP *Always carefully select fruit used for decoration and check that the fruit is perfect and free of any bruising, as this will quickly spoil the decoration. Wipe them with a damp cloth to remove any dust. A more even effect can be achieved if the stalks are still firmly attached to the fruit.*

Caramel shapes

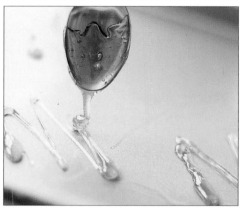

The caramel used for making baskets is also suitable for making fancy shapes to decorate ice cream sundaes. Instead of drizzling the caramel onto aluminum foil-covered oranges, drizzle shapes such as treble clefs, graduated zig zags, spirals, curly scribbles, initials, stars or hearts onto a lightly oiled baking sheet. Vary the sizes, from small decorations about 2 inches long to larger 4 inch long shapes.

Using colored chocolate

1 Pipe random lines of melted dark chocolate onto a piece of nonstick baking parchment. Overpipe with piped white chocolate. Using pink liquid food coloring, tint a little of the melted white chocolate.

2 Pipe a third layer of chocolate squiggles, this time in pink, onto the dark and white layers. Chill in the refrigerator until set.

3 Break the colored shapes into jagged fragments of varying sizes and stick them into ice cream to decorate. They look particularly good on top of ice cream sundaes.

Frosted flowers

1 Lightly beat an egg white, then brush a very thin layer onto edible flowers, such as pansies, violas, nasturtiums, tiny rose buds or petals. Herb flowers can also be used, as can strawberries, seedless grapes or cherries.

2 Sprinkle the flower or fruit with superfine sugar and let dry on a large plate. Use on the day of making.

Citrus curls

1 Using a zester, pare the zest of an orange, lemon or lime, removing just the colored zest of the skin and leaving the bitter white pith on the fruit.

2 Dust the citrus curls with a little superfine sugar and use them to sprinkle on citrus-based frozen desserts such as lemon sorbet.

Corkscrews

1 Use a cannelle knife to pare long strips of orange, lemon or lime zest. The strips should be as long as possible and very narrow.

2 Twist the strips of zest tightly around toothpicks so that they curl into corkscrews. Slide the sticks out and hang the corkscrew curls over the edge of ice cream dishes.

Meringue dainties

1 Make a meringue mixture using 2 eggs and a generous ½ cup sugar. Spoon it into a large piping bag fitted with either a small plain ¼-inch or a ⅜-inch nozzle.

2 Pipe heart shapes, zigzags, shooting stars or geometric shapes onto baking sheets lined with nonstick baking parchment.

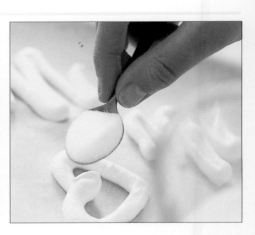

3 Sprinkle the shapes lightly with sugar and bake at low heat until they are firm enough to be lifted off the paper easily. Cool, then store in a cake pan for up to 1 week or until needed.

Decorative effects with sauces

Spooning sauces onto ice cream is a quick and simple method of decorating ice cream and can look particularly pretty on ice cream sundaes, but sauces can also be piped in decorative shapes and patterns or used to create elaborate or dramatic backdrops against which to display your favorite ice creams.

Creating teardrops

1 Spoon a little Melba sauce on the bottom of a plate, tilt to cover then pipe or spoon small dots of unwhipped heavy cream around the edge of the plate.

2 Draw a skewer or toothpick through the dots to form teardrops. Scoop the ice cream into the center of the plate.

Feathering

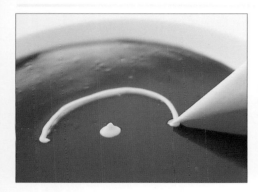

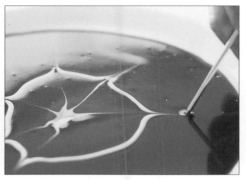

Piping zigzag lines

1 Spoon a little chocolate or butterscotch sauce onto a plate, then pipe a central dot and one or more circles of melted white chocolate or heavy cream on the sauce, starting at the center and working outward.

2 Draw a skewer or toothpick in lines from the center of the plate to the rim, like the spokes of a wheel. Or mark lines in alternate directions for a spider's web effect.

Arrange scoops of ice cream on a plate. Spoon a little cooled chocolate sauce into a piping bag, snip the tip, and pipe long zigzag lines onto the plate and ice cream. For added effect, dust with a little sifted cocoa powder.

Piped border

Decorative squiggles

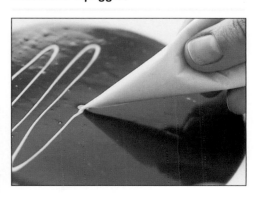

1 Pipe a swirly border of sieved strawberry or apricot jam around the edge of a plate. Alternatively, use melted white or dark chocolate and let chocolate set.

2 Using the jam or chocolate as a border, flood the center of the design with fruit, chocolate or butterscotch sauce, or cream. Arrange the ice cream on top, keeping it within the border.

Spoon a little butterscotch or chocolate sauce on a flat plate and tilt the plate to cover the bottom completely. Spoon melted white chocolate into a waxed paper bag, snip off the tip and pipe squiggly lines on the sauce. Let set, then arrange the ice cream.

the recipes

This section contains over 150 recipes for the most exquisite ice cream desserts. Beautifully presented with easy-to-follow steps, they range from the classic flavors in ice creams and sorbets to imaginative low-fat, elegant and even hot ice cream desserts. With new and exciting flavors and combinations, every recipe will bring certain success.

classic sorbets, ices & granitas

After a rich main course, nothing refreshes the palate better than a clean-tasting sorbet or ice. Stock the freezer when fruits are plentiful to make effortless desserts throughout the year. Slushy granitas are especially easy; use robust flavorings such as coffee and ginger.

Lemon Sorbet

This is probably the most classic sorbet of all. Refreshingly tangy and deliciously smooth, it quite literally melts in the mouth.

SERVES SIX

INGREDIENTS

1 cup SUGAR

1¼ cups WATER

4 LEMONS, well scrubbed

1 EGG WHITE

SUGARED LEMON ZEST,
to decorate

1 Put the sugar and water into a saucepan and bring to a boil, stirring occasionally until the sugar has just dissolved.

2 Using a swivel vegetable peeler pare the zest thinly from two of the lemons so that it falls right into the pan.

3 Simmer for 2 minutes without stirring, then take the pan off the heat. Let cool, then chill.

4 Squeeze the juice from all the lemons and add it to the syrup

BY HAND: Strain the syrup into a shallow freezerproof container, reserving the zest. Freeze the mixture for 4 hours, until it is mushy.

USING AN ICE CREAM MAKER: Strain the syrup and lemon juice and churn the mixture until thick.

5 BY HAND: Scoop the sorbet into a food processor and beat it until smooth. Lightly whisk the egg white with a fork until it is just frothy. Spoon the sorbet back into the container, beat in the egg white and return the mixture to the freezer for 4 hours.

USING AN ICE CREAM MAKER: Add the egg white to the mixture and continue to churn for 10–15 minutes, until firm enough to scoop.

6 Scoop into bowls or glasses and decorate with sugared lemon zest.

COOK'S TIP *Cut one third off the top of a lemon and retain as a lid. Squeeze the juice out of the larger portion. Remove any membrane and use the shell as a ready-made container. Scoop or pipe sorbet into the shell, top with lid and add lemon leaves or small bay leaves. Serve on a bed of crushed ice, allowing one lemon per person.*

VARIATION *Sorbet can be made from any citrus fruit. As a guide you will need 1¼ cups fresh fruit juice and the pared zest of half the squeezed fruits. Use 4 oranges or 2 oranges and 2 lemons, or, for grapefruit sorbet, use the zest of one ruby grapefruit and the juice of two. For lime sorbet, combine the zest of three limes with the juice of six.*

Pear and Sauternes Sorbet

Based on a traditional sorbet that would have been served between
savory courses, this fruity sorbet is delicately flavored with Sauternes wine,
spiked with brandy.

SERVES SIX

INGREDIENTS

1½ pounds RIPE PEARS

¼ cup SUGAR

1 cup WATER
plus ¼ cup extra

1 cup SAUTERNES WINE,
plus extra to serve

2 tablespoons BRANDY

juice of ½ LEMON

1 EGG WHITE

FRESH MINT SPRIGS,
dusted with confectioners' sugar,
to decorate

1 Quarter the pears, peel them and cut out the cores. Slice them into a saucepan and add the sugar and ¼ cup of the measured water. Cover and simmer for 10 minutes or until the pears are just tender.

2 Put the pear mixture in a food processor or blender and process until smooth, then scrape into a bowl. Let cool, then chill.

3 Stir the wine, brandy and lemon juice into the chilled pear purée with the remaining water.

4 BY HAND: Pour the mixture into a plastic or other freezerproof container, freeze for 4 hours, then beat in a food processor or blender until smooth. Return the sorbet to the container.

USING AN ICE CREAM MAKER: Simply churn the pear mixture in an ice cream maker until thick.

5 Lightly whisk the egg white with a fork until just frothy. Either add to the sorbet in the ice cream maker, or stir into the sorbet in the container. Churn or return to the freezer until the sorbet is firm enough to scoop. Serve the sorbet in dessert glasses, with a little extra Sauternes poured over each portion. Decorate with the sugared mint sprigs.

COOK'S TIP *Sorbets that contain alcohol tend to take a long time to freeze, especially when made in an ice cream maker. To save time, transfer it to a container as soon as it thickens and finish freezing it in the freezer. If you make the sorbet by hand, freeze the mixture in a stainless steel roasting pan to begin with. Transfer the sorbet to a plastic container only after the egg white has been added.*

Red Berry Sorbet

This vibrant red sorbet seems to capture the true flavor of summer. Pick your own berries, if you can, and use them as soon as possible.

SERVES SIX

INGREDIENTS

¼ cup SUGAR

scant 1 cup WATER

5 cups MIXED RIPE BERRIES, hulled, including STRAWBERRIES, and RASPBERRIES

juice of ½ LEMON

1 EGG WHITE

small whole and halved STRAWBERRIES and STRAWBERRY LEAVES and FLOWERS, to decorate

1 Put the sugar and water into a saucepan and bring to a boil, stirring until the sugar has dissolved. Pour the syrup into a bowl, let cool, then chill.

2 Purée the fruits in a food processor or blender, then press through a sieve into a large bowl. Stir in the syrup and lemon juice.

3 BY HAND: Pour the mixture into a plastic or other freezerproof container and freeze for 4 hours, until mushy. Transfer to a food processor, process until smooth, then return to the container. Lightly whisk the egg white and stir into the mixture. Freeze for 4 hours.

USING AN ICE CREAM MAKER: Churn until thick, then add the whisked egg white. Continue to churn until firm enough to scoop.

4 Scoop onto plates or bowls, and decorate with fresh strawberries, leaves and flowers.

VARIATION *For a fruity sorbet with a hidden kick, add 3 tablespoons vodka or cassis. Don't be too generous with the spirits, or the sorbet will not freeze firm.*

Black Currant Sorbet

Wonderfully sharp and bursting with flavor, this is a very popular sorbet. If you find it a bit tart, add a little more sugar before freezing.

SERVES SIX

INGREDIENTS

5 cups BLACK CURRANTS, trimmed

1½ cups WATER

¼ cup SUGAR

1 EGG WHITE

SPRIGS OF BLACK CURRANTS, to decorate

1 Put the black currants in a saucepan and add ⅔ cup of the measured water.

2 Cover the pan and simmer for 5 minutes or until the fruit is soft. Cool slightly, then purée in a food processor or blender.

3 Set a large sieve over a bowl, pour the purée into the sieve, then press it through the mesh with the back of a spoon.

4 Pour the remaining measured water into the clean pan. Add the sugar and bring to a boil, stirring until the sugar has dissolved. Pour the syrup into a bowl. Cool, then chill. Mix the black currant purée and sugar syrup together.

5 BY HAND: Spoon into a plastic or other freezerproof container and freeze until mushy. Lightly whisk the egg white until just frothy. Spoon the sorbet into a food processor, process until smooth, then return it to the container and stir in the egg white. Freeze for 4 hours or until firm.

USING AN ICE CREAM MAKER: Churn until thick. Add the egg white and continue churning until it is firm enough to scoop.

6 Serve decorated with the black currant sprigs.

Strawberry and Lavender Sorbet

Delicately perfumed with just a hint of lavender,
this delightful pastel pink sorbet is perfect
for a special-occasion dinner.

SERVES SIX

INGREDIENTS

¼ cup SUGAR

1¼ cups WATER

6 FRESH LAVENDER FLOWERS

5 cups STRAWBERRIES, hulled

1 EGG WHITE

LAVENDER FLOWERS, to decorate

1 Bring the sugar and water to a boil in a saucepan, stirring until the sugar has dissolved.

2 Take the pan off the heat, add the lavender flowers and let infuse for 1 hour. If time permits, chill the syrup before using.

3 Purée the strawberries in a food processor or in batches in a blender, then press the purée through a large sieve into a bowl.

4 BY HAND: Pour the purée into a plastic container, strain in the syrup and freeze for 4 hours, until mushy. Transfer to a food processor and process until smooth. Whisk the egg white until frothy, and stir into the sorbet. Spoon the sorbet back into the container and freeze until firm.

USING AN ICE CREAM MAKER: Pour the strawberry purée into the bowl and strain in the lavender syrup. Churn until thick. Add the whisked egg white to the ice cream maker and continue to churn until the sorbet is firm enough to scoop.

5 Serve in scoops, piled into tall glasses, and decorate with sprigs of lavender flowers.

COOK'S TIP *The size of the lavender flowers can vary; if they are very small you may need to use eight. To double check, taste a little of the cooled lavender syrup. If you think the flavor is a little mild, add 2–3 more flowers, reheat and cool again before using.*

Minted Earl Grey Sorbet

Originally favored by the Georgians at grand summer balls, this refreshing, slightly tart sorbet is perfect for a lazy afternoon in the garden.

SERVES SIX

INGREDIENTS

1 cup SUGAR

1¼ cups WATER

1 LEMON, well scrubbed

3 tablespoons EARL GREY TEA LEAVES

2 cups BOILING WATER

1 EGG WHITE

2 tablespoons chopped fresh MINT LEAVES

FRESH MINT SPRIGS or FROSTED MINT, to decorate

1 Put the sugar and water into a saucepan and bring the mixture to a boil, stirring until the sugar has dissolved.

2 Thinly pare the zest from the lemon so that it falls right into the pan of syrup. Simmer for 2 minutes, then pour into a bowl. Cool, then chill.

3 Put the tea into a pan and pour in the boiling water. Cover and let stand for 5 minutes, then strain into a bowl. Cool, then chill.

4 BY HAND: Pour the tea into a plastic or other freezerproof container. Strain in the chilled syrup. Freeze for 4 hours.

USING AN ICE CREAM MAKER: Combine the tea and syrup and churn the mixture until thick.

5 BY HAND: Lightly whisk the egg white until just frothy. Scoop the sorbet into a food processor, process until smooth and mix in the mint and egg white. Spoon back into the container and freeze for 4 hours, until firm.

USING AN ICE CREAM MAKER: Add the mint to the mixture. Lightly whisk the egg white until just frothy, then put it in the ice cream maker and continue to churn until firm enough to scoop.

6 Serve in scoops, decorated with a few fresh or frosted mint leaves.

COOK'S TIP *If you only have Earl Grey tea bags these can be used instead, but add enough to make scant 2 cups strong tea.*
Make frosted mint leaves by dipping the leaves in egg white and sprinkling them with superfine sugar.

Coffee Granita

The most famous of all granitas, this originated in Mexico. It consists of full-bodied coffee frozen into tiny ice flakes.

SERVES SIX

INGREDIENTS

5 tablespoons good quality
GROUND COFFEE

4 cups BOILING WATER

¼ cup SUGAR

⅔ cup HEAVY CREAM
(optional)

1 Spoon the coffee into a French press coffee maker or pitcher, pour in the boiling water and let stand for 5 minutes. Plunge the coffee maker or strain from the pitcher. Pour the coffee into a large plastic container, to a maximum depth of 1 inch.

2 Add the sugar and stir until it has dissolved completely. Let the mixture cool.

3 Cover and freeze for 2 hours or until the coffee mixture around the sides of the container is starting to become mushy.

4 Using a fork, break up the ice crystals and mash the mixture finely. Return the granita to the freezer for 2 hours more, beating every 30 minutes, until the ice becomes fine, even crystals.

5 After the final beating return the now slushy granita to the freezer. When ready to serve, spoon the granita into glass dishes. Whip the cream and pass it separately, if desired.

COOK'S TIP *If you taste the coffee before freezing, don't be alarmed by its strength; the change from liquid to ice mysteriously dulls the flavor, so the finished taste is just right.*

Raspberry Granita

This vibrant bright red granita looks spectacular. Served solo, it is an excellent dessert for anyone on a fat-free diet. For something a little more indulgent, serve with whole berries and creme fraiche or whipped cream.

SERVES SIX

INGREDIENTS

½ cup SUGAR

1¼ cups WATER

3½ cups RASPBERRIES, hulled, plus extra, to decorate

juice of 1 LEMON

little SIFTED CONFECTIONERS' SUGAR, for dusting

1 Put the sugar and water in a large saucepan and bring to a boil, stirring occasionally until the sugar has dissolved. Pour the sugar syrup into a bowl, let cool, then chill.

2 Purée the raspberries in a food processor or in batches in a blender. Spoon the purée into a fine sieve set over a large bowl. Press the purée through the sieve with the back of the spoon and then discard the seeds.

3 Scrape the purée into a large measuring cup, stir in the sugar syrup and lemon juice and add cold water until you have 4 cups.

4 Pour the mixture into a large plastic container so that the depth is no more than 1 inch. Cover and freeze for 2 hours, until the mixture around the sides of the container is mushy.

5 Using a fork, break up the ice crystals and mash finely. Return to the freezer for 2 hours, beating every 30 minutes, until the ice forms fine, even crystals.

6 Spoon into tall glass dishes and decorate with extra raspberries dusted with a little sifted confectioners' sugar, if desired.

COOK'S TIP *For a granita with a little extra oomph, stir in 3 tablespoons cassis, but don't be tempted to add more or the granita will not freeze. If you miss one of the beatings, don't panic. Set the granita aside at room temperature for 10–15 minutes to soften slightly, then beat thoroughly with a fork until it is the desired consistency. Return it to the freezer and continue with the recipe.*

Watermelon Granita

Pastel pink flakes of ice, subtly blended with the citrus freshness of lime and the delicate flavor of watermelon, make this granita a rare treat for the eye and the tastebuds.

2 Discard most of the seeds, scoop the flesh into a food processor and process briefly until smooth. Alternatively, use a blender, and process the watermelon quarters in small batches.

3 Strain the purée into a large plastic container. Discard the seeds. Pour in the chilled syrup, lime zest and juice and mix well.

4 Cover and freeze for 2 hours, until the mixture around the sides of the container is mushy. Mash the ice finely with a fork and return the granita to the freezer.

5 Freeze for 2 more hours mashing the mixture every 30 minutes, until the granita has a fine slushy consistency. Scoop it into dishes and serve with the wedges of extra lime.

VARIATION *To serve this granita cocktail-style, dip the rim of each glass serving dish in a little water or beaten egg white, then dip it into sugar. Spoon in the granita, pour in a little Cointreau, Tequila or white rum and decorate with lime wedges or thin strips of lime zest removed with a cannelle knife and twisted around a toothpick.*

SERVES SIX

INGREDIENTS

⅔ cup SUGAR

¼ cup WATER

1 whole WATERMELON, about 4–4½ pounds

FINELY GRATED ZEST and JUICE of 2 LIMES, plus LIME WEDGES, for serving

1 Bring the sugar and water to a boil in a saucepan, stirring until the sugar has dissolved. Pour into a bowl. Cool, then chill. Cut the watermelon into quarters.

Tequila and Orange Granita

Full of flavor, this distinctive Mexican granita will have guests clamoring for more. Serve simply with wedges of citrus fruit, or spoon on a little grenadine.

SERVES SIX

INGREDIENTS

½ cup SUGAR

1¼ cups WATER

6 ORANGES, well scrubbed

6 tablespoons TEQUILA

ORANGE and LIME WEDGES to decorate

1 Put the sugar and water into a saucepan. Using a vegetable peeler, thinly pare the zest from three of the oranges, letting it fall into the pan. Bring to a boil, stirring to dissolve the sugar. Pour the syrup into a bowl, cool, then chill.

2 Strain the syrup into a shallow plastic container. Squeeze all the oranges, strain the juice into the syrup, then stir in the tequila. Check that the mixture is no more than 1 inch deep; transfer to a larger container if needed.

3 Cover and freeze for 2 hours, until the mixture around the sides of the container is mushy. Mash well with a fork and return the granita to the freezer.

4 Freeze for 2 more hours, mashing the mixture with a fork every 30 minutes, until the granita has a fine slushy consistency. Scoop it into dishes and serve with the orange and lime wedges.

COOK'S TIP *If you don't have any tequila, make the granita with vodka, Cointreau, or even white rum. Don't be tempted to add more than the recommended amount; too much alcohol will stop the granita from freezing.*

Ruby Grapefruit Granita

This is slightly sharper than the other granitas, but is very refreshing. It's the ideal choice for serving after a rich or very filling main course.

SERVES SIX

INGREDIENTS

1 cup SUGAR

1¼ cups WATER

4 RUBY GRAPEFRUIT

TINY MINT LEAVES,
to decorate

1 Put the sugar and water into a saucepan. Bring the water to a boil, stirring until the sugar has dissolved. Pour the syrup into a bowl, cool, then chill.

COOK'S TIP *Grapefruit shells make very good serving dishes. For a more modern treatment, consider the effect you would like to achieve when halving the grapefruit. They look great when tilted at an angle. Having squeezed the juice and removed the membrane, trim a little off the base of each shell so that it will remain stable when filled with granita.*

2 Cut the grapefruit in half. Squeeze the juice, taking care not to damage the grapefruit shells. Set these aside. Strain the juice into a large plastic container. Stir in the chilled syrup, making sure that the depth of the mixture does not exceed 1 inch.

3 Cover and freeze for 2 hours or until the mixture around the sides of the container is mushy. Using a fork, break up the ice crystals and mash the granita finely.

4 Freeze for 2 more hours, mashing the mixture every 30 minutes, until the granita consists of fine, even crystals.

5 Select the six best grapefruit shells for use as the serving dishes. Using a sharp knife, remove the grapefruit pulp, leaving the shells as clean as possible.

6 Scoop the sorbet into the grapefruit shells, decorate with the tiny mint leaves and serve.

Ginger Granita

This full-bodied granita is a must for ginger lovers. Served solo, it is a simple and inexpensive dessert, yet is stylish enough to serve to the most sophisticated guests.

SERVES SIX

INGREDIENTS

¼ cup SUGAR

4 cups WATER

3 ounces GINGER ROOT

a little GROUND CINNAMON,
to decorate

1 Put the sugar and water into a saucepan. Bring to a boil, stirring until the sugar has dissolved. Take the pan off the heat.

2 Peel the ginger, chop it finely, then stir it into the hot sugar syrup. Set aside for at least 1 hour to infuse and cool, then pour into a bowl and chill.

3 Strain the chilled syrup into a large, shallow plastic container, making sure the depth is no more than 1 inch. Cover and freeze for 2 hours or until the mixture around the sides of the container has become mushy.

4 Using a fork, break up the ice crystals and mash finely. Return the granita to the freezer for 2 more hours, beating every 30 minutes, until the ice becomes soft and very fine with evenly sized ice crystals.

COOK'S TIP *You will be able to maintain the right texture for an hour or so, but after that it will become too firm. To serve, spoon into tall glasses and dust with ground cinnamon.*

5 After the final beating, return the now slushy granita to the freezer. Serve in tall glasses decorated with ground cinnamon.

VARIATION *Whip ⅔ cup heavy cream and pipe it on top of each portion of granita. Decorate with crystallized ginger.*

Damson Ice

Use ripe fruits for natural sweetness. If you can't find damsons, use another deep-red variety of plum or extra-juicy Victoria plums.

SERVES SIX

INGREDIENTS

1¼ pounds RIPE DAMSONS, washed

scant 2 cups WATER

⅔ cup SUGAR

1 Put the damsons into a saucepan and add ⅔ cup of the water. Cover and simmer for 10 minutes or until the damsons are tender.

2 Pour the remaining water into a second saucepan. Add the sugar and bring to a boil, stirring until the sugar has dissolved. Pour the syrup into a bowl, let cool, then chill.

3 Break up the cooked damsons in the pan with a wooden spoon and scoop out any pits. Pour the fruit and juices into a large sieve set over a bowl. Press the fruit through the sieve and discard the skins and any remaining pits from the sieve.

4 BY HAND: Pour the damson purée into a shallow plastic container. Stir in the syrup and freeze for 6 hours, beating once or twice to break up the ice crystals.

USING AN ICE CREAM MAKER: Mix the purée with the syrup and churn until firm enough to scoop.

5 Spoon into tall glasses or dishes and serve with wafer cookies.

VARIATIONS *Apricot ice can be made in the same way. Flavor the water ice with a little lemon or orange zest or add a broken cinnamon stick to the pan when poaching the fruit.*

Apple and Cider Ice

This very English combination has a subtle apple flavor with just a hint of cider. As the apple purée is very pale, almost white, add a few drops of green food coloring to echo the pale green skin of the Granny Smith apples.

SERVES SIX

INGREDIENTS

1¼ pounds GRANNY
SMITH APPLES

¼ cup SUGAR

1¼ cups WATER

1 cup STRONG DRY CIDER

few drops of GREEN FOOD
COLORING
(optional)

strips of thinly pared
LIME ZEST, to decorate

1 Quarter, core and roughly chop the apples. Put them into a saucepan. Add the sugar and half the water. Cover and simmer for 10 minutes or until the apples are soft.

2 Press the mixture through a sieve placed over a bowl. Discard the apple skins and seeds. Stir the cider and the remaining water into the apple purée and add a little coloring, if desired.

3 BY HAND: Pour into a shallow plastic container and freeze for 6 hours, beating with a fork once or twice to break up the ice crystals.

USING AN ICE CREAM MAKER: Churn until firm enough to scoop.

4 Scoop into dishes and decorate with twists of thinly pared lime zest.

COOK'S TIP *Add the food coloring gradually, making the mixture a little darker than you would like the finished sorbet to be, as freezing lightens the color slightly.*

classic

vanilla,
chocolate
& coffee
ice creams

This chapter provides the best classic vanilla ice cream recipes, plus some imaginative variations using ingredients such as brandied fruits, crumbled cookies, saffron and cinnamon. The principle flavors of chocolate, coffee and caramel are many people's favorite ice creams, making this selection the ultimate collection of classic ice creams.

Classic Vanilla Ice Cream

Nothing beats the creamy simplicity of true vanilla ice cream. Vanilla beans are expensive, but well worth buying for the superb flavor they impart.

2 Lift up the vanilla bean. Holding it over the pan, scrape out the black seeds with a small knife so that they fall back into the milk. Set the vanilla bean aside and bring the milk back to a boil.

4 When the custard thickens and is smooth, pour it back into the bowl. Cool it, then chill.

SERVES FOUR

INGREDIENTS

1 VANILLA BEAN

1¼ cups LOW-FAT MILK

4 EGG YOLKS

6 tablespoons CASTER SUGAR

1 teaspoon CORNSTARCH

1¼ cups HEAVY CREAM

1 Using a small knife slit the vanilla bean lengthwise. Pour the milk into a heavy saucepan, add the vanilla bean and bring to a boil. Remove from heat and let sit for 15 minutes to let the flavors infuse.

3 Whisk the egg yolks, sugar and cornstarch in a bowl until the mixture is thick and foamy. Gradually pour in the hot milk, whisking constantly. Return the mixture to the pan and cook over low heat, stirring constantly.

5 BY HAND: Whip the cream until it has thickened but still falls from a spoon. Fold it into the custard and pour into a plastic or other freezerproof container. Freeze for 6 hours or until firm enough to scoop, beating twice with a fork, or in a food processor.

USING AN ICE CREAM MAKER: Stir the cream into the custard and churn the mixture until thick

6 Scoop into dishes, bowls or cones—or eat straight from the container.

COOK'S TIP *Don't throw the vanilla bean away after use. Instead, rinse it in cold water, dry and store in the sugar jar. After a week or so the sugar will take on the wonderful aroma and flavor of the vanilla and will be delicious sprinkled on berries. Use it to sweeten whipped cream, custard, cookies and shortbread.*

Brown Bread Ice Cream

This very English ice cream is flecked with tiny clusters of crisp, crunchy caramelized brown bread crumbs and tastes a bit like the more modern cookies-and-cream ice creams.

SERVES FOUR TO SIX

INGREDIENTS

4 EGG YOLKS

6 tablespoons SUGAR

1 teaspoon CORNSTARCH

1¼ cups LOW-FAT MILK

3 tablespoons BUTTER

1½ cups FRESH
BROWN BREAD CRUMBS

¼ cup LIGHT BROWN SUGAR

1 teaspoon NATURAL
VANILLA EXTRACT

1¼ cups HEAVY CREAM

1 Whisk the egg yolks, sugar and cornstarch together in a bowl until thick and pale. Pour the milk into a heavy saucepan, bring it just to a boil, then gradually pour it onto the egg yolk mixture, whisking constantly.

2 Return the mixture to the pan and cook over low heat, stirring constantly, until the custard thickens and is smooth. Pour it back into the bowl, let cool, then chill.

COOK'S TIP *Watch the bread crumbs carefully when frying. Like almonds, they have a habit of burning if you turn your back on them for a moment, and burnt crumbs will give the ice cream a bitter taste. The crumbs should darken only slightly.*

3 Melt the butter in a large frying pan. Add the bread crumbs, stir until evenly coated in butter, then sprinkle on the sugar. Cook gently for 4–5 minutes, stirring until lightly browned. Remove from heat and let sit until cool and crisp.

4 BY HAND: Add the vanilla extract to the custard and mix well. Whip the cream until thick, then fold into the custard. Pour into a plastic or other freezerproof container. Freeze for 4 hours, beating once with a fork to break up the crystals.

USING AN ICE CREAM MAKER: Add the vanilla to the custard and mix well. Stir in the cream. Transfer to the ice cream maker and churn until thick.

5 BY HAND: Break up the bread crumbs with your fingers. Beat the ice cream briefly, then stir in the bread crumbs. Return the container to the freezer and leave until firm enough to scoop.

USING AN ICE CREAM MAKER: Rub the bread crumbs between your fingers to break up any lumps. Stir the bread crumbs into the mixture, and churn for 5–10 minutes, until ready to serve in scoops.

Crème Fraîche and Honey Ice Cream

This delicately flavored vanilla ice cream is delicious either served on its own or with slices of hot apple or cherry pie.

SERVES FOUR

INGREDIENTS

4 EGG YOLKS

¼ cup FLOWER HONEY

1 teaspoon CORNSTARCH

1¼ cups LOW-FAT MILK

1½ teaspoons VANILLA EXTRACT

generous 1 cup CRÈME FRAÎCHE

NASTURTIUM, PANSY or HERB FLOWERS, to decorate

1 Whisk the egg yolks, honey and cornstarch in a bowl until thick and foamy. Pour the milk into a heavy saucepan, bring to a boil, then gradually pour onto the yolk mixture, whisking constantly.

2 Return the mixture to the pan and cook over low heat, stirring constantly, until the custard thickens and is smooth. Pour it back into the bowl, then chill.

3 BY HAND: Stir in the vanilla and crème fraîche. Pour into a plastic or other freezerproof container. Freeze for 6 hours or until firm enough to scoop, beating once or twice with a fork or in a food processor to break up the ice crystals.

USING AN ICE CREAM MAKER: Stir the vanilla and crème fraîche into the custard mix and churn until thick and firm enough to scoop.

4 Serve in glass dishes and decorate with nasturtiums, pansies or herb flowers.

COOK'S TIP *Measure the honey carefully and use level spoonfuls; if you are over-generous, the honey flavor will dominate and the ice cream will be too sweet.*

Tutti Frutti Ice Cream

This Italian fruit ice cream takes its name from an expression meaning "all the fruits."
Four fruits have been used here, but you can make up your own blend of candied fruits,
including papaya and mango.

SERVES FOUR TO SIX

INGREDIENTS

1¼ cups LOW-FAT MILK

1 VANILLA BEAN

4 EGG YOLKS

6 tablespoons SUGAR

1 teaspoon CORNSTARCH

1¼ cups WHIPPING CREAM

⅔ cup MULTI-COLORED
CANDIED CHERRIES

⅓ cup SLICED CANDIED
LIME and ORANGE PEEL

⅓ cup CANDIED
PINEAPPLE

1 Pour the milk into a heavy saucepan. Using a small, sharp knife slit the vanilla bean lengthwise, add it to the milk and bring to a boil. Immediately remove the pan from heat and leave the milk for 15 minutes to let the flavor infuse.

2 Lift up the vanilla bean. Holding it over the pan of milk, scrape out the small black seeds with a narrow-bladed knife so that they fall into the milk. Set the vanilla bean aside, for later re-use, and bring the flavored milk back to a boil over low heat.

3 Meanwhile, whisk the egg yolks, sugar and cornstarch in a bowl until thick and foamy. Gradually whisk in the flavored milk.

4 Pour the milk mixture back into the pan. Cook over low heat, stirring constantly, until the custard thickens. Pour it back into the bowl and cover. Cool, then chill.

5 BY HAND: Whip the cream until it has thickened but is still soft enough to fall from a spoon, then fold it into the custard.

USING AN ICE CREAM MAKER: Mix the thickened custard with the cream. There is no need to whip the cream first. Churn the custard and cream mixture until it is thick.

6 BY HAND: Pour the mixture into a plastic or other freezerproof container. Freeze for 4 hours, beating once with a fork or electric mixer to break up the ice crystals. If you prefer, break up the crystals by blending the mixture briefly in a food processor.

7 Finely chop the candied cherries, peel and pineapple and fold into the ice cream. Return to the freezer for 2–3 hours or churn in the ice cream maker for 5–10 minutes, until firm enough to scoop.

VARIATION *Steep the candied fruits in a little Kirsch for 3 hours before adding.*

Cookies and Cream

This wickedly indulgent ice cream is a version of a favorite with many people
who grew up loving creme-filled cookies and ice cream.

SERVES FOUR TO SIX

INGREDIENTS

4 EGG YOLKS

6 tablespoons SUGAR

1 teaspoon CORNSTARCH

1¼ cups LOW-FAT MILK

1 teaspoon VANILLA
EXTRACT

1¼ cups WHIPPING CREAM

5 ounces CHUNKY CHOCOLATE
AND HAZELNUT COOKIES,
crumbled into pieces

1 Whisk the egg yolks, sugar and cornstarch in a bowl until the mixture is thick and foamy. Pour the milk into a heavy saucepan, bring it just to a boil, then pour it onto the yolk mixture, whisking constantly.

2 Return to the pan and cook over low heat, stirring until the custard thickens and is smooth. Pour it back into the bowl and cover closely. Let cool, then chill.

3 BY HAND: Stir the vanilla into the custard. Whip the cream until it is thickened but is still soft enough to fall from a spoon.

USING AN ICE CREAM MAKER: Stir the vanilla into the custard. Stir in the whipping cream and churn until thick.

4 BY HAND: Fold the cream into the chilled custard, then pour into a plastic or other freezerproof container. Freeze for 4 hours,

beating once with a fork, electric beater or in a food processor to break up the ice crystals. Beat one more time, then fold in the cookie chunks. Cover and return to the freezer until firm.

USING AN ICE CREAM MAKER: Churn until thick enough to scoop then scrape the ice cream into a freezerproof container. Fold in the cookie chunks and freeze for 2–3 hours, until firm.

COOK'S TIP *Experiment with different types of cookies to find the type that gives the best results.*

Brandied Fruit and Rice Ice Cream

Based on a favorite Victorian ice cream, this rich dessert combines spicy rice pudding with a creamy egg custard flecked with brandy-soaked fruits. The mixture is then frozen until it is just firm enough to scoop.

SERVES FOUR TO SIX

INGREDIENTS

⅓ cup PRUNES

⅓ cup DRIED APRICOTS

¼ cup CANDIED CHERRIES

2 tablespoons BRANDY

⅔ cup LIGHT CREAM

For the rice mixture

generous ¼ cup RICE

scant 2 cups WHOLE MILK

1 CINNAMON STICK, halved, plus extra CINNAMON STICKS, to decorate

4 CLOVES

For the custard

4 EGG YOLKS

6 tablespoons SUGAR

1 teaspoon CORNSTARCH

1¼ cups WHOLE MILK

2 Put the rice, milk and whole spices in a saucepan. Bring to a boil, then simmer gently for 30 minutes, stirring occasionally, until most of the milk has been absorbed. Lift out the spices and leave the rice cool

3 Whisk the egg yolks, sugar and cornstarch in a bowl until thick and foamy. Heat the milk in a heavy pan, then gradually pour it onto the yolks, whisking constantly. Pour back into the pan and cook, stirring, until the custard thickens. Let cool, then chill.

1 Chop the prunes, apricots and candied cherries finely and put them in a bowl. Pour in the brandy. Cover and let soak for 3 hours or overnight if possible.

4 BY HAND: Mix the chilled custard, rice and cream together. Pour into a plastic or other freezerproof container and freeze for 4–5 hours, until mushy then beat the ice cream lightly with a fork to break up the ice crystals.

USING AN ICE CREAM MAKER: Mix the chilled custard, rice and cream together. Churn until thick.

5 BY HAND: Fold in the fruits, then freeze for 2–3 hours, until firm enough to scoop.

USING AN ICE CREAM MAKER: Spoon the ice cream into a freezerproof container and fold in the fruits. Freeze for 2–3 hours, until firm.

6 Serve the ice cream in scoops decorated with cinnamon sticks.

COOK'S TIP *As the brandy-soaked fruits are so soft, it is better to remove the ice cream from the ice cream maker, fold in the fruits and then freeze the mixture in a container until firm enough to scoop. This way, the fruits do not disintegrate and their colors are preserved. If you make the ice cream by hand, do not process it to break up ice crystals or the texture of the rice will be lost.*

Cinnamon and Coffee Parfait

This French-style ice cream is flecked with cinnamon and mixed with just a hint of coffee. As it is made with a boiling sugar syrup, it doesn't require beating during freezing, so can be poured right into freezerproof serving dishes.

SERVES SIX

INGREDIENTS

1 tablespoon INSTANT COFFEE GRANULES

2 tablespoons BOILING WATER

1½ teaspoons GROUND CINNAMON

4 EGG YOLKS

generous ½ cup SUGAR

½ cup COLD WATER

1¼ cups HEAVY CREAM, lightly whipped

scant 1 cup CRÈME FRAÎCHE

extra GROUND CINNAMON to decorate

2 Put the sugar in a small saucepan, add the cold water and heat gently, stirring occasionally, until the sugar has dissolved.

3 Increase the heat and boil for 4–5 minutes without stirring until the syrup registers 239°F on a candy thermometer. Alternatively, test by dropping a little of the syrup into a cup of cold water. Pour out the water. If the syrup can be molded into a soft ball, it is ready.

4 Put the bowl of egg yolks over the pan of simmering water and whisk in the sugar syrup. Whisk until the mixture is very thick and then remove from heat. Continue whisking until it is cool.

5 Whisk the coffee and cinnamon into the yolk mixture, then fold in the cream. Pour into a container or individual freezerproof glass dishes. Freeze for 4 hours or until firm. If frozen in a container, scoop into bowls and decorate with a dusting of cinnamon.

COOK'S TIP *Test the syrup regularly. When it is almost ready the syrup will fall slowly from the spoon. If the syrup fails to form a ball when tested in cold water, boil it for a few more minutes; if the syrup forms strands that snap, it is overdone and you must start again.*

1 Spoon the coffee into a heatproof bowl, stir in the boiling water until dissolved, then stir in the cinnamon. Put the egg yolks in a large heatproof bowl and whisk them lightly until frothy. Bring a medium saucepan of water to a boil and lower the heat so that it simmers gently.

Gingered Semi-freddo

This Italian ice cream is much like soft serve ice cream when it comes to texture. Made with a boiled sugar syrup rather than a traditional egg custard and generously speckled with chopped stem ginger, this delicious ice cream will stay soft when frozen.

SERVES SIX

INGREDIENTS

4 EGG YOLKS

generous ½ cup SUGAR

½ cup COLD WATER

1¼ cups HEAVY CREAM

⅔ cup DRAINED STEM GINGER, finely chopped, plus extra slices, to decorate

3 tablespoons WHISKEY (optional)

1 Put the egg yolks in a large heatproof bowl and whisk until frothy. Bring a saucepan of water to a boil and simmer gently.

2 Mix the sugar and measured cold water in a saucepan and heat gently, stirring occasionally, until the sugar has dissolved.

3 Increase the heat and boil for 4–5 minutes without stirring, until the syrup registers 239°F on a candy thermometer. Alternatively, test by dropping a little of the syrup into a cup of cold water. Pour out the water. You should be able to mold the syrup into a ball.

4 Put the bowl of egg yolks over the pan of simmering water and whisk in the sugar syrup. Continue whisking until the mixture is very thick. Remove from heat and whisk until cool.

5 Whip the cream and lightly fold it into the yolk mixture, with the chopped ginger and whiskey, if using. Pour into a plastic or other freezerproof container and freeze for 1 hour.

6 Stir the semi-freddo to bring any ginger that has sunk to the bottom of the container to the top, then return to the freezer for 5–6 hours, until firm. Scoop into dishes or chocolate shells (see Cook's Tip). Decorate with slices of ginger.

COOK'S TIP *Semi-freddo looks wonderful in chocolate shells, made by spreading melted chocolate over squares of nonstick baking parchment and then draping them over upturned tumblers. Peel the paper off when the chocolate has set and turn the shells the right way up before filling.*

Classic Dark Chocolate Ice Cream

Rich, dark and wonderfully luxurious, this ice cream can be served solo or drizzled with warm chocolate sauce. If you are making it in advance, don't forget to soften the ice cream before serving so that the full flavor of the chocolate comes through.

SERVES FOUR TO SIX

INGREDIENTS

4 EGG YOLKS

6 tablespoons SUGAR

1 teaspoon CORNSTARCH

1¼ cups LOW-FAT MILK

7 ounces DARK CHOCOLATE

1¼ cups WHIPPING CREAM

SHAVED CHOCOLATE, to decorate

1 Whisk the egg yolks, sugar and cornstarch in a bowl until thick and foamy. Pour the milk into a saucepan, bring it just to a boil, then gradually whisk it into the yolk mixture.

2 Return the mixture to the pan and cook over low heat, stirring constantly, until the custard thickens and is smooth. Take the pan off the heat.

3 Break the chocolate into small pieces and stir into the hot custard until it has melted. Let cool, then chill.

4 BY HAND: Whip the cream until it has thickened but still falls from a spoon. Fold into the custard, then pour into a plastic or other freezerproof container. Freeze for 6 hours or until firm enough to scoop, beating once or twice with a fork or in a food processor.

USING AN ICE CREAM MAKER: Mix the chocolate custard with the whipping cream. Churn until firm enough to scoop.

5 Serve in scoops, decorated with chocolate shavings.

COOK'S TIP *For the best flavor use a good quality chocolate with at least 75% cocoa solids, such as top-of-the-line Belgian dark chocolate or Continental-style dark cooking chocolate.*

Chocolate Double Mint Ice Cream

Full of body and flavor, this creamy, smooth ice cream combines the sophistication of dark chocolate with the satisfying coolness of fresh chopped mint. Crushed peppermints provide extra crunch.

SERVES FOUR

INGREDIENTS

4 EGG YOLKS

6 tablespoons SUGAR

1 teaspoon CORNSTARCH

1¼ cups LOW-FAT MILK

7 ounces DARK CHOCOLATE,
broken into squares

¼ cup PEPPERMINTS

¼ cup CHOPPED FRESH MINT

1¼ cups WHIPPING CREAM

sprigs of FRESH MINT dusted with
CONFECTIONERS' SUGAR,
to decorate

1 Put the egg yolks, sugar and cornstarch in a bowl and whisk until thick and foamy. Pour the milk into a heavy saucepan, bring to a boil, then gradually whisk into the yolk mixture.

2 Scrape the mixture back into the pan and cook over low heat, stirring constantly, until the custard thickens and is smooth. Scrape it back into the bowl, add the chocolate, a little at a time, and stir until melted. Cool, then chill.

3 Put the peppermints in a strong plastic bag and crush them with a rolling pin. Stir them into the custard with the chopped mint.

4 BY HAND: Whip the cream until it has thickened, but is still soft enough to fall from a spoon. Fold it into the custard, scrape the mixture into a plastic or other freezerproof container and freeze for 6–7 hours, beating once or twice with a fork or electric beater to break up the ice crystals.

USING AN ICE CREAM MAKER: Combine the custard and cream and churn the mixture until firm enough to scoop.

5 Serve the ice cream in scoops and decorate with mint sprigs dusted with sifted confectioners' sugar.

COOK'S TIP *If you freeze the ice cream in a container, don't beat it in a food processor when breaking up the ice crystals or the crunchy texture of the crushed peppermints will be lost.*

Dark Chocolate and Hazelnut Praline Ice Cream

For nut lovers and chocoholics everywhere, this luxurious combination is the ultimate indulgence. For a change, you might like to try using other types of nuts for the praline instead.

SERVES FOUR TO SIX

INGREDIENTS

4 EGG YOLKS

1 teaspoon CORNSTARCH

scant 1 cup SUGAR

1¼ cups LOW-FAT MILK

5 ounces DARK CHOCOLATE, broken into squares

1 cup HAZELNUTS

¼ cup WATER

1¼ cups WHIPPING CREAM

1 Put the egg yolks in a bowl and add the cornstarch, with half the sugar. Whisk until thick and foamy. Bring the milk just to a boil in a heavy saucepan, then gradually pour it onto the yolk mixture, whisking constantly. Scrape back into the pan and cook over low heat, stirring constantly, until the custard has thickened and is smooth.

2 Take the pan off the heat and stir the chocolate into the hot custard, a few squares at a time. Cool, then chill. Brush a baking sheet with oil and set it aside.

3 Meanwhile put the hazelnuts, remaining sugar and measured water in a large, heavy frying pan. Place over low heat and heat without stirring until the sugar has dissolved.

4 Increase the heat slightly and cook until the syrup surrounding the nuts has turned pale golden. Quickly pour the mixture onto the oiled baking sheet and let sit until the praline cools and hardens.

5 BY HAND: Whip the cream until it has thickened but is still soft enough to fall from a spoon. Fold it into the custard and pour the mixture into a freezerproof container. Freeze for 4 hours, beating once with a fork or in a food processor to break up the ice crystals.

USING AN ICE CREAM MAKER: Pour the chocolate custard into the ice cream maker and add the cream. Churn for 25 minutes, until thick and firm enough to scoop.

6 Break the praline into pieces. Reserve a few pieces for decoration and finely chop the rest.

7 BY HAND: Beat it once more, then fold in the chopped praline. Freeze for 2–3 hours or until firm.

USING AN ICE CREAM MAKER: Scrape the ice cream into a container and stir in the praline. Freeze for 2–3 hours or until firm enough to scoop.

8 Scoop onto plates and decorate with the reserved praline.

Triple Chocolate Terrine

This variation on the popular Neapolitan layered ice cream is made with smooth, dark, milk and white chocolate. Serve it in slices, sandwiched between rectangular wafer cookies or in a pool of warm dark chocolate sauce.

SERVES EIGHT TO TEN

INGREDIENTS

6 EGG YOLKS

½ cup SUGAR

1 teaspoon CORNSTARCH

scant 2 cups LOW-FAT MILK

4 ounces DARK CHOCOLATE, broken into squares

4 ounces MILK CHOCOLATE, broken into squares

4 ounces WHITE CHOCOLATE, broken into squares

½ teaspoon VANILLA EXTRACT

scant 2 cups WHIPPING CREAM

1 Whisk the egg yolks, sugar and cornstarch in a bowl until thick and foamy. Pour the milk into a heavy saucepan and bring it to a boil. Gradually pour it onto the yolk mixture, whisking constantly, then return the mixture to the pan and cook over low heat, stirring constantly, until the custard thickens and is smooth.

2 Divide the custard equally among three bowls of equal size. Add the dark chocolate to one bowl, the milk chocolate to another and the white chocolate and vanilla to the third.

3 Stir with separate spoons until the chocolate has melted. Cool, then chill. Line a 10 x 3 x 3-inch terrine or large loaf pan with plastic wrap.

4 BY HAND: Whip the cream until it has just thickened but still falls from a spoon, divide among the bowls and fold into the custard. Pour each flavor into a separate freezerproof container and freeze for 3–4 hours, until thickened. Beat with a fork or electric mixer until smooth.

USING AN ICE CREAM MAKER: Stir a third of the cream into each bowl, then churn the milk chocolate custard mixture until thick. Return the remaining bowls of flavored custard and cream to the refrigerator.

5 BY HAND: Spoon the milk chocolate ice cream into the lined pan, level the surface using the back of a spoon and freeze until firm. Spoon the white chocolate ice cream into the pan, level the surface and freeze until firm. Repeat the process with the dark chocolate ice cream, making sure the surface is smooth and level.

USING AN ICE CREAM MAKER: Churn the white chocolate ice cream until thick and smooth then spoon it into the pan. Level the surface and freeze until firm. Continue in the same way with the white chocolate and, finally, with the dark chocolate

6 Cover the terrine with plastic wrap, then freeze it overnight. To serve, remove the plastic wrap cover, then invert onto a plate. Peel off the plastic wrap and serve in slices.

COOK'S TIP *Make sure each layer of ice cream is firm before adding another, or the layers may merge. If you have made the ice cream by hand, the dark chocolate layer may need to be softened at room temperature before spreading.*

Chunky Chocolate Ice Cream

The three different chocolates in this decadent ice cream make it so delectable that it will rapidly disappear unless you hide it in the back of the freezer.

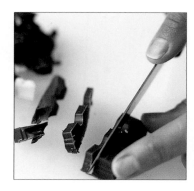

SERVES FOUR TO SIX

INGREDIENTS

4 EGG YOLKS

6 tablespoons SUGAR

1 teaspoon CORNSTARCH

1¼ cups LOW-FAT MILK

7 ounces MILK CHOCOLATE

2 ounces DARK CHOCOLATE, plus extra, to decorate

2 ounces WHITE CHOCOLATE

1¼ cups WHIPPING CREAM

1 Whisk the egg yolks, sugar and cornstarch in a bowl until the mixture is thick and foamy. Pour the milk into a large, heavy saucepan. Heat the milk and bring it just to a boil, then gradually pour it onto the egg yolk mixture, whisking constantly.

2 Return the custard mixture to the pan and cook over low heat, stirring constantly with a wooden spoon, until the custard thickens and is smooth.

3 Pour the custard back into the bowl. Break 5 ounces of the milk chocolate into squares, stir these into the hot custard, then cover closely. Let cool, then chill. Chop the remaining milk, dark and white chocolate finely and reserve to use as decoration.

4 BY HAND: Whip the cream until it has thickened but is still soft enough to fall from a spoon.

USING AN ICE CREAM MAKER: Mix the chocolate custard and the whipping cream and churn for 25–30 minutes until thick.

5 BY HAND: Fold the whipped cream into the custard, pour into a plastic or other freezerproof container and freeze for 4 hours, beating once with a fork or electric beater or in a food processor.

USING AN ICE CREAM MAKER: Scoop the churned ice cream into a plastic container.

6 BY HAND: Beat the ice cream one more time. Fold in the pieces of chocolate and freeze for at least 2–3 hours or until firm enough to scoop. Decorate with more pieces of chocolate.

USING AN ICE CREAM MAKER: Fold in the pieces of chocolate and freeze for 2–3 hours, until firm enough to scoop. Decorate with more pieces of chocolate.

COOK'S TIP *For maximum flavor, use good quality Belgian chocolate or your favorite chocolate bar; avoid using low-quality chocolate.*

Chocolate Ripple Ice Cream

SERVES FOUR TO SIX

INGREDIENTS

4 EGG YOLKS

6 tablespoons SUGAR

1 teaspoon CORNSTARCH

1¼ cups LOW-FAT MILK

9 ounces DARK CHOCOLATE,
broken into squares

2 tablespoons BUTTER, diced

2 tablespoons LIGHT
CORN SYRUP

6 tablespoons LIGHT CREAM or
CREAM and MILK MIXED

1¼ cups WHIPPING CREAM

WAFER COOKIES,
to serve

This creamy, dark chocolate ice cream, unevenly rippled with wonderful swirls of rich chocolate sauce, will stay deliciously soft even after freezing. Not that it will remain in the freezer for long!

1 Put the egg yolks, sugar and cornstarch in a bowl and whisk until thick and foamy. Pour the milk into a heavy saucepan, bring it just to a boil, then gradually pour it onto the yolk mixture, whisking constantly.

2 Return the mixture to the pan and cook over low heat, stirring constantly, until the custard thickens and is smooth. Pour it back into the bowl and stir in 5 ounces of the chocolate, until melted. Cover the chocolate custard closely, let it cool, then chill.

3 Put the remaining chocolate into a saucepan and add the butter. Spoon in the corn syrup. Heat gently, stirring, until the chocolate and butter have melted.

4 Stir in the light cream or cream and milk mixture. Heat gently, stirring, until smooth, then let the chocolate sauce cool.

5 BY HAND: Whip the cream until it has thickened, but is still soft enough to fall from a spoon. Fold it into the custard, pour into a plastic or other freezerproof container and freeze for 5 hours, until thick, beating once with a fork or electric beater or in a food processor. Beat the ice cream in the container one more time.

USING AN ICE CREAM MAKER: Stir the cream into the custard and churn the mixture for 20–25 minutes, until thick.

6 Add alternate spoonfuls of ice cream and chocolate sauce to a 6-cup plastic container. Freeze for 5–6 hours, until firm. Serve with wafers.

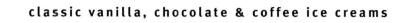

Chocolate and Brandy Parfait

This parfait is traditionally made with a mixture of chocolate and coffee, but here it is blended with cocoa powder for extra strength. Melted Belgian chocolate and a generous shot of brandy are the secrets of its superb flavor.

SERVES SIX

INGREDIENTS

3 tablespoons UNSWEETENED COCOA POWDER

¼ cup BOILING WATER

5 ounces DARK CHOCOLATE, broken into squares

4 EGG YOLKS

½ cup SUGAR

½ cup WATER

1¼ cups HEAVY CREAM

4–5 tablespoons BRANDY

drizzled WHITE CHOCOLATE RINGS, to decorate

1 Mix the cocoa into a paste with the boiling water. Put the chocolate into a heatproof bowl. Bring a pan of water to a boil, remove refrigerator and place the bowl on top until the chocolate melts. In a separate bowl, whisk the yolks until frothy.

2 Heat the sugar and measured water gently in a saucepan, stirring occasionally, until dissolved, then boil for 4–5 minutes, without stirring, until it registers 239°F on a candy thermometer. You can also test by dropping a little syrup into cold water. The syrup should make a soft ball.

3 Quickly whisk the syrup into the yolks. Lift the bowl of chocolate off the pan and bring the water to a simmer. Place the bowl with the yolk mixture on top and whisk until very thick. Lift it off the pan and continue whisking until cool.

4 Whisk in the cocoa mixture, then fold in the melted chocolate. Whip the cream lightly and fold it in, with the brandy. Pour the mixture into 6–8 freezerproof serving dishes, then freeze for 4 hours or until firm. Decorate with white chocolate rings, made by drizzling melted white chocolate on nonstick baking parchment and letting it set.

COOK'S TIP *If you are not sure whether the syrup is ready, it is better to use it sooner rather than later. If it is overboiled it will set like a rock when added to the cool yolks.*

Double White Chocolate Ice Cream

Chunks of white chocolate are a bonus in this delicious ice cream. Serve it scooped in waffle cones dipped in dark chocolate, for a sensational treat.

SERVES EIGHT

INGREDIENTS

4 EGG YOLKS

6 tablespoons SUGAR

1 teaspoon CORNSTARCH

1¼ cups LOW-FAT MILK

9 ounces WHITE CHOCOLATE, chopped

2 teaspoons VANILLA EXTRACT

1¼ cups WHIPPING CREAM

8 CHOCOLATE DIPPED CONES, to serve

1 Whisk the egg yolks, sugar and cornstarch in a bowl until the mixture is thick and foamy. Pour the milk into a heavy saucepan, bring it to a boil, then gradually pour it onto the yolk mixture, whisking constantly.

2 Return the custard mixture to the saucepan and cook over low heat, stirring constantly, until the custard thickens and is smooth. Pour the hot custard back into the same bowl.

3 Add 5 ounces of the chopped white chocolate to the hot custard, with the vanilla. Gently stir until the chocolate has melted, let cool, then chill.

4 **BY HAND:** Whip the cream until it has thickened but still falls from a spoon. Fold it into the custard and pour into a plastic or other freezerproof container. Freeze for 4 hours, beating once with a fork or electric beater or in a food processor. Beat the ice cream again, then stir in the remaining chocolate and return to the freezer for 2 hours.

USING AN ICE CREAM MAKER: Stir the cream into the custard, then churn the mixture until thick. Add the remaining chocolate and churn for 5–10 minutes, until firm. Serve in chocolate dipped cones.

VARIATION *If you prefer, scoop the ice cream into glass dishes and decorate with white chocolate curls or extra diced chocolate. Ice cream served this way won't go quite as far, so will only serve 4–6.*

Dark Chocolate Sherbet

This dark chocolate sherbet is a cross between a sorbet and a low-fat ice cream, and is ideal for chocoholics who are trying to count calories.

SERVES FOUR TO SIX

INGREDIENTS

2½ cups LOW-FAT MILK

⅓ cup GOOD QUALITY UNSWEETENED COCOA POWDER (such as VAN HOUTEN)

½ cup SUGAR

1 teaspoon INSTANT COFFEE GRANULES

CHOCOLATE-COVERED RAISINS, to decorate

1 Heat the milk in a saucepan. Meanwhile, put the cocoa in a bowl. Add a little of the hot milk to the cocoa and mix into a paste.

2 Add the remaining milk to the cocoa mixture, stirring constantly, then pour the chocolate milk back into the saucepan. Bring to a boil, stirring continuously.

3 Take the pan off the heat and stir in the sugar and the coffee granules. Pour into a pitcher, let cool, then chill well.

4 BY HAND: Pour the mixture into a plastic or other freezerproof container and freeze for 6 hours, until firm, beating once or twice with a fork, electric mixer or in a food processor to break up the ice crystals. Let soften slightly before scooping into dishes. Sprinkle each portion with a few chocolate-covered raisins.

ICE CREAM MAKER: Churn the chilled mixture until very thick. Scoop into dishes. Sprinkle each portion with a few chocolate-covered raisins.

COOK'S TIP *Use good quality cocoa and don't overheat the milk mixture, or the finished ice may taste bitter. If there are any lumps of cocoa in the milk, beat the mixture with a balloon whisk to remove them.*

Tiramisu

This favorite Italian combination is not usually served as a frozen dessert, but it does make a delicious ice cream. Like the more traditional version, it tastes very rich, despite the fact that virtually fat-free fromage frais is a major ingredient.

SERVES FOUR

INGREDIENTS

¼ cup SUGAR

⅔ cup WATER

generous 1 cup MASCARPONE

scant 1 cup VIRTUALLY FAT-FREE FROMAGE FRAIS

1 teaspoon VANILLA EXTRACT

2 teaspoons INSTANT COFFEE, dissolved in 2 tablespoons BOILING WATER

2 tablespoons COFFEE LIQUEUR or BRANDY

3 ounces LADYFINGERS

UNSWEETENED COCOA POWDER, for dusting

CHOCOLATE CURLS, to decorate

1 Put ½ cup of the sugar into a small saucepan. Add the water and bring to a boil, stirring until the sugar has dissolved. Let the syrup cool, then chill it.

2 Put the mascarpone into a bowl. Beat it with a spoon until it is soft, then stir in the fromage frais. Add the chilled sugar syrup, a little at a time, then stir in the vanilla.

3 BY HAND: Spoon the mixture into a plastic or other freezerproof container and freeze for 4 hours, beating once with a fork, electric mixer or in a food processor to break up the ice crystals.

USING AN ICE CREAM MAKER: Churn the mascarpone mixture until it is thick but too soft to scoop.

4 Meanwhile, put the instant coffee mixture in a small bowl, sweeten with the remaining sugar, then add the liqueur or brandy. Stir well and let cool.

5 Crumble the cookies into small pieces and toss them in the coffee mixture. If you have made the ice cream by hand, beat it again.

6 Spoon a third of the ice cream into a 3¾-cup plastic container, spoon on half the cookies, then top with half the remaining ice cream.

7 Sprinkle on the last of the coffee-soaked cookies, then cover with the remaining ice cream. Freeze for 2–3 hours, until firm enough to scoop. Dust with cocoa powder and spoon into glass dishes. Decorate with chocolate curls, and serve.

Classic Coffee Ice Cream

This bittersweet blend is a must for those who like their coffee strong and dark with just a hint of cream.

When serving, decorate with the chocolate-covered coffee beans that are available at some larger

supermarkets and candy stores.

4 BY HAND: Whip the cream until it has thickened but still falls from a spoon. Fold into the custard, add the coffee, then pour into a plastic or other freezerproof container. Freeze for 6 hours, until firm, beating once or twice with a fork, electric mixer or in a food processor to break up the crystals.

ICE CREAM MAKER: Mix the coffee and cream with the chilled custard, then churn the mixture until firm enough to scoop.

5 Scoop the ice cream into glass dishes, sprinkle with chocolate-covered coffee beans and serve.

SERVES FOUR TO SIX

INGREDIENTS

6 tablespoons FINE COFFEE GROUNDS

1 cup BOILING WATER

4 EGG YOLKS

6 tablespoons SUGAR

1 teaspoon CORNSTARCH

1¼ cups LOW-FAT MILK

⅔ cup HEAVY CREAM

CHOCOLATE-COVERED COFFEE BEANS, to decorate

1 Put the coffee in a French press coffee maker or pitcher and pour in the boiling water. Let cool, then strain and chill until needed.

2 Whisk the egg yolks, sugar and cornstarch in a bowl until the mixture is thick and foamy. Pour the milk into a heavy saucepan, bring to a boil, then gradually pour onto the yolk mixture, whisking constantly.

3 Return the mixture to the pan and cook over low heat, stirring constantly, until the custard thickens and is smooth. Pour it back into the bowl and cover closely with plastic wrap. Cool, then chill.

COOK'S TIP *If you only have coffee beans, put ¼ cup in a mortar and crush with a pestle. Bring 1¼ cups low-fat milk to a boil, and infuse crushed beans for 15 minutes. Strain and use the flavored milk to make the custard.*

Coffee Caramel Swirl

A wonderful combination of creamy vanilla, marbled with coffee-flavored caramel. Serve on its own or as a sundae with classic coffee and chocolate ice cream.

SERVES FOUR TO SIX

INGREDIENTS

For the caramel sauce

2 teaspoons CORNSTARCH

5¼-ounce can EVAPORATED MILK

6 tablespoons BROWN SUGAR

4 teaspoons INSTANT COFFEE GRANULES

1 tablespoon BOILING WATER

For the ice cream

4 EGG YOLKS

6 tablespoons SUGAR

1 teaspoon CORNSTARCH

1¼ cups LOW-FAT MILK

1 teaspoon VANILLA EXTRACT

1¼ cups WHIPPING CREAM

1 To make the sauce, put cornstarch and a little evaporated milk in a small, heavy saucepan and mix into a smooth paste. Add the sugar and remaining evaporated milk. Cook over low heat, stirring until the sugar has dissolved, then increase the heat and cook, stirring continuously, until slightly thickened and just beginning to darken in color.

2 Take the pan off the heat. Mix the coffee with the boiling water and stir into the sauce. Cool the sauce quickly by plunging the bottom of the pan into cold water.

3 Whisk the egg yolks, sugar and cornstarch together until thick and foaming. Bring the milk just to a boil in a heavy saucepan, then gradually whisk into the yolk mixture. Return to the pan and cook over low heat, stirring continuously, until thickened and smooth. Pour back into the bowl, stir in the vanilla and let cool.

4 BY HAND: Whip the cream until thickened but still soft enough to fall from a spoon. Fold into custard then pour into a plastic container and freeze for 4 hours, beating once, halfway through, with a fork, electric beater or food processor.

USING AN ICE CREAM MAKER: Combine the custard and cream and churn until thick but not firm enough to scoop.

5 BY HAND: Beat the ice cream again to break up any ice crystals.

USING AN ICE CREAM MAKER: Transfer the semi-frozen churned ice cream to a plastic container.

6 Beat the caramel sauce well and drizzle it thickly onto the ice cream. Marble together by roughly running a knife through the mixture. Cover and freeze the ice cream for 4-5 hours, until it is firm enough to scoop. Serve in scoops in bowls or plates.

COOK'S TIP *If the sauce is too thick to drizzle, gently warm the bottom of the pan for a few seconds, stirring well.*

VARIATION *The sauce is also delicious drizzled on plain vanilla ice cream.*

classic fruit & nut ice creams

From classic fruit-flavored ice creams to those speckled with chopped toasted nuts, this chapter imaginatively introduces the most widely used ice cream flavors. Fresh fruit purées, liqueured dried fruits and satisfying nuts transform a basic ice cream into something very special.

Simple Strawberry Ice Cream

Capture the essence of childhood summers with this easy-to-make ice cream.
Whipping cream is better than heavy cream for this recipe, as
it doesn't overwhelm the taste of the fresh fruit.

SERVES FOUR TO SIX

INGREDIENTS

4 cups STRAWBERRIES,
hulled

½ cup CONFECTIONERS' SUGAR

juice of ½ LEMON

1¼ cups WHIPPING CREAM

extra STRAWBERRIES,
to decorate

1 Purée the strawberries in a food processor or blender until smooth, then add the confectioners' sugar and lemon juice and process again to mix. Press the purée through a sieve into a bowl. Chill until very cold.

2 BY HAND: Whip the cream until it is just thickened but still falls from a spoon. Fold into the purée, then pour into a plastic container or other freezerproof container. Freeze for 6 hours, until firm, beating twice with a fork, electric beater or in a food processor to break up the ice crystals.

USING AN ICE CREAM MAKER: Churn the purée until thick, then pour in the cream and churn until thick enough to scoop. Scoop into dishes and decorate with a few extra strawberries.

COOK'S TIP *If possible, taste the strawberries before buying them. Halve large strawberries for decoration.*

VARIATION *Raspberry or any other berries can be used to make this ice cream.*

Gooseberry and Clotted Cream Ice Cream

*Gooseberries are hard to find but are delicious in this ice cream. Look for clotted cream
at specialty or gourmet food stores. The delicious, slightly tart flavor of this combination
goes particularly well with tiny, melt-in-your-mouth meringues.*

SERVES FOUR TO SIX

INGREDIENTS

4 cups GOOSEBERRIES,
trimmed

¼ cup WATER

6 tablespoons SUGAR

⅔ cup WHIPPING CREAM

a few drops of GREEN FOOD
COLORING (optional)

½ cup CLOTTED CREAM

FRESH MINT SPRIGS,
to decorate

MERINGUES, to serve

1 Put the gooseberries in a
saucepan and add the water and
sugar. Cover and simmer for
10 minutes or until soft. Transfer
to a food processor or blender and
process into a smooth purée. Press
through a sieve placed over a bowl.
Cool, then chill.

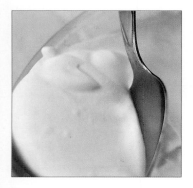

2 BY HAND: Chill the purée in a
plastic container. Whip the cream
until it is thick but still falls from a
spoon. Fold into the purée with the
green food coloring, if using.
Freeze for 2 hours, then beat with
a fork, electric mixer or in a food
processor, to break up. Return
to the freezer for 2 hours.

3 BY HAND: Beat the ice cream
again, then fold in the clotted
cream. Freeze for 2–3 hours.

USING AN ICE CREAM MAKER:
Mix the chilled purée with the
whipping cream, add a few drops
of green food coloring, if using,
and churn until thickened and
semi-frozen. Add the clotted cream
and continue to churn until thick
enough to scoop.

4 To serve, scoop the ice cream
into dishes or small plates,
decorate with fresh mint sprigs
and add a few small meringues
to each serving.

COOK'S TIP *Just a small amount of
clotted cream adds a surprising
richness to this simple ice cream. If the
gooseberry purée is very tart, you can
add extra sugar when mixing in the
whipping cream.*

Blackberry Ice Cream

There could scarcely be fewer ingredients in this delicious, vibrant ice cream. If you make the ice cream in a machine, don't be tempted to add the cream with the fruit, or the mixture will become buttery by the time it has been churned and is stiff enough to scoop.

SERVES FOUR TO SIX

INGREDIENTS

5 cups BLACKBERRIES, hulled, plus extra, to decorate

6 tablespoons SUGAR

2 tablespoons WATER

1¼ cups WHIPPING CREAM

CRISP DESSERT COOKIES, to serve

1 Put the blackberries in a pan and add the water and sugar. Cover and simmer for 5 minutes, until just soft.

2 Transfer the fruit to a sieve placed over a bowl and press it through the mesh, using a wooden spoon. Let cool, then chill.

3 BY HAND: Whip the cream until it is just thick but still soft enough to fall from a spoon, then mix it with the chilled fruit purée. Pour the mixture into a plastic or other freezerproof container and freeze for 2 hours.

USING AN ICE CREAM MAKER: Churn the chilled purée for 10–15 minutes, until it is thick, then gradually pour in the cream. There is no need to whip the cream first.

4 BY HAND: Mash the mixture with a fork, or beat it in a food processor to break up the ice crystals. Return it to the freezer for 4 more hours, beating the mixture again after 2 hours.

USING AN ICE CREAM MAKER: Continue to churn the ice cream until it is firm enough to scoop.

5 Scoop into dishes and decorate with extra blackberries. Serve with crisp dessert cookies.

VARIATION *Frozen blackberries can be used for the purée. You will need to increase the cooking time to 10 minutes and stir occasionally. Black currants can be used instead of blackberries. A combination of blackberries and peeled and sliced apples also works well.*

Banana and Toffee Ice Cream

The addition of sweetened condensed milk helps to bring out the natural flavor of the bananas and, surprisingly, the ice cream is not excessively sweet.

SERVES FOUR TO SIX

INGREDIENTS

3 RIPE BANANAS

juice of 1 LEMON

12½-ounce can SWEETENED CONDENSED MILK

⅔ cup WHIPPING CREAM

5 ounces TOFFEE

chopped TOFFEE, to decorate

1 Process the bananas into a purée in a food processor or blender, then add the lemon juice and process briefly to mix. Scrape the purée into a plastic or other freezerproof container.

2 Pour in the condensed milk, stirring with a metal spoon, then add the cream. Mix well, cover and freeze for 4 hours or until thick.

3 Chop the toffee finely, using a sharp knife. If this proves difficult, put it in a double plastic bag and hit with a rolling pin.

4 Beat the semi-frozen ice cream with a fork or electric mixer to break up the ice crystals, then stir in the toffee. Return the ice cream to the freezer for 3–5 hours or until firm. Scoop onto a plate or into a bowl and decorate with chopped toffee. Serve immediately.

COOK'S TIP *Because of the consistency of the sweetened condensed milk, this ice cream takes a long time to freeze and is best made by hand rather than by machine. To reduce the initial freezing time, start chilling the mixture in a stainless steel roasting pan, transferring to a plastic container only after adding the toffee. If you are making this ice cream for small children, you may prefer to leave the toffee out or use chopped chocolate instead.*

Apricot and Amaretti Ice Cream

Prolong the very short season of fresh apricots by transforming them into this superb ice cream with crushed amaretti cookies and whipped cream.

SERVES FOUR TO SIX

INGREDIENTS

1¼ pounds FRESH APRICOTS, halved and pitted

juice of 1 ORANGE

¼ cup SUGAR

1¼ cups WHIPPING CREAM

2 ounces AMARETTI COOKIES

1 Put the apricots, orange juice and sugar in a saucepan. Cover and simmer for 5 minutes, until the fruit is tender. Let cool.

2 Lift out one third of the fruit and set it aside on a plate. Transfer the remaining contents of the pan to a food processor or blender and process into a smooth purée.

3 BY HAND: Whip the cream until it is just thick but still soft enough to fall from a spoon. Gradually add the fruit purée, folding it into the mixture. Pour into a plastic or other freezerproof container and freeze for 4 hours, beating once with a fork, electric mixer or in a food processor.

USING AN ICE CREAM MAKER: Churn the apricot purée until it is slushy, then gradually add the cream. Continue to churn until the ice cream is thick, but not firm enough to scoop.

4 BY HAND: Beat for a second time. Crumble in the amaretti cookies.

USING AN ICE CREAM MAKER: Scrape the ice cream into a container. Crumble in the amaretti cookies.

5 Add the reserved apricots and gently fold these ingredients into the ice cream. Freeze for 2–3 hours or until firm enough to scoop.

COOK'S TIP *Chill the fruit purée if you have time; this will speed up the churning or freezing process. If you have some amaretto liqueur, fold in 3 tablespoons with the cookies.*

Peach and Cardamom Frozen Yogurt

SERVES FOUR

INGREDIENTS

8 CARDAMOM PODS

6 PEACHES,
total weight about 1¼ pounds,
halved, and pitted

6 tablespoons SUGAR

2 tablespoons WATER

scant 1 cup
PLAIN, ORGANIC YOGURT

The velvety texture of this smooth peach ice cream spiced with cardamom suggests that it is made with cream, but the secret ingredient is actually yogurt—great for those watching their waistline.

1 Put the cardamom pods on a board and crush them with the bottom of a ramekin, or in a mortar and pestle.

2 Chop the peaches roughly and put them in a saucepan. Add the crushed cardamom pods, with their black seeds, and the sugar and water. Cover and simmer for 10 minutes or until the fruit is tender. Let cool.

3 Transfer the peach mixture to a food processor or blender, process until smooth, then press through a sieve placed over a bowl.

4 BY HAND: Add the yogurt to the sieved purée and combine in the bowl.

5 BY HAND: Pour into a plastic container and freeze for 5–6 hours, until firm, beating once or twice with a fork, electric beater or in a processor to break up the ice crystals.

USING AN ICE CREAM MAKER: Churn the purée until thick, then scrape it into a plastic or other container. Stir in the yogurt and freeze until firm enough to hold a scoop shape.

6 Scoop the ice cream onto a large platter, and serve immediately.

COOK'S TIP *Use plain, organic yogurt for its extra mild taste, which will not overwhelm the delicate taste of the peaches. Use a melon baller to make miniature scoops in individual dishes.*

Mango and Passion Fruit Gelato

Fresh and fruity, this tropical ice cream has a delicate perfume. Passion fruit tend to vary in size. If you can locate the large ones, four will be plenty for this dish.

2 Turn the slices inside out so that the pieces of mango stand proud of the skin, then scoop them into a food processor or blender, using a spoon. Finally, cut the remaining flesh off of the pits and add it to the rest.

3 Process the mango flesh until smooth, then add the grated lime zest, lime juice and sugar and process briefly.

4 **BY HAND:** Whip the cream until it is just thick but will still fall from a spoon. Fold in the puréed mango and lime mixture, then pour into a plastic or other freezerproof container. Freeze for 4 hours, until semi-frozen.

USING AN ICE CREAM MAKER: Churn the fruit mixture for 10–15 minutes, then add the cream and continue to churn until the mixture is thick but still too soft to scoop. Scrape it into a plastic container.

5 Cut the passion fruit in half and scoop the seeds and pulp into the ice cream mixture, mix well and freeze for 2 hours, until firm enough to scoop.

SERVES FOUR

INGREDIENTS

4 LARGE MANGOES

grated zest and juice of 1 LIME

¼ cup SUGAR

1¼ cups WHIPPING CREAM

4–6 PASSION FRUIT

1 Cut a thick slice from either side of the pit on each unpeeled mango. Using a sharp knife, make criss-cross cuts in the mango flesh, cutting down as far as the skin.

Pineapple Ice Cream

Look for pineapples that are labeled "extra sweet." This variety has bright sunflower-yellow flesh that is naturally sweet and juicy. It is ideal for making the most wonderful ice cream.

SERVES FOUR TO SIX

INGREDIENTS

2 EXTRA-SWEET PINEAPPLES

1¼ cups WHIPPING CREAM

¼ cup SUGAR

 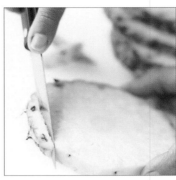

1 Slice one pineapple in half through the leafy top, then scoop out the flesh from both halves, keeping the shells intact. Stand them upside down to drain, wrap in plastic wrap and chill until needed.

2 Trim the top off the remaining pineapple, cut the flesh into slices, then cut off the skin and any "eyes." Remove the core from each slice, then finely chop the flesh from both pineapples.

3 Purée 11 ounces of the pineapple in a food processor or blender. Set aside the remaining chopped pineapple.

4 **BY HAND:** Whip the cream until it is just thick but still falls from a spoon. Fold in the purée and sugar, then pour into a plastic or other freezerproof container. Freeze for 6 hours, beating twice with a fork, electric mixer or in a food processor.

USING AN ICE CREAM MAKER: Churn the pineapple purée with the sugar for 15–20 minutes. Mix in the cream and churn until thick but still too soft to scoop.

5 **BY HAND:** Fold in 1½ cups of the chopped pineapple and freeze for 2–3 hours.

USING AN ICE CREAM MAKER: Add the pineapple to the ice cream maker and continue to churn the ice cream until it is stiff enough to serve in scoops.

6 Serve the ice cream in scoops in the pineapple shells. Pass any remaining pineapple separately.

VARIATION *This ice cream is also delicious mixed with meringues: crumble four meringue nests into the ice cream mixture when adding the finely chopped pineapple.*

Apricot Parfait

Creamy, delicately flavored French-style ice cream conceals a hidden layer of poached apricots. If you don't have time to make the caramel, top each serving with a spoonful of extra thick heavy cream and some thin strips of extra apricot.

SERVES SIX

INGREDIENTS

scant 1 cup DRIED APRICOTS

1¼ cups APPLE JUICE

6 tablespoons
LIGHT BROWN SUGAR

4 EGG YOLKS

generous ½ cup SUGAR

½ cup WATER

⅔ cup WHIPPING CREAM

grated zest and juice of ½ LEMON

4 Chop these apricots roughly and divide them among six freezerproof ramekins. Purée the remaining apricots and juice until smooth.

5 Whisk the egg yolks in a large, heatproof bowl until frothy. Put the sugar and water in a pan, heat gently until the sugar has dissolved, then boil for 4–5 minutes, until the syrup registers 239°F on a candy thermometer. Alternatively, test by dropping a little of the syrup into a cup of cold water. Pour out the water. The syrup should mold into a soft ball.

6 Quickly whisk the hot syrup into the egg yolks. Put the bowl over a saucepan of simmering water and whisk the mixture until it is thick.

7 Lift the bowl off the pan and continue whisking the mixture until it is cool and the whisk leaves a trail when lifted.

8 Whip the cream lightly, fold it into the yolk mixture, then gently fold in the apricot purée, with the lemon zest and juice.

9 Pour the parfait mixture into the six ramekins and freeze for 4 hours, until firm. When ready to serve, roughly break the caramelized sugar into pieces and use to decorate the parfaits.

1 Put the apricots in a saucepan. Pour in the apple juice and soak for 3–4 hours. Meanwhile, line a baking sheet with aluminum foil. Using an inverted ramekin as a guide, draw six circles on the foil. Brush with a little oil.

2 Preheat the broiler to its lowest setting. Sprinkle the brown sugar into the marked circles. Place under the grill, on its lowest shelf setting and leave for 3–4 minutes, until the sugar has dissolved and caramelized. Let cool and harden.

3 Simmer the soaked apricots for 10 minutes until they are soft and plump. Let cool, then lift out nine apricots with a slotted spoon.

Rum Raisin Ice Cream

An old favorite. For children, this ice cream always seems so much more sophisticated than mere vanilla.

The longer you can let the raisins soak in the rum,

the stronger the flavor will be.

SERVES FOUR TO SIX

INGREDIENTS

scant 1 cup
LARGE RAISINS

¼ cup DARK RUM

4 EGG YOLKS

6 tablespoons LIGHT
BROWN SUGAR

1 teaspoon CORNSTARCH

1¼ cups LOW-FAT MILK

1¼ cups WHIPPING CREAM

COOKIES or
ICE CREAM CONES, to serve

4 BY HAND: Whip the cream until it is just thick but still falls from a spoon. Fold it into the custard and pour the mixture into a plastic or other freezerproof container. Freeze for 4 hours, beating once with a fork, electric mixer or in a food processor. Then beat again.

USING AN ICE CREAM MAKER: Pour the cream into the custard, then churn until thick. Transfer to a plastic container.

1 Put the raisins in a bowl, add the rum and mix well. Cover and let soak for 3–4 hours or overnight if possible.

2 Whisk the egg yolks, brown sugar and cornstarch in a large bowl until the mixture is thick and foamy. Pour the milk into a heavy-based saucepan, and bring it to just below the boiling point.

3 Gradually whisk the milk into the eggs, then pour the mixture back into the pan. Cook over low heat, stirring constantly, until the custard thickens and is smooth. Take off the heat and let cool.

5 Fold the soaked raisins into the ice cream, cover and freeze for 2–3 hours or until firm enough to scoop. Serve in bowls or tall glasses with cookies, or serve simply in ice cream cones.

COOK'S TIP *If you scoop it into cones, the ice cream will serve 6–8 people. If you don't have any dark rum, white rum, brandy or even whiskey can be used instead.*

Rhubarb and Ginger Ice Cream

A fruit so highly favored by Queen Victoria; two varieties of rhubarb were grown and named after her and her consort Prince Albert. The classic combination of gently poached rhubarb and chopped ginger is brought up to date by blending it with mascarpone to make this pretty blush-pink ice cream.

SERVES FOUR TO SIX

INGREDIENTS

5 pieces of STEM GINGER

1 pound trimmed RHUBARB, sliced

½ cup SUGAR

2 tablespoons WATER

⅔ cup MASCARPONE

⅔ cup WHIPPING CREAM

WAFER CUPS, to serve (optional)

VARIATION *If the rhubarb purée is rather pale, add a few drops of pink coloring when mixing in the cream.*

1 Using a sharp knife, roughly chop the stem ginger and set it aside. Put the rhubarb slices into a saucepan and add the sugar and water. Cover and simmer for 5 minutes, until the rhubarb is just tender and still bright pink.

2 Transfer the mixture to a food processor or blender, process until smooth, then let cool. Chill if time permits.

3 BY HAND: Combine the mascarpone, cream and ginger with the rhubarb purée.

USING AN ICE CREAM MAKER: Churn the rhubarb purée for 15–20 minutes, until it is thick.

4 BY HAND: Pour the mixture into a plastic or other freezerproof container and freeze for 6 hours or until firm, beating once or twice during the freezing time to break up the ice crystals.

USING AN ICE CREAM MAKER: Put the mascarpone into a bowl, soften it with a wooden spoon, then gradually beat in the cream. Add the chopped ginger, then transfer to the ice cream maker and churn until the ice cream is firm. Serve as scoops in bowls or wafer baskets.

Nougat Ice Cream

Taking its inspiration from the delicious candy served in France as one of the 13 traditional Christmas desserts, this is a superb ice cream, especially when served with chilled liqueurs as ice cream petits fours.

SERVES SIX TO EIGHT

INGREDIENTS

½ cup HAZELNUTS

½ cup PISTACHIOS

⅓ cup CANDIED PEEL, in large pieces

6–8 sheets RICE PAPER

3 EGG WHITES

1¼ cups CONFECTIONERS' SUGAR, sifted

1¼ cups HEAVY CREAM

2 teaspoons ORANGE FLOWER WATER

4 Take off the heat and continue whisking until soft peaks form. In a separate bowl, whip the cream and orange flower water lightly, then fold in the meringue.

5 Spoon half the meringue mixture into the lined cake pan, easing it into the corners.

6 Sprinkle the meringue with half the nuts and candied peel. Cover with the remaining meringue mixture.

7 Sprinkle with the remaining nuts and fruit. Cover with two more sheets of rice paper and freeze for at least 6 hours or overnight, until completely firm.

8 Carefully turn the ice cream out of the pan and peel off the plastic wrap. If the bottom of the ice cream is soft, cover it with the remaining two sheets of rice paper, pressing it onto the ice cream so that it sticks. Cut into small squares or triangles, arrange on individual plates and serve.

VARIATION *Use toasted blanched almonds instead of pistachios if you prefer. The meringue can be flavored with rose water or grated lemon zest instead of orange flower water.*

1 Spread out the hazelnuts on a baking sheet and brown them lightly under a hot broiler. Mix them with the pistachios and chop all the nuts roughly. Slice the candied peel thinly, then cut the slices into bite-size slivers.

2 Line the bottom and sides of an 11 x 7 x 1½-inch cake pan with plastic wrap, then with four of the pieces of rice paper, folding the paper into the corners and overlapping the sheets slightly.

3 Put the egg whites and confectioners' sugar into a large, heatproof bowl. Place it over a saucepan of simmering water. Whisk for 5 minutes or until the meringue is very thick.

Maple and Pecan Ice Cream

This all-American ice cream is even more delicious when it is served with extra maple syrup and topped with whole pecans.

SERVES FOUR TO SIX

INGREDIENTS

1 cup PECANS

4 EGG YOLKS

¼ cup SUGAR

1 teaspoon CORNSTARCH

1¼ cups LOW-FAT MILK

¼ cup MAPLE SYRUP

1¼ cups WHIPPING CREAM

extra MAPLE SYRUP AND PECANS, to serve

1 Cut the pecans in half lengthwise, spread them out on a baking sheet and broil them under a moderate heat for 2–3 minutes, until lightly browned. Remove from heat and let cool.

2 Place the egg yolks, sugar and cornstarch into a bowl and whisk until thick and foamy. Pour the milk into a heavy-based saucepan, bring to a boil, then gradually whisk it into the yolk mixture.

3 Return the mixture to the pan and cook over low heat, stirring constantly, until the custard thickens and is smooth.

4 Pour the custard back into the bowl, and stir in the maple syrup. Let cool, then chill.

5 BY HAND: Whip the cream until it is thick but still falls from a spoon. Fold it into the custard and pour into a plastic or other freezerproof container. Freeze for 4 hours, beating once with a fork, electric mixer or in a food processor to break up the ice crystals. After this time, beat it again.

USING AN ICE CREAM MAKER: Stir the cream into the custard, then churn the mixture until thick. Scrape into a plastic container.

6 Fold in the nuts. Freeze for 2–3 hours, until firm enough to scoop into dishes. Pour extra maple syrup on each portion and top with extra pecans.

COOK'S TIP *Avoid "maple-flavored" syrup; the flavor is harsher and tends to taste synthetic. Look for "pure maple syrup" on the label.*

Rocky Road Ice Cream

This classic ice cream is a mouthwatering combination of roughly crushed praline, rich vanilla custard and whipping cream.

SERVES FOUR TO SIX

INGREDIENTS

4 EGG YOLKS

1 teaspoon CORNSTARCH

generous 1 cup SUGAR

1¼ cups LOW-FAT MILK

2 teaspoons VANILLA EXTRACT

OIL, for greasing

½ cup MACADAMIA NUTS

½ cup HAZELNUTS

½ cup SLICED ALMONDS

¼ cup WATER

1¼ cups WHIPPING CREAM

1 Put the egg yolks in a bowl and stir in the cornstarch, with 6 tablespoons of the sugar. Whisk until the mixture has turned thick and foamy. Pour the milk into a heavy saucepan, bring it to a boil, then gradually whisk it into the yolk mixture in the bowl.

2 Return the mixture to the pan. Cook over low heat, stirring constantly until the custard thickens and is smooth. Pour it back into the bowl and stir in the vanilla. Let cool, then chill.

3 Grease a large baking sheet with oil. Put the remaining sugar in a large, heavy frying pan, sprinkle the nuts on top and pour in the water. Heat gently, without stirring, until the sugar has dissolved completely, then boil the syrup for 3–5 minutes, until it is just beginning to turn golden.

4 Quickly pour the nut mixture onto the oiled baking sheet and let cool and harden.

5 BY HAND: Whip the cream until it is thick but still falls from a spoon. Fold it into the custard and pour into a plastic or other freezerproof container. Freeze for 4 hours, beating once with a fork, electric mixer or in a food processor, and then beat it again.

USING AN ICE CREAM MAKER: Stir the cream into the custard and churn until stiff but too soft to scoop. Scrape into a container.

6 Smash the praline with a rolling pin to break off about a third. Reserve this for the decoration. Put the rest of the praline into a strong plastic bag and hit it several times with a rolling pin until it breaks into bite-size pieces.

7 Fold the crushed praline into the ice cream and freeze it for 2–3 hours, until firm. Scoop into glasses and decorate with the reserved praline, broken into large pieces.

COOK'S TIP *If you can't locate macadamia nuts, use extra hazelnuts. If the nuts fail to brown evenly when you are making the praline in the frying pan, don't stir the syrup. Instead, tilt the pan first one way, then the other.*

Cashew and Orange Flower Ice Cream

Delicately perfumed with orange flower water and a little orange zest, this nutty, lightly sweetened ice cream evokes images of desserts that are popular in the Middle East.

SERVES FOUR TO SIX

INGREDIENTS

4 EGG YOLKS

6 tablespoons SUGAR

1 teaspoon CORNSTARCH

1¼ cups LOW-FAT MILK

1¼ cups WHIPPING CREAM

1¼ cups CASHEWS, finely chopped

1 tablespoon ORANGE FLOWER WATER

grated zest of ½ ORANGE, plus CURLS OF THINLY PARED ORANGE ZEST, to decorate

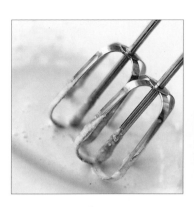

1 Whisk the egg yolks, sugar and cornstarch in a bowl until thick and foamy. Pour the milk into a heavy saucepan, gently bring it to a boil, then gradually whisk it into the egg yolk mixture.

2 Return to the pan and cook over low heat, stirring constantly until smooth. Pour back into the bowl. Cool, then chill.

3 Heat the cream in a saucepan. When it boils, stir in the chopped cashews. Let cool.

4 Stir the orange flower water and grated orange zest into the chilled custard. Process the nut cream in a food processor or blender until it forms a fine paste, then stir it into the custard mixture.

5 BY HAND: Pour the mixture into a plastic or other freezerproof container and freeze for 6 hours, beating twice with a fork or whisk with an electric mixer to break up the ice crystals.

USING AN ICE CREAM MAKER: Churn the mixture until it is firm enough to scoop.

6 To serve, scoop the ice cream into dishes and decorate each portion with an orange zest curl.

COOK'S TIP *For a more intense flavor, roast the cashews before chopping them. Thinly pare the orange zest, then wrap each strip in turn around a toothpick and leave it for a minute or two.*

Pistachio Ice Cream

This favorite owes its enduring popularity to its delicate pale green color and distinctive yet subtle flavor. Buy the pistachios as you need them, as they quickly get stale if left in the cupboard.

SERVES FOUR TO SIX

INGREDIENTS

4 EGG YOLKS

6 tablespoons SUGAR

1 teaspoon CORNSTARCH

1¼ cups LOW-FAT MILK

1 cup PISTACHIOS, plus a few extra, to decorate

1¼ cups WHIPPING CREAM

a little GREEN FOOD COLORING

CHOCOLATE DIPPED WAFFLE CONES, to serve (optional)

1 Place the egg yolks, sugar and cornstarch in a bowl and whisk until the mixture is thick and foamy.

2 Pour the milk into a heavy saucepan, gently bring it to a boil, then gradually whisk it into the egg yolk mixture.

3 Return the mixture to the saucepan and cook it over low heat, stirring constantly, until the custard thickens and is smooth. Pour it back into the bowl, set aside to cool, then chill in the refrigerator until needed.

4 Shell the pistachios and put them in a food processor or blender. Add 2 tablespoons of the cream and grind the mixture to a coarse paste.

5 Pour the rest of the cream into a small saucepan. Bring it to a boil, stir in the coarsely ground pistachios, then let cool.

6 Mix the chilled custard and pistachio cream together and tint the mixture delicately with a few drops of food coloring.

7 BY HAND: Pour the tinted custard and pistachio mixture into a plastic or other freezerproof container. Freeze for 6 hours, beating once or twice with a fork or in an electric mixer to break up the ice crystals. Scoop the ice cream into cones or dishes to serve and sprinkle each portion with a few extra pistachios.

USING AN ICE CREAM MAKER: Churn the mixture until firm enough to scoop. Serve in cones or dishes, sprinkled with extra pistachios.

COOK'S TIP *If you make the ice cream by hand, it is important not to beat the frozen mixture in a food processor or the pistachios will become too finely ground. Bought waffle cones can be decorated by dipping them in melted chocolate and sprinkling them with extra chopped pistachios.*

cream-free & low-fat frozen desser

S Whether for dietary reasons or simply
by choice, many people do not like to
indulge in rich traditional ice creams.
On the following pages are some
intensely flavored desserts using
low-fat and dairy-free ingredients. With
recipes that range from a smooth
creamy coconut ice cream
to a refreshing orange
frozen yogurt, there is a frozen dessert
to suit everyone.

Kulfi

This famous Indian ice cream is traditionally made by slowly boiling milk until it has reduced to about one third of the original amount. Although you can save time by using condensed milk, nothing beats this delicious ice cream when made in the authentic manner.

SERVES FOUR

INGREDIENTS

6¼ cups WHOLE MILK

3 CARDAMOM PODS

2 tablespoons SUGAR

½ cup PISTACHIOS, skinned, plus a few to decorate

a few PINK ROSE PETALS, to decorate

1 Pour the milk into a large, heavy saucepan. Bring to a boil, lower the heat and simmer gently for 1 hour, stirring occasionally.

2 Put the cardamom pods in a mortar and crush them with a pestle. Add the pods and the seeds to the milk and continue to simmer for 1–1½ hours or until the milk has reduced to about 2 cups.

3 Strain the milk into a pitcher, stir in the sugar and let cool.

4 Grind half the pistachios to a smooth powder in a blender, nut grinder or cleaned coffee grinder. Cut the remaining pistachios into thin slivers and set them aside for decoration. Stir the ground nuts into the milk mixture.

5 Pour the milk and pistachio mixture into four kulfi molds. Freeze overnight until firm.

6 To unmold the kulfi, half fill a plastic container or bowl with very hot water, stand the molds in the water and count to ten. Immediately lift out the moulds and invert them on a baking sheet.

7 Transfer the ice creams to a platter or individual plates. To decorate, sprinkle sliced pistachios on the ice creams and then the rose petals. Serve immediately.

COOK'S TIP *Stay in the kitchen while the milk is simmering, so that you can control the heat to keep the milk gently bubbling without boiling over. If you don't have any kulfi molds, use popsicle molds without the tops or even disposable plastic cups. If the kulfi won't turn out, dip a cloth in very hot water, wring it out and place it on the tops of the molds to soften the ice cream, or plunge the molds back into hot water for a few more seconds.*

Dondurma Kaymalki

This sweet, pure white ice cream comes from the Middle East, where it is traditionally thickened with sahlab and flavored with orange flower water and mastic, a resin used in chewing gum. As sahlab and mastic are both difficult to obtain in the West, cornstarch and condensed milk have been used instead.

SERVES FOUR TO SIX

INGREDIENTS

3 tablespoons CORNSTARCH

2½ cups WHOLE MILK

7½-ounce can SWEETENED
CONDENSED MILK

1 tablespoon HONEY

2 teaspoons ORANGE
FLOWER WATER

a few JORDAN ALMONDS,
to serve

1 Put the cornstarch in a saucepan and mix into a smooth paste with a little of the milk. Stir in the remaining milk and the condensed milk and bring the mixture to a boil, stirring until it has thickened and is smooth. Pour the mixture into a bowl.

2 Stir in the honey and orange flower water. Cover with a plate to prevent the formation of a skin, let cool, then chill.

3 BY HAND: Pour the mixture into a plastic or other freezerproof container and freeze for 6–8 hours, beating twice with a fork, electric mixer or in a food processor to break up the ice crystals.

USING AN ICE CREAM MAKER: Churn until firm enough to scoop.

4 To serve, scoop into dishes and serve with a few Jordan almonds.

VARIATION *Rose water can be used instead of orange flower water. If you have made the ice cream by hand, remember to transfer it to the refrigerator about half an hour before you are ready to scoop.*

Date and Tofu Ice Cream

All you skeptics who claim to hate tofu, prepare to be converted by this creamy date and apple ice cream.

Generously spiced with cinnamon, it not only tastes good but is packed with soy protein,

contains no added sugar, is low in fat and free from all dairy products.

SERVES FOUR

INGREDIENTS

1½ cups PITTED DATES

2½ cups APPLE JUICE

1 teaspoon GROUND CINNAMON

10½-ounce package CHILLED TOFU, drained and cubed

⅔ cup UNSWEETENED SOY MILK

1 Put the dates in a saucepan. Pour in 1¼ cups of the apple juice and let soak for 2 hours. Simmer for 10 minutes, then let cool. Using a slotted spoon, lift out one-quarter of the dates, chop roughly and set aside.

2 Purée the remaining dates in a food processor or blender. Add the cinnamon and process with enough of the remaining apple juice to make a smooth paste.

3 Add the cubes of tofu, a few at a time, processing after each addition. Finally, add the remaining apple juice and the soy milk.

4 BY HAND: Pour the mixture into a plastic or other freezerproof container and freeze for 4 hours, beating once with a fork, electric mixer or in a food processor to break up the ice crystals. After this time, beat again with a fork to ensure a smooth texture.

USING AN ICE CREAM MAKER: Churn the mixture until very thick, but not thick enough to scoop. Scrape into a plastic container.

5 Stir in most of the chopped dates and freeze for 2–3 hours, until firm.

6 Scoop into dessert glasses and decorate with the remaining chopped dates.

COOK'S TIP *As tofu is a nondairy product it will not blend completely, so don't be concerned if the mixture contains tiny flecks of tofu.*

Coconut Ice Cream

Despite its creamy taste, this ice cream contains neither cream nor eggs and is very refreshing. Serve it with scoops of Red Berry Sorbet.

SERVES FOUR TO SIX

INGREDIENTS

⅔ cup WATER

½ cup SUGAR

2 LIMES

14-fluid-ounce can COCONUT MILK

TOASTED COCONUT SHAVINGS, to decorate (see Cook's Tip)

1 Put the water in a small saucepan. Add the sugar and bring to a boil, stirring constantly, until the sugar has all dissolved. Remove the pan from heat and let the syrup cool, then chill well.

2 Grate the limes finely, taking care to avoid the bitter pith. Squeeze them and pour the juice and zest into the pan of syrup. Add the coconut milk.

3 BY HAND: Pour the mixture into a plastic or other freezerproof container and freeze for 5–6 hours, until firm, beating twice with a fork, electric beater or in a food processor to break up the crystals. Scoop into dishes and decorate with toasted coconut shavings.

ICE CREAM MAKER: Churn the mixture until firm enough to scoop. Serve in dishes, decorated with the toasted coconut shavings.

COOK'S TIP *Use the flesh from a coconut to make a pretty decoration. Having rinsed the flesh with cold water, cut off thin slices using a swivel-bladed vegetable peeler. Toast the slices under a medium broiler until the coconut has curled and the edges have turned golden. Cool slightly, then sprinkle the shavings on the coconut ice cream.*

Banana Gelato

This mild, creamy banana ice cream is made with soy milk, making it good for children who are lactose intolerant or allergic to dairy products.

SERVES FOUR TO SIX

INGREDIENTS

½ cup SUGAR

⅔ cup WATER

1 LEMON

3 RIPE BANANAS

1¼ cups VANILLA-FLAVORED SOY MILK

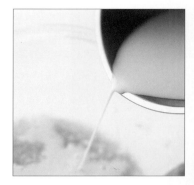

1 Put the sugar and water in a saucepan and bring to a boil, stirring until the sugar has dissolved. Set the syrup aside to cool.

2 Squeeze the lemon. Put the bananas in a bowl and mash with a fork. Slowly add the lemon juice.

3 BY HAND: Stir in the cooled sugar syrup and the vanilla-flavored soy dessert. Pour the mixture into a large plastic container and freeze for 6–7 hours, until firm, beating twice during that time with a fork, electric mixer or in a food processor to break up the ice crystals. Scoop into dishes and serve.

USING AN ICE CREAM MAKER: Stir in the cooled sugar syrup and the soy dessert. Churn the mixture until thick, then scrape it into a freezerproof container and freeze for 3–4 hours, until firm. Scoop into dishes and serve.

COOK'S TIP *This recipe makes 4 cups of gelato, so if you are using an ice cream maker with only a small capacity, it may be wise to churn the mixture in two batches. Check your manufacturer's handbook.*

Honeyed Goat's Milk Gelato

Goat's milk is more widely available than it used to be and is more easily tolerated by some individuals than cow's milk. It makes a surprisingly rich frozen dessert.

SERVES FOUR

INGREDIENTS

6 EGG YOLKS

¼ cup SUGAR

2 teaspoons CORNSTARCH

2½ cups GOAT'S MILK

¼ cup HONEY

POMEGRANATE SEEDS, to decorate

1 Whisk the egg yolks, sugar and cornstarch in a bowl until pale and thick. Pour the goat's milk into a heavy saucepan, bring it to a boil, and then gradually whisk it into the yolk mixture.

2 Return the custard mixture to the saucepan and cook over low heat, stirring constantly, until the custard thickens and is smooth. Pour it back into the clean bowl.

3 Stir the honey into the milk mixture. Let cool, then chill.

4 BY HAND: Pour the mixture into a plastic or other freezerproof container and freeze for 6 hours, until firm enough to scoop, beating twice with a fork, electric beater or in a food processor to break up the ice crystals.

USING AN ICE CREAM MAKER: Churn the chilled mixture until thick enough to scoop.

5 To serve, scoop into dessert glasses and decorate with a few pomegranate seeds.

COOK'S TIP *Make sure the spoon measures are level or the honey flavor will be too dominant.*

VARIATION *This ice cream is also delicious with a little ginger; stir in ¼ cup finely chopped stem ginger when the ice cream is partially frozen.*

Raspberry Sherbet

Traditional sherbets are made in much the same way as sorbets but with added milk. This modern low-fat version is made from raspberry purée blended with sugar syrup and virtually fat-free fromage frais, then flecked with crushed raspberries.

SERVES SIX

INGREDIENTS

¼ cup SUGAR

⅔ cup WATER

3½ cup RASPBERRIES, plus extra, to serve

generous 2 cups VIRTUALLY FAT-FREE FROMAGE FRAIS

1 Put the sugar and water in a small saucepan and bring to a boil, stirring until the sugar has dissolved. Pour into a pitcher and cool.

2 Put 2½ cups of the raspberries in a food processor or blender. Process into a purée, then press through a sieve placed over a large bowl to remove the seeds. Stir the sugar syrup into the raspberry purée and chill the mixture until it is very cold.

3 Add the fromage frais to the purée and whisk until smooth.

4 BY HAND: Pour the mixture into a plastic or other freezerproof container and freeze for 4 hours, beating once with a fork, electric beater or in a food processor to break up the ice crystals. After this time, beat it again.

USING AN ICE CREAM MAKER: Churn the mixture until it is thick but too soft to scoop. Scrape into a freezerproof container.

5 Crush the remaining raspberries between your fingers and add them to the partially frozen ice cream. Mix lightly, then freeze for 2–3 hours, until firm. Scoop the ice cream into dishes and serve with extra raspberries.

COOK'S TIP *If you intend to make this in an ice cream maker, check your handbook before you begin churning as this recipes makes 3¾ cups of mixture. If this is too much for your machine, make it in two batches or by hand.*

Orange Frozen Yogurt

Serve this refreshing low-fat frozen yogurt simply, in cones, or scoop it into meringue baskets and decorate it with blueberries and mint for a more sophisticated treat.

3 BY HAND: Spoon the yogurt into a bowl, gradually add the chilled orange juice and syrup mixture and mix well. Pour the mixture into a plastic container. Freeze for 6 hours or until firm, beating twice with a fork or in a food processor to break up the ice crystals.

USING AN ICE CREAM MAKER: Churn the orange mixture until thick, but not thick enough to scoop. Switch off the machine, remove the paddle, if necessary, add the yogurt and mix well. Replace the paddle and continue to churn the ice cream for 15–20 minutes, until thick. Scrape it into a plastic or other freezerproof container and freeze until firm.

4 Scoop the frozen yogurt into cones or meringue nests and decorate with blueberries and mint.

COOK'S TIP *Meringue nests are not difficult to make, but if you do not have the time, bought ones are a perfectly acceptable alternative.*

SERVES SIX

INGREDIENTS

6 tablespoons WATER

2 teaspoons POWDERED GELATIN

½ cup SUGAR

1 cup "FRESHLY SQUEEZED" ORANGE JUICE from a carton or bottle

generous 2 cups PLAIN, ORGANIC YOGURT

CONES or MERINGUE NESTS, BLUEBERRIES and FRESH MINT SPRIGS, to serve

1 Put 2 tablespoons of the water in a small bowl and sprinkle the powdered gelatin on top. Set aside until spongy. Meanwhile, put the sugar in a small saucepan, add the remaining water and heat through gently until the sugar has dissolved completely.

2 Take off the heat, add the gelatin and stir until dissolved. Cool, stir in the orange juice and chill for 15–30 minutes.

bombes & terrines

Layered, marbled or speckled with fruit and nuts, bombes and terrines make stunning frozen desserts that reveal a feast of color and texture when cut into. Uncomplicated to assemble, but requiring plenty of freezing time, they're best made several days in advance, ready and waiting for that special occasion.

Cassata

Cassata is an irresistible Italian ice cream, usually made of three layers and frozen in a bombe mold.

This version, layered in a terrine, combines the complementary flavors of pistachio,

vanilla and tutti frutti.

SERVES EIGHT

INGREDIENTS

6 EGG YOLKS

generous 1 cup SUGAR

1 tablespoon CORNSTARCH

2½ cups MILK

2½ cups HEAVY CREAM

¼ cup PISTACHIOS

½ teaspoon ALMOND EXTRACT

dash each of GREEN and RED
FOOD COLORING

¼ cup CANDIED PEEL,
finely chopped

¼ cup CANDIED CHERRIES,
finely chopped

1 teaspoon VANILLA EXTRACT

1 Whisk the egg yolks, sugar, cornstarch and a little of the milk in a bowl until pale and creamy. Bring the remaining milk and the cream to a boil in a large, heavy saucepan.

2 Immediately pour into the egg yolk mixture in a steady stream, whisking well. Pour back into the saucepan and cook over very low heat, stirring until thickened. Do not let the mixture boil. Remove from heat and divide into three equal amounts. Cover and let cool.

3 Put the pistachios in a bowl. Cover with boiling water and let sit for 1 minute. Drain the nuts and spread between several thicknesses of paper towels. Rub between the paper to loosen the skins.

4 Pick out the nuts, rubbing off any remaining skins. Roughly chop and add to one bowl with the almond extract and a drop of green food coloring.

5 Stir the candied peel, and cherries and a drop of red food coloring into the second bowl. Stir the vanilla into the third. Line a dampened 2 pound terrine or loaf pan with nonstick baking parchment.

6 BY HAND: Pour the mixtures into 3 separate containers and freeze them until thickened, beating twice with a fork or a food processor.

Put the frozen pistachio ice cream into the prepared pan, then the vanilla and the tutti frutti. Freeze overnight until firm.

USING AN ICE CREAM MAKER:
Churn the pistachio ice cream in an ice cream maker and spread into the prepared pan. Level the surface. Place in the freezer while preparing the remaining ice creams. Follow the same procedure with the vanilla and then the tutti frutti ice cream. Freeze overnight until firm.

7 To serve, dip the terrine or pan in very hot water for 2–3 seconds, then place a long serving plate upside down on top of it. Holding together, turn them over. Lift up the container. Peel off the lining paper. Serve the cassata in slices.

Coconut Mousse

Unlike most frozen desserts, this is neither cream nor custard based. Instead, creamed coconut is folded into a very light Italian-style meringue, producing a deliciously airy, mousse-like texture. Cream is added, but it does not dominate.

SERVES SIX

INGREDIENTS

4 EGG WHITES

¾ cup SUGAR

1½ cups FRESHLY GRATED COCONUT, grated

1¼ cups HEAVY CREAM

1 tablespoon LEMON JUICE

TOASTED COCONUT SHAVINGS, to decorate

For the sauce

6 PASSION FRUIT

½ teaspoon CORNSTARCH

⅔ cup FRESH ORANGE JUICE

1 tablespoon SUGAR

3 tablespoons KIRSCH

1 Dampen six ⅔-cup metal molds, then line them with plastic wrap. Put the egg whites and sugar in a large, heatproof bowl over a pan of gently simmering water. Beat with an electric beater until the meringue mixture is very thick.

2 Remove from heat and continue beating for about 2 minutes, until the beater leaves a thick trail when lifted.

3 Fold in the grated coconut. In a separate bowl, whip the cream until it forms soft peaks. Using a large metal spoon, fold the cream and lemon juice into the meringue. Spoon into the prepared molds.

4 To level, draw a knife across the top of each mold. Cover with plastic wrap and freeze for at least 4 hours or overnight.

5 Make the sauce. Cut each passion fruit in half and scoop the seeds and pulp into a small saucepan. Blend the cornstarch with a little of the orange juice in a cup. Stir into the passion fruit mixture, with the remaining orange juice and the sugar. Heat gently, stirring constantly, until the mixture thickens slightly. Let cool, then stir in the kirsch.

6 To serve, dip each mold into very hot water for 1 second. Invert the molds on dessert plates, lift off the molds and peel off the plastic wrap. Spoon on a little sauce, decorate with coconut shavings and serve.

COOK'S TIP *Lightly toasting the coconut shavings greatly increases the flavor and works well with the sweetness of the meringue. Spread the coconut shavings onto a lined metal baking sheet and place under a hot broiler for just a few minutes. Don't leave them for any longer, as they will burn very easily.*

Tropical Fruit and Ginger Bombes

A very simple frozen dessert, shaped like miniature Christmas puddings in squares of muslin. Serve with fresh tropical fruit, passion fruit sauce, or compote.

SERVES SIX

INGREDIENTS

½ cup DRIED MANGO, finely chopped

½ cup DRIED PAPAYA, finely chopped

½ cup DRIED PINEAPPLE, finely chopped

2 tablespoons finely chopped CANDIED GINGER, or STEM GINGER, chopped

¼ cup COINTREAU or other ORANGE-FLAVORED LIQUEUR

generous 1 cup RICOTTA CHEESE

generous 1 cup MASCARPONE CHEESE

3 tablespoons HEAVY CREAM

1 tablespoon CONFECTIONERS' SUGAR

1 Cut six 9-inch squares of muslin and set them aside. Mix the dried fruit and ginger in a bowl. Add the liqueur and leave to stand for 1–2 hours. Lightly mix the ricotta and mascarpone in a bowl until evenly mixed but not runny.

2 Add the steeped fruits and ginger, with any remaining liqueur, to the ricotta mixture, then gently stir in the cream and confectioners' sugar until combined. Spoon one-sixth of the mixture into the center of each muslin square.

3 Bring the edges of the muslin up around one portion of filling squeezing fairly tightly so the mixture forms a ball. Secure with string. Make five more bombes in the same way. Freeze for at least 3 hours.

4 To serve, place the bombes on dessert plates and remove the muslin if liked.

Raspberry Cranachan Bombe

SERVES EIGHT

INGREDIENTS

3 cups RASPBERRY SORBET

2½ cups HEAVY CREAM

¼ cup HONEY

5 tablespoons WHISKEY

½ cup OATS, toasted

1 Soften the sorbet by letting it stand at room temperature for about 20 minutes. Meanwhile, chill a 6¼-cup bombe mold or pudding mold.

2 Using a large spoon, evenly pack the sorbet onto the bottom and up the sides of the mold. If this proves difficult and the sorbet starts to slide around, freeze it for about 10 minutes before continuing. Return the bombe mold to the freezer.

The flavors in this recipe stem from a traditional Scottish dessert made of whiskey and honey-flavored cream with toasted oats and raspberries.

3 Whip the cream with the honey and whiskey until it forms soft peaks, then fold in the oats. Spoon into the sorbet-lined mold and level the surface. Cover with plastic wrap and freeze overnight.

4 To serve, loosen the edges of the mold with a knife. Dip the mold very briefly in hot water then invert onto a serving plate. Serve in wedges.

VARIATION *Cointreau or another orange-flavored liqueur could be used instead of whiskey. If preferred, ¾ cup finely chopped and toasted hazelnuts could be substituted for the oats.*

Layered Chocolate and Chestnut Bombes

These delicious little bombes look especially delicious if they are served on plates that have been drizzled with melted semi-sweet chocolate, but if you're short on time you can create a very decorative effect simply by dusting the plates with cocoa powder or sprinkling grated chocolate on top .

SERVES SIX

INGREDIENTS

3 EGG YOLKS

6 tablespoons SUGAR

2 teaspoons CORNSTARCH

1¼ cups MILK

4 ounces PLAIN CHOCOLATE, broken into pieces, plus 2 ounces, to decorate

½ cup SWEETENED CHESTNUT PURÉE

2 tablespoons BRANDY or COINTREAU

generous ½ cup MASCARPONE CHEESE

1 teaspoon VANILLA EXTRACT

scant 2 cups HEAVY CREAM

1 Whisk the egg yolks in a bowl with the sugar, cornstarch and a little of the milk. Bring the remaining milk to a boil in a heavy saucepan. Pour the milk onto the egg mixture, whisking well. Return to the pan and cook over very low heat, stirring, until thickened. Do not boil the custard or it may curdle. Divide the custard equally among three bowls.

2 Add 4 ounces of the chocolate to one bowl and let sit until melted, stirring frequently until smooth. If the chocolate fails to melt completely, and the bowl is suitable, microwave very briefly.

3 If the chestnut purée is firm, beat it until softened, then stir it into the second bowl, with the brandy or Cointreau. Add the mascarpone and the vanilla to the third bowl of custard. Cover each custard closely with a circle of waxed paper and let cool.

4 Whip the cream until it forms soft peaks. Fold a third of it into each of the cooled custard mixtures. Spoon the chestnut mixture into six ⅔-cup plain or fluted individual molds and level the surface.

5 Spoon the chocolate mixture onto the chestnut mixture in the molds and level the surface. Spoon the vanilla mixture onto the chocolate. Cover and freeze for 6 hours or overnight.

6 To serve, melt the chocolate for decoration in a heatproof bowl set over a pan of gently simmering water. Transfer to a paper piping bag and snip off the tip. Alternatively, use a piping bag fitted with a writing nozzle.

7 Scribble lines of the melted chocolate on the serving plates to decorate. Loosen the edge of each mold with a knife. Dip each mold very briefly in hot water, then invert onto a flat surface. Using a rounded knife, carefully transfer the molds to the serving plates. Let stand for 10 minutes at room temperature to let the ice cream soften before serving.

VARIATION *If you can't get sweetened chestnut purée, use the same amount of unsweetened purée and add an extra 2 tablespoons sugar.*

Caramel and Pecan Terrine

The combination of caramel and nuts in this dessert is really delicious. Take care that the syrup does not become too dark or the ice cream will taste bitter.

SERVES SIX

INGREDIENTS

generous ½ cup SUGAR

5 tablespoons WATER

scant 2 cups HEAVY CREAM

2 tablespoons CONFECTIONERS' SUGAR

¼ cup PECANS, toasted

1 Heat the sugar and water in a small, heavy saucepan until the sugar dissolves. Boil rapidly until the sugar has turned pale golden. Remove from heat and let stand until the syrup develops a rich brown color.

2 Pour 6 tablespoons of the cream onto the caramel. Heat to make a smooth sauce. Let cool.

3 Dampen a 1 pound loaf pan, then line the bottom and sides with plastic wrap. Whip another ⅔ cup of the cream with the confectioners' sugar until it forms soft peaks. Then whip the remaining cream in a separate bowl and stir in the caramel sauce and pecans.

4 Spoon a third of the caramel cream into the prepared pan and spread with half the plain whipped cream. Spread half of the remaining caramel cream on top, then top with the last of the plain cream. Finally add the remaining caramel cream and level the surface. Freeze for 6 hours.

5 To serve, dip the pan in very hot water for 2 seconds, invert onto a serving plate and peel off the plastic wrap. Serve sliced.

COOK'S TIP *Watch the caramel syrup closely after removing it from heat. If it starts to turn too dark, dip the bottom of the pan in cold water to stop the cooking process. If the syrup remains very pale, return the pan to the heat and cook the syrup for a little longer.*

Marzipan and Kumquat Terrine

Tangy poached kumquats make a perfect contrast to the sweet almond paste in this frozen terrine. Any leftover kumquats keep well in the refrigerator for a week, making a lovely topping for vanilla ice cream.

SERVES SIX

INGREDIENTS

3 cups KUMQUATS

generous ½ cup SUGAR

⅔ cup WATER

2 EGG YOLKS

2 teaspoons CORNSTARCH

1¼ cups WHOLE MILK

7 ounces GOLDEN MARZIPAN, grated

½ teaspoon ALMOND EXTRACT

1¼ cups WHIPPING CREAM

1 Cut the kumquats in half and scoop out the seeds with the tip of a knife. Heat the sugar and water gently in a heavy saucepan until the sugar dissolves. Add the kumquats and cook gently for about 10 minutes, until tender. Let the syrup cool.

2 . Whisk the egg yolks in a bowl with the cornstarch and 4 tablespoons of the syrup until smooth. In a heavy saucepan, bring the milk just to a boil, then gradually pour it onto the egg yolk mixture, whisking constantly.

3 Return to the pan and cook over low heat for 2 minutes, stirring constantly, until the custard has thickened. Do not let it boil or the custard may curdle. Transfer the custard to a bowl and stir in the marzipan and almond extract. Cover the surface closely with waxed paper to prevent the formation of a skin on the surface, and set aside until cool.

4 Line a small terrine or loaf pan with plastic wrap and set aside. Put a generous third of the kumquats into a food processor. Pour in another 4 tablespoons of the kumquat syrup and blend until smooth and pulpy.

5 BY HAND: Whip the cream until thickened and fold into the custard with the kumquat pulp. Pour into the lined pan and freeze overnight.

USING AN ICE CREAM MAKER: Stir the cream and pulp into the custard and churn until thick. Pour into the pan and freeze for 4 hours.

6 Transfer the pan to the refrigerator about 1 hour before serving to let it soften slightly. Invert onto a plate and remove the pan. Peel off the plastic wrap and serve the ice cream topped with the remaining kumquats.

Spicy Pumpkin and Orange Bombe

Pumpkin has a subtle flavor that is truly transformed with the addition of

citrus fruits and spices. Here, the delicious mixture is encased in syrupy sponge cake

and served with an orange and whole spice syrup.

SERVES EIGHT

INGREDIENTS

For the sponge cake

½ cup UNSALTED BUTTER, softened

½ cup SUGAR

1 cup SELF-RISING FLOUR

½ teaspoon BAKING POWDER

2 EGGS

For the ice cream

1 ORANGE

scant 1½ cups SUGAR

1¼ cups WATER

2 CINNAMON STICKS, halved

2 teaspoons WHOLE CLOVES

2 tablespoons ORANGE FLOWER WATER

14-ounce can UNSWEETENED PUMPKIN PURÉE

1¼ cups HEAVY CREAM

2 pieces STEM GINGER, grated

CONFECTIONERS' SUGAR, for dusting

1 Preheat the oven to 350°F. Grease and line a 1 pound loaf pan. Beat the softened butter, sugar, flour, baking powder and eggs in a bowl until creamy.

2 Scrape the mixture into the prepared pan, level the surface and bake for 30–35 minutes, until firm in the center. Let cool.

3 Make the ice cream. Pare thin strips of zest from the orange, scrape off any white pith, then cut the strips into very fine shreds. Squeeze the orange and set the juice aside. Heat the sugar and water in a small, heavy saucepan until the sugar dissolves. Bring to a boil and boil rapidly without stirring for 3 minutes.

4 Stir in the orange shreds, juice, cinnamon and cloves and heat gently for 5 minutes. Strain the syrup, reserving the orange shreds and spices. Measure 1¼ cups of the syrup and reserve. Return the spices to the remaining syrup and stir in the orange flower water. Pour into a pitcher and set aside to cool.

5 Beat the pumpkin purée with ¼ cup of the measured strained syrup until evenly combined. Stir in the cream and ginger. Cut the cake into ½-inch slices. Dampen a 6¼-cup pudding mold and line it with plastic wrap. Pour the remaining strained syrup into a shallow dish.

6 Dip the cake slices briefly in the syrup and use to line the prepared mold, placing the syrupy coated sides against the bowl. Trim the pieces to fit where necessary, so that the lining is even and any gaps are filled. Chill.

7 BY HAND: Pour the pumpkin mixture into a shallow container and freeze until firm. Scrape the ice cream into the sponge-lined mold, level the surface and freeze until firm, preferably overnight.

USING AN ICE CREAM MAKER: Churn the pumpkin mixture until very thick, then scrape it into the sponge-lined mold. Level the surface and freeze until firm, preferably overnight.

8 To serve, invert the ice cream onto a serving plate. Lift off the bowl and peel off the plastic wrap. Dust with the confectioners' sugar and serve in wedges with the spiced syrup spooned on top.

COOK'S TIP *If you prefer a smooth syrup, strain to remove the cinnamon sticks and cloves before spooning it onto the bombe.*

Rippled Nectarine and Brown Sugar Terrine

A delicious combination of nectarine ice cream, cream cheese and brown sugar, swirled together

attractively and set in the corner of a tilted square cake pan for

an interesting triangular shape.

SERVES SIX TO EIGHT

INGREDIENTS

¼ cup LIGHT BROWN SUGAR

1½ teaspoons HOT WATER

scant 1 cup CREAM CHEESE

1 cup CONFECTIONERS' SUGAR

6 tablespoons MILK

3 RIPE NECTARINES

2 teaspoons LEMON JUICE

scant ½ cup HEAVY CREAM

1 Line one half of a 8-inch square cake pan with plastic wrap, pressing into the corners. Dissolve the sugar in the water, stirring until it forms a syrup. Beat the cream cheese in a bowl with a quarter of the confectioners' sugar until softened and smooth, then beat in the milk.

2 Slice the nectarines in half, cut out the pits, then put the nectarines in a food processor. Add the lemon juice and remaining confectioners' sugar and process to a purée.

3 Whip the cream, then fold in the purée. Prop up the pan at an angle of 45°. Spoon a third of the nectarine purée into the pan. Place spoonfuls of the cream cheese mixture onto the purée.

4 Drizzle with half the brown sugar syrup. Spoon half the remaining nectarine mixture into the pan, then spoon on the remaining cream cheese and syrup. Finally, spoon on the remaining nectarine mixture.

5 Using a teaspoon handle, fold the mixtures together in about six strokes to lightly ripple the ingredients. Freeze overnight, keeping the pan propped at the same angle in the freezer until solid, then lay the pan flat.

6 Transfer the terrine to the refrigerator about 30 minutes before serving so that it softens. Turn out onto a serving plate and peel off the plastic wrap. Serve in slices.

COOK'S TIP *Before making this dessert, check that the pan will fit at an angle in the freezer. If not, use a 2 pound loaf pan instead.*

Mocha, Prune and Armagnac Terrines

A really simple frozen dessert that is perfect for entertaining. Just remember to allow time for the prunes to soak in the Armagnac.

SERVES SIX

INGREDIENTS

½ cup PITTED PRUNES, chopped

6 tablespoons Armagnac

½ cup SUGAR

⅔ cup WATER

3 tablespoons COFFEE BEANS

5 ounces PLAIN CHOCOLATE, broken into pieces

1¼ cups HEAVY CREAM

UNSWEETENED COCOA POWDER, for dusting

1 Put the prunes in a small bowl. Pour over 5 tablespoons of the Armagnac and let soak for at least 3 hours at room temperature, or overnight in the refrigerator. Line the bottoms of six ½-cup ramekins with circles cut from waxed paper.

2 Put the sugar and the measured water in a heavy saucepan and heat gently until the sugar dissolves, stirring occasionally. Add the soaked prunes and any of the Armagnac that remains in the bowl; simmer the prunes gently in the syrup for 5 minutes.

3 Using a slotted spoon, lift the prunes out of the pan and set them aside. Add the coffee beans to the syrup and simmer gently for 5 minutes.

4 Lift out the coffee beans and put about a third of them in a bowl. Spoon on ½ cup of the syrup and stir in the remaining Armagnac.

5 Add the chocolate to the pan containing the remaining syrup and let sit until melted. Whip the cream until it just holds its shape. Using a large metal spoon, fold the chocolate mixture and prunes into the cream until just combined. Spoon the mixture into the lined ramekins, cover and freeze for at least 3 hours.

6 To serve, loosen the edges of the ramekins with a knife, then dip in very hot water for 2 seconds and invert onto serving plates. Decorate the plates with coffee bean syrup and cocoa powder.

COOK'S TIP *Both the individual terrines and the coffee bean syrup can be made several days in advance if you want to avoid last-minute cooking. Cover the syrup and store it in the refrigerator.*

VARIATION *Armagnac has a smoother, fruitier flavor than ordinary brandy, although brandy makes a good substitute. Real coffee lovers might even like to substitute Kahlúa or another coffee-based liqueur.*

Coconut and Lemongrass Ice Cream

Lemongrass adds a tantalizing fragrance to ice creams and sorbets.

If you can't get fresh, use the dried stalks or preserved stalks in jars.

SERVES FIVE TO SIX

INGREDIENTS

4 LEMONGRASS STALKS

1⅔ cups COCONUT MILK

3 EGG YOLKS

½ cup SUGAR

2 teaspoons CORNSTARCH

⅔ cup WHIPPING CREAM

finely grated zest of 1 LIME

For the lime syrup

6 tablespoons SUGAR

5 tablespoons WATER

1 LIME, very thinly sliced,
plus 2 tablespoons LIME JUICE

1 Cut the lemongrass stalks in half lengthwise and bruise the stalks with a rolling pin. Put them in a heavy saucepan, add the coconut milk and bring to just below the boiling point. Remove from heat and let infuse for 30 minutes. Then remove the lemongrass.

2 Whisk the egg yolks in a bowl with the sugar and cornstarch until smooth. Gradually add the coconut milk, whisking constantly.

3 Return to the saucepan and heat gently, stirring until the custard thickens. Remove from heat and strain into a clean bowl. Cover with waxed paper and chill.

4 BY HAND: Lightly whip the cream, add the grated lime zest and fold into the custard. Pour into a container and freeze for 3–4 hours, beating twice as it thickens. Spoon into dariole molds and return to the freezer for 3 hours.

USING AN ICE CREAM MAKER: Stir the cream and lime zest into the custard. Churn until thick, then spoon into 5–6 dariole molds. Freeze for at least 3 hours.

5 Heat the sugar and water in a heavy saucepan until the sugar dissolves. Boil for 5 minutes without stirring. Reduce the heat, add the lime slices and juice and simmer for 5 more minutes. Cool.

6 To turn out, loosen with a knife and briefly dip in very hot water Serve with syrup and lime slices.

Walnut Castles

This recipe is loosely based on a classic Indian Kulfi, using finely

chopped walnuts instead of the more familiar pistachios.

SERVES SIX

INGREDIENTS

9 cups WHOLE MILK

15 whole CARDAMOM PODS

6 tablespoons SUGAR

1 cup WALNUTS,
finely chopped

2 tablespoons ROSEWATER

1 tablespoon LEMON JUICE

CHOPPED WALNUTS,
to decorate

1 Put the milk and cardamom pods in a large, heavy saucepan. Bring to a boil, then simmer vigorously without boiling over. Continue until reduced to about 3 cups.

2 Strain the milk into a bowl, discarding the cardamom pods. Add the sugar, chopped walnuts and rosewater and let cool, then stir in the lemon juice.

BY HAND: Pour the mixture into a shallow container and freeze until thickened and firm.

USING AN ICE CREAM MAKER:
Churn the mixture until thick. Spoon into six ½-cup dariole molds or plastic cups and freeze overnight.

3 To serve, briefly dip the molds in very hot water, then turn out onto individual dessert plates. Serve with chopped walnuts sprinkled on top.

tortes & gâteaux

Frozen tortes and gâteaux are an impressive finale to any dinner gathering, yet they're so convenient for the cook. Encased or layered with cake, meringue or crisp cookies, these delicious recipes provide an extensive collection of both classic and modern flavors.

Zabaglione Ice Cream Torte

For anyone who likes zabaglione, the famous, creamy Italian dessert, this simple frozen version is an absolute must! Its taste and texture are just as good, and there's no last-minute whisking to worry about.

SERVES TEN

INGREDIENTS

6 ounces AMARETTI COOKIES

½ cup DRIED APRICOTS, finely chopped

5 tablespoons UNSALTED BUTTER, melted

For the ice cream

5 tablespoons LIGHT BROWN SUGAR

5 tablespoons WATER

5 EGG YOLKS

1 cup HEAVY CREAM

5 tablespoons MADEIRA OR CREAM SHERRY

For the apricot compote

generous ½ cup DRIED APRICOTS

2 tablespoons LIGHT BROWN SUGAR

⅔ cup WATER

1 Put the cookies in a strong plastic bag and crush finely with a rolling pin. Transfer to a bowl and stir in the apricots and melted butter until evenly combined.

2 Using a dampened teaspoon, pack the mixture evenly onto the bottom and up the sides of a 9½-inch loose-bottomed tart pan about 1½ inches deep. Chill.

3 Make the Ice Cream. Put the sugar and water in a small, heavy saucepan and heat, stirring, until the sugar has dissolved. Bring to a boil and boil for 2 minutes without stirring. Meanwhile, bring a large saucepan of water to the simmering point. Put the yolks in a heatproof bowl to fit over the pan without touching the water.

4 Off the heat, whisk the egg yolks until pale, then gradually whisk in the sugar syrup. Put the bowl over the pan of simmering water and continue to whisk for about 10 minutes or until the mixture leaves a trail when the whisk is lifted.

5 Remove the bowl from heat and continue whisking for another 5 minutes or until the mixture is cold. In a separate bowl, whip the cream with the Madeira or sherry until it stands in peaks.

6 Using a large metal spoon, fold the cream into the whisked mixture. Spoon it into the cookie shell, level the surface, cover and freeze overnight.

7 To make the compote, simmer the apricots and sugar in the water until the apricots are plump and the juices are syrupy, adding a little more water if necessary. Let cool.

8 Serve the torte in slices with a little of the compote spooned onto each portion.

Chocolate and Brandied Fig Torte

A seriously rich torte for chocolate lovers. If you are not fond of figs, use dried prunes, dates or apricots instead.

SERVES EIGHT

INGREDIENTS

1½ cups DRIED FIGS

¼ cup BRANDY

7 ounces GINGERSNAP COOKIES

¾ cup UNSALTED BUTTER, softened

⅔ cup MILK

9 ounces SEMI-SWEET CHOCOLATE, broken into pieces

3 tablespoons SUGAR

UNSWEETENED COCOA POWDER, for dusting

LIGHTLY WHIPPED CREAM or CRÈME FRAÎCHE, to serve

1 Chop the figs and put them in a bowl, pour in the brandy and let sit for 2–3 hours, until most of the brandy has been absorbed. Break the cookies into large chunks, put them in a strong plastic bag and crush them with a rolling pin.

2 Melt half the butter and stir in the cookie crumbs until combined. Pack onto the bottom and up the sides of an 8-inch loose-bottomed tart pan, which is about 1¼ inches deep. Chill.

3 Pour the milk into a saucepan, add the chocolate pieces and heat gently until the chocolate has melted and the mixture is smooth, stirring frequently. Pour the chocolate mixture into a bowl and let cool.

4 In a separate bowl, beat the remaining butter with the caster sugar until the mixture is pale and creamy.

5 Add the chocolate mixture, whisking until it is well mixed. Fold in the figs, and any remaining brandy, and spoon the mixture into the cookie case. Level the surface, cover and freeze overnight.

6 Transfer the torte to the refrigerator about 30 minutes before serving so that the filling softens slightly. Dust lightly with cocoa powder and serve in slices, with lightly whipped cream or crème fraîche.

Rhubarb and Ginger Wine Torte

Rhubarb is not often used in frozen desserts, but this luxurious torte uses it in a classic partnership with ginger.
The result is a refreshingly tart flavor, making it the perfect
choice for those who prefer less sweet desserts.

SERVES EIGHT

INGREDIENTS

1¼ pounds RHUBARB, trimmed

½ cup SUGAR

2 tablespoons WATER

scant 1 cup CREAM CHEESE

⅔ cups HEAVY CREAM

¼ cup STEM GINGER,
finely chopped

a few drops of PINK FOOD
COLORING (optional)

1 cup GINGER WINE

6 ounces LADYFINGERS

FRESH MINT or
LEMON BALM SPRIGS,
dusted with confectioners' sugar,
to decorate

1 Chop the rhubarb roughly and put it in a saucepan with the sugar and water. Cover and cook very gently for 5–8 minutes, until the rhubarb is just tender. Process in a food processor or blender until smooth, then let cool.

2 Beat the cream cheese in a bowl until softened. Stir in the cream, rhubarb purée and ginger, then a little food coloring, if desired. Line a 6–8-cup loaf pan with plastic wrap.

3 BY HAND: Pour the mixture into a shallow container and freeze until firm.

USING AN ICE CREAM MAKER:
Churn in an ice cream maker until firm.

4 Pour the ginger wine into a shallow dish. Spoon a thin layer of ice cream on the bottom of the pan. Working quickly, dip the ladyfingers in the ginger wine, then lay them lengthwise onto the ice cream in a single layer (*left*). Trim the ladyfingers to fit.

5 Spread another layer of ice cream on the cookies. Repeat the process, adding two to three more layers and finishing with ice cream. Cover and freeze overnight.

6 Transfer to the refrigerator 30 minutes before serving, to soften the torte slightly. Briefly dip in very hot water, then invert it onto a flat dish. Peel off the plastic wrap and decorate.

COOK'S TIP *Taste the rhubarb mixture just before churning it and add a little confectioners' sugar if you find the flavor too tart.*

Christmas Torte

Not everyone likes traditional Christmas pudding. This is an exciting alternative, but don't feel that you have to limit it to the festive season. Packed with dried fruit and nuts, it is perfect for any special occasion and looks and tastes sensational.

SERVES EIGHT TO TEN

INGREDIENTS

¼ cup DRIED CRANBERRIES

scant ½ cup PITTED PRUNES

⅓ cup GOLDEN RAISINS

¼ cup PORT

2 pieces STEM GINGER,
finely chopped

2 tablespoons UNSALTED
BUTTER

3 tablespoons LIGHT
BROWN SUGAR

scant 2 cups FRESH WHITE
BREAD CRUMBS

2½ cups HEAVY CREAM

2 tablespoons CONFECTIONERS'
SUGAR

1 teaspoon GROUND ALLSPICE

¼ cup BRAZIL NUTS,
finely chopped

SUGARED BAY LEAVES (see
Cook's Tip) and FRESH
CHERRIES, to decorate

1 Put the cranberries, prunes and golden raisins in a food processor and process briefly. Transfer them into a bowl and add the port and ginger. Let absorb the port for 2 hours.

2 Melt the butter in a frying pan. Add the sugar and heat gently until the sugar has dissolved. Add the bread crumbs, stir lightly, then fry over low heat for about 5 minutes, until lightly colored and turning crisp. Let cool.

3 Transfer the bread crumbs to a food processor or blender and process into finer crumbs. Sprinkle a third into a 7-inch loose-bottomed springform pan and freeze.

4 Whip the cream with the confectioners' sugar and allspice until the mixture is thick but not yet standing in peaks. Fold in the brazil nuts with the dried fruit mixture and any port that has not been absorbed.

5 Spread a third of the mixture onto the bread crumb base in the tin, taking care not to dislodge the crumbs. Sprinkle with another layer of the bread crumbs. Repeat the layering, finishing with a layer of the cream mixture. Freeze the torte overnight.

6 Make the sugared bay leaves. Chill the torte for about 1 hour before serving, decorated with sugared bay leaves and fresh cherries.

COOK'S TIP *To make the sugared bay leaves wash and dry the leaves, then paint both sides with beaten egg white. Sprinkle with superfine sugar. Let dry on waxed paper for 2–3 hours.*

Pistachio and Nougat Torte

Pistachios, nougat, honey and rose water make a perfect blend of flavors in this quick and easy torte. Transfer to the refrigerator about an hour before serving.

SERVES EIGHT

INGREDIENTS

¼ cup PISTACHIOS

5 ounces NOUGAT

1¼ cups WHIPPING CREAM

6 tablespoons HONEY

2 tablespoons ROSEWATER

generous 1 cup FROMAGE FRAIS

8 TRIFLE SPONGE CAKES

CONFECTIONERS' SUGAR, for dusting

FRESH RASPBERRIES, POACHED APRICOTS or CHERRIES, to serve (optional)

1 Soak the pistachios in boiling water for 2 minutes. Drain them thoroughly, then rub them between pieces of paper towel to remove the skins. Peel off any skins that remain, then chop them roughly.

2 Using a small sharp knife or scissors cut the nougat into small pieces. Pour the cream into a bowl, add the honey and rose water and whip until it is just beginning to hold its shape.

3 Stir in the fromage frais, chopped pistachios and nougat, and mix well. Slice the sponge cakes horizontally into three very thin layers.

4 Line a 6–6½-inch square loose-bottomed cake pan with waxed paper or plastic wrap. Arrange a layer of cake pieces on the bottom, trimming the pieces to fit.

5 Pack the prepared filling into the pan and level the surface. Cover with the remaining sponges, then cover and freeze overnight.

6 To serve, invert the torte onto a serving plate and dust with confectioners' sugar. Serve with raspberries, poached apricots or cherries, if desired.

White Chocolate and Brownie Torte

This is a deliciously easy dessert, guaranteed to appeal to just about everyone! If you can't buy good-quality brownies, use moist chocolate cake.

SERVES TEN

INGREDIENTS

11 ounces WHITE CHOCOLATE, broken into pieces

2½ cups HEAVY CREAM

9 ounces RICH CHOCOLATE BROWNIES

UNSWEETENED COCOA POWDER, for dusting

1 Dampen the sides of an 8-inch springform pan and line with a strip of waxed paper. Put the chocolate in a small pan. Add ⅔ cup of the cream and heat very gently until the chocolate has melted. Stir until smooth, then pour into a bowl and let cool.

2 Break the chocolate brownies into pieces and place these on the bottom of the pan. Pack them down lightly to make a fairly dense layer.

3 Whip the remaining cream until it forms peaks, then fold in the white chocolate mixture. Spoon into the pan to cover the layer of brownies, then tap the pan gently on the work surface to level the chocolate mixture. Cover and freeze overnight.

4 Transfer the torte to the refrigerator about 45 minutes before serving. Decorate with a light dusting of cocoa powder before serving.

Strawberry and Lemon Curd Gâteau

Layer two favorite flavors in this fresh fruit gâteau, which is perfect for summer entertaining and takes only minutes to assemble.

SERVES EIGHT

INGREDIENTS

½ cup UNSALTED BUTTER, softened

generous ½ cup SUGAR

2 EGGS

1 cup SELF-RISING FLOUR

½ teaspoon BAKING POWDER

To finish

2¼ cups STRAWBERRY ICE CREAM

1¼ cups HEAVY CREAM

scant 1 cup GOOD QUALITY LEMON CURD

2 tablespoons LEMON JUICE

5 cups STRAWBERRIES, hulled

2 tablespoons SUGAR

3 tablespoons COINTREAU or other ORANGE-FLAVORED LIQUEUR

1 Preheat the oven to 350°F. Grease and line a 9-inch round springform cake pan. In a mixing bowl, beat the butter with the sugar, eggs, flour and baking powder until creamy.

2 Spoon the mixture into the prepared pan and bake for about 20 minutes or until just firm. Let cool for 5 minutes, then turn the cake out onto a wire rack. Cool completely. Wash and dry the cake pan, so it is ready to use again.

3 Line the sides of the clean cake pan with a strip of nonstick baking parchment. Using a sharp knife, carefully slice off the top of the cake where it has formed a crust. Save this for another purpose.

4 Place the cake in the pan, cut-side down. Freeze the cake for 10 minutes, then spread the strawberry ice cream evenly onto the cake and freeze until firm.

5 Pour the cream into a bowl, whip it until it forms soft peaks, then fold in the lemon curd and lemon juice. Spoon the mixture onto the strawberry ice cream. Cover and freeze overnight.

6 About 45 minutes before you intend to serve the dessert, decorate it and make the sauce. Cut half the strawberries into thin slices. Put the rest in a food processor or blender and add the sugar and liqueur. Purée the mixture to make a sauce.

7 Arrange the sliced strawberries on the frozen gâteau. Serve with the sauce spooned on top.

Zucotto

An Italian-style dessert with a rich ricotta, fruit, chocolate and nut filling, zucotto is encased in a moist, chocolate and liqueur-flavored cake.

SERVES EIGHT

INGREDIENTS

3 EGGS

6 tablespoons SUGAR

⅔ cup ALL-PURPOSE FLOUR

¼ cup UNSWEETENED COCOA POWDER

6 tablespoons KIRSCH

generous 1 cup RICOTTA CHEESE

½ cup CONFECTIONERS' SUGAR

2 ounces SEMI-SWEET CHOCOLATE, finely chopped

½ cup BLANCHED ALMONDS, chopped and toasted

scant ½ cup CANDIED CHERRIES, quartered

2 pieces STEM GINGER, finely chopped

⅔ cup HEAVY CREAM

UNSWEETENED COCOA POWDER, for dusting

1 Preheat the oven to 350°F. Grease and line a 9-inch cake pan. Whisk the eggs and sugar in a heatproof bowl over a pan of simmering water until the whisk leaves a trail. Remove the bowl from heat and continue to whisk the mixture for 2 minutes.

2 Sift the flour and cocoa into the bowl and fold it in with a large metal spoon. Spoon the mixture into the prepared pan and bake for about 20 minutes, until just firm. Let cool

3 Cut the cake horizontally into three layers. Set aside 2 tablespoons of the kirsch. Drizzle the remaining kirsch onto the layers.

4 Beat the ricotta in a bowl until softened. Beat in the confectioners' sugar, chocolate, almonds, cherries, ginger and reserved kirsch.

5 Pour the cream into a separate bowl and whip it lightly. Using a large metal spoon, fold the cream into the ricotta mixture. Chill. Cut an 8-inch circle from one cake layer, using a plate as a guide, and set it aside.

6 Use the remaining cake to make the case for the zucotto. Cut the cake to fit the bottom of a 12½–15-cup freezerproof mixing bowl. Cut more cake for the sides of the bowl, arranging the pieces together until they are about one third of the way up.

7 Spoon the ricotta filling into the bowl up to the height of the cake, and level the surface.

8 Fit the reserved circle of cake on top of the filling. Trim off the excess cake around the edges. Cover and freeze overnight

9 Transfer the zucotto to the refrigerator 45 minutes before serving, so that the filling softens slightly. Invert it onto a serving plate. Peel off the plastic wrap. Dust with cocoa powder. Serve in slices.

Raspberry Mousse Gâteau

A lavish amount of raspberries gives this gâteau its vibrant color and flavor. Make it at the height of summer, when raspberries are plentiful and full of flavor.

3 Let cool, then remove the cake from the pan and place it on a wire rack. Wash and dry the pan.

4 Line the sides of the clean pan with a strip of waxed paper and carefully lower the cake back into it. Freeze until the raspberry filling is ready.

5 Set aside a generous 1 cup of the raspberries. Put the remainder in a clean bowl, stir in the confectioners' sugar and process into a purée in a food processor or blender. Sieve the purée into a bowl, then stir in the whiskey, if using.

6 Whip the cream to form soft peaks. Whisk the egg whites until they are stiff. Using a large metal spoon, fold the cream, then the egg whites into the raspberry purée.

7 Spread half the raspberry mixture onto the cake. Sprinkle on with the reserved raspberries. Spread the remaining raspberry mixture on top and level the surface. Cover and freeze the gâteau overnight.

8 Transfer the gâteau to the refrigerator at least 1 hour before serving. Remove it from pan, place on a serving plate. Serve in slices.

SERVES EIGHT TO TEN

INGREDIENTS

2 EGGS

¼ cup SUGAR

½ cup ALL-PURPOSE FLOUR

2 tablespoons UNSWEETENED COCOA POWDER

3½ cups RASPBERRIES

1 cup CONFECTIONERS' SUGAR

¼ cup WHISKEY (optional)

1¼ cups WHIPPING CREAM

2 EGG WHITES

1 Preheat the oven to 350°F. Grease and line a 9-inch springform cake pan. Whisk the eggs and sugar in a heatproof bowl set over a pan of gently simmering water until the whisk leaves a trail when lifted. Remove the bowl from heat and continue to whisk the mixture for 2 minutes.

2 Sift the flour and cocoa powder over the mixture and fold it in with a large metal spoon. Spoon the mixture into the pan and spread it gently to the edges. Bake for 12–15 minutes, until just firm.

Rich Chocolate Mousse Gâteau

Because this gâteau is heavily laced with liqueur, you can easily get away with bought cake. The mousse is rich, so serve small portions.

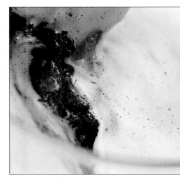

SERVES TWELVE

INGREDIENTS

14 ounces MOIST CHOCOLATE CAKE

5 tablespoons COINTREAU or other ORANGE-FLAVORED LIQUEUR

finely grated zest and juice of 1 ORANGE

11 ounces SEMI-SWEET CHOCOLATE, broken into pieces

¼ cup UNSWEETENED COCOA POWDER

3 tablespoons LIGHT CORN SYRUP

3 EGGS

1¼ cups WHIPPING CREAM

⅔ cup HEAVY CREAM, LIGHTLY WHIPPED

UNSWEETENED COCOA POWDER, for dusting

1 Cut the cake into ¼-inch thick slices. Set a third aside, and use the remainder to make a shell for the mousse. Line the bottom of a 9-inch springform or loose-bottomed cake pan with cake, trimming to fit neatly, then use more for the sides, making a shell about 1½-inches deep.

2 Mix 2 tablespoons of the liqueur with the orange juice and drizzle onto the cake shell.

3 Put the chocolate in a heatproof bowl. Add the cocoa powder, syrup and remaining liqueur and place the bowl over a pan of gently simmering water. Let sit until the chocolate has melted, then remove from heat. Stir until smooth.

4 Whisk the eggs with the orange zest in a mixing bowl until they are thick and pale. Whip the whipping cream until it forms soft peaks.

5 Fold the chocolate mixture into the whisked eggs, using a large metal spoon, then fold in the cream. Scrape the mixture into the cake shell and level the surface.

6 Cover with the reserved chocolate cake, trimming the pieces to fit. Cover and freeze overnight.

7 Transfer the gâteau to the refrigerator 30 minutes before serving. Invert onto a plate, spread with heavy cream and dust with cocoa powder.

Maple and Walnut Meringue Gâteau

This simple dessert is a feast for all meringue lovers.
Before serving, let it thaw slightly in the
refrigerator to enjoy the full flavor.

SERVES TEN TO TWELVE

INGREDIENTS

4 EGG WHITES

scant 1 cup LIGHT BROWN
SUGAR

1¼ cups WALNUT PIECES

2½ cups HEAVY CREAM

⅔ cup MAPLE SYRUP,
plus extra, to serve

1 Preheat the oven to 275°F. Draw
three 9-inch circles on separate
sheets of nonstick baking parchment.
Invert the paper onto three baking
sheets. Whisk the egg whites in a
greasefree bowl until stiff.

2 Whisk in the sugar, about
1 tablespoon at a time, whisking
well after each addition until the
meringue is stiff and glossy. Spread
to within ½ inch of the edge of
each marked circle. Bake for about
1 hour or until crisp, swapping the
baking sheets around halfway
through cooking. Let cool.

3 Set aside 3 tablespoons of the
walnuts. Finely chop the remainder.
Whip the cream with the maple
syrup until it forms soft peaks. Fold
in the chopped walnuts. Use about
a third of the mixture to sandwich
the meringues together on a flat,
freezerproof serving plate.

4 Using a rounded knife, spread
the remaining cream mixture on
the top and sides of the gâteau.
Sprinkle with the reserved walnuts
and freeze overnight.

5 Transfer the gâteau to the
refrigerator about 1 hour before
serving so that the cream filling
softens slightly. Drizzle a little of
the extra maple syrup on top just
before serving. Serve in slices.

Berry and Crushed Meringue Gâteau

This recipe takes five minutes to make but looks and
tastes as though a lot of preparation went into it.
Use really good vanilla ice cream.

SERVES SIX

INGREDIENTS

3½ cups MIXED SMALL
STRAWBERRIES, RASPBERRIES
or RED CURRANTS

2 tablespoons CONFECTIONERS'
SUGAR

3 cups CLASSIC VANILLA
ICE CREAM

6 MERINGUE NESTS
(or 4 ounces meringue)

1 Dampen a 2-pound loaf pan and
line it with plastic wrap. If using
strawberries, chop them into small
pieces. Put them in a bowl and add
the raspberries or red currants and
confectioners' sugar. Toss until the
fruit is beginning to break up, but
do not let it become mushy.

2 Put the ice cream in a bowl and
break it up with a fork. Crumble
the meringues into the bowl and
add the berry mixture.

3 Fold all the ingredients together
until evenly combined and lightly
marbled. Pack into the prepared
pan and press down gently to level.
Cover and freeze overnight. To
serve, invert onto a plate and peel
off the plastic wrap. Serve in slices.

Brandied Apple Charlotte

Loosely based on a traditional Apple Charlotte, this frozen version combines brandy-steeped dried apple with a spicy ricotta cream to make an unusual and very tasty dessert.

SERVES EIGHT TO TEN

INGREDIENTS

¼ cup DRIED APPLES

5 tablespoons BRANDY

¼ cup UNSALTED BUTTER

½ cup LIGHT BROWN SUGAR

½ teaspoon GROUND ALLSPICE

¼ cup WATER

½ cup GOLDEN RAISINS

11 ounces MADEIRA CAKE, cut into ½-inch slices

generous 1 cup RICOTTA CHEESE

2 tablespoons LEMON JUICE

⅔ cup HEAVY or WHIPPING CREAM

CONFECTIONERS' SUGAR and FRESH MINT SPRIGS, to decorate

1 Roughly chop the dried apples, then transfer them to a clean bowl. Pour in the brandy and set aside for about 1 hour, until most of the brandy has been absorbed.

2 Melt the butter in a frying pan. Add the sugar and stir over low heat for 1 minute. Add the ground allspice, water and soaked apples, with any remaining brandy. Cook gently for 5 minutes or until the apples are tender. Stir in the golden raisins and let cool.

3 Use the Madeira slices to line the sides of an 8-inch square or 8-inch round springform or loose-bottomed cake pan. Place in the freezer while you make the filling.

4 Beat the ricotta in a bowl until it has softened, then stir in the apple mixture and lemon juice. Whip the cream in a separate bowl and fold it in. Spoon the mixture into the lined pan and level the surface. Cover and freeze overnight.

5 Transfer the charlotte to the refrigerator 1 hour before serving. Invert it onto a serving plate, dust with sugar. Decorate with mint sprigs.

Chocolate, Rum Raisin Roulade

SERVES SIX

INGREDIENTS

This richly flavored dessert can be assembled and frozen a week or two in advance. Use vanilla, chocolate or coffee ice cream if you prefer, though all versions will be just as enjoyably indulgent.

For the roulade

4 ounces SEMI-SWEET CHOCOLATE, broken into pieces

4 EGGS, separated

generous ½ cup SUGAR

UNSWEETENED COCOA POWDER and CONFECTIONERS' SUGAR, for dusting

For the filling

⅔ cup HEAVY CREAM

1 tablespoon CONFECTIONERS' SUGAR

2 tablespoons RUM

1¼ cups RUM RAISIN ICE CREAM

1 Make the roulade. Preheat the oven to 350°F. Grease a 13 x 9-inch jelly roll pan and line with nonstick baking parchment. Grease the parchment. Melt the chocolate in a heatproof bowl set over a pan of simmering water. In a separate bowl, whisk the egg yolks with the sugar until thick and pale.

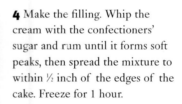

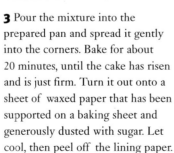

2 Stir the melted chocolate into the yolk mixture. Whisk the egg whites in a greasefree bowl until stiff. Stir a quarter of the whites into the yolk mixture to lighten it, then fold in the remainder.

3 Pour the mixture into the prepared pan and spread it gently into the corners. Bake for about 20 minutes, until the cake has risen and is just firm. Turn it out onto a sheet of waxed paper that has been supported on a baking sheet and generously dusted with sugar. Let cool, then peel off the lining paper.

4 Make the filling. Whip the cream with the confectioners' sugar and rum until it forms soft peaks, then spread the mixture to within ½ inch of the edges of the cake. Freeze for 1 hour.

5 Using a teaspoon, scoop up long curls of the ice cream and lay an even layer on the cream.

6 Starting from a narrow end carefully roll up the sponge, using the paper to help. Slide the roulade off the paper-lined baking sheet and onto a long plate that is freezerproof. Cover and freeze overnight. Transfer to the refrigerator 30 minutes before serving. Serve dusted with cocoa powder and confectioners' sugar.

Lime Cheesecake

This cheesecake has a deliciously tangy, sweet flavor, but needs no gelatin to set the filling, unlike most unbaked cheesecakes. It is not difficult to prepare and looks pleasantly summery with its citrus decoration.

SERVES TEN

INGREDIENTS

6 ounces ALMOND COOKIES

5 tablespoons UNSALTED BUTTER

8 LIMES

½ cup SUGAR

6 tablespoons WATER

scant 1 cup COTTAGE CHEESE

generous 1 cup MASCARPONE CHEESE

1¼ cups HEAVY CREAM

1 Lightly grease the sides of an 8-inch springform pan and line with a strip of waxed paper. Break up the almond cookies slightly, put them in a strong plastic bag and crush them with a rolling pin.

2 Melt the butter in a small pan and stir in the cookie crumbs until evenly combined. Spoon the mixture into the pan and pack it down with the back of a spoon. Freeze the cookie mixture while you make the filling.

3 Finely grate the zest and squeeze the juice from five of the limes. Heat the sugar and water in a small saucepan, stirring until the sugar dissolves. Bring to a boil and boil for 2 minutes without stirring, then remove the syrup from heat, stir in the lime juice and zest and let cool.

4 Press the cottage cheese through a fine sieve into a large bowl. Beat in the mascarpone cheese, then the lime syrup.

BY HAND: Lightly whip the cream and fold into the cheese mixture. Pour into a shallow container and freeze until thick.

USING AN ICE CREAM MAKER: Add the cream and churn in an ice cream maker until thick.

5 Meanwhile, cut a slice off either end of each of the remaining limes, stand them on a board and slice off the skins. Cut them into very thin slices.

6 Arrange the lime slices around the sides of the pan, pressing them against the paper.

7 Pour the cheese mixture onto the cookie crust in the pan and level the surface. Cover and freeze the cheesecake overnight.

8 About 1 hour before you are going to serve the cheesecake, carefully transfer it to a serving plate and put it in the refrigerator to soften slightly.

Butterscotch Tart

Dark brown sugar gives this dessert its deliciously smooth butterscotch flavor. Remember to chill the
evaporated milk for a couple of hours before you are ready to make the filling.
This will ensure that it is smooth.

SERVES EIGHT

INGREDIENTS

For the case

3½ ounces GINGERSNAP COOKIES

¼ cup GROUND HAZELNUTS,
toasted

¼ cup UNSALTED BUTTER,
melted

For the filling

1¼ cups EVAPORATED MILK,
chilled

⅔ cup DARK BROWN SUGAR

1 EGG WHITE

⅔ cup HEAVY CREAM

CHOPPED TOASTED HAZELNUTS
and BROWN SUGAR,
to decorate

1 Break up the cookies slightly, put them in a strong plastic bag and crush them with a rolling pin. Put them in a bowl and add the toasted nuts and the butter. Mix until evenly combined.

2 Press onto the bottom and slightly up the sides of a 9½-inch loose-bottomed tart pan or freezerproof pie pan that is about 1½ inches deep.

3 Whisk the evaporated milk and sugar in a large bowl until the mixture is pale and thick and leaves a thick trail when the whisk is lifted.

4 In a separate greasefree bowl, whisk the egg white until stiff. Whip the heavy cream separately until it forms soft peaks.

5 Using a large metal spoon, fold first the cream and then the egg white into the whisked evaporated milk and sugar. Pour the mixture into the cookie crust. Cover and freeze overnight.

6 To serve, sprinkle the tart with hazelnuts and brown sugar and cut in thin wedges.

COOK'S TIP *Ground and chopped pecans, walnuts or almonds can be used instead of the hazelnuts.*

hot
ice cream desserts

Nothing beats the soft, melting texture of ice cream as it seeps into deliciously warm pastry or mingles with the juices of a hot fruit compote, bringing out the flavor of both. The following chapter includes quick-and-easy desserts and make-ahead desserts. Serve immediately to enjoy the lingering warmth.

Baby Baked Alaskas with Liqueured Apricots

Just as effective as a traditional baked Alaska, these individual desserts are concealed under their own little meringue mountains.

SERVES SIX

INGREDIENTS

3 tablespoons SUGAR

¼ cup WATER

generous ½ cup DRIED APRICOTS, roughly chopped

2 tablespoons COINTREAU or other ORANGE-FLAVORED LIQUEUR

2¼ cups VANILLA, HONEY or any NUT-FLAVORED ICE CREAM

6 LARGE ALMOND or GINGER COOKIES

3 EGG WHITES

scant 1 cup SUGAR

1 Heat the sugar and water in a small, heavy saucepan, stirring occasionally, until the sugar has dissolved. Add the apricots and simmer gently for 5 minutes, until they have absorbed most of the syrup. Stir in the liqueur and let chill.

2 Freeze six small dariole molds or metal pudding molds for 15 minutes. At the same time, remove the ice cream from the freezer and set aside for 15 minutes to soften slightly.

VARIATION *Feel free to experiment and substitute your favorite liqueur for the orange one recommended here. You can also use any other dried fruits instead of the apricots, if desired.*

3 Using a teaspoon, pack most of the ice cream into the molds, leaving a deep cavity in the center of each. Return each mold to the freezer once completed.

5 Dip each mold in very hot water for 1–2 seconds, then invert. Slide a cookie under each ice cream and transfer to a baking sheet. Place in the freezer.

4 When all the molds have been lined with ice cream, remove them from the freezer again and fill the centers with the apricots. Cover the apricots with more ice cream and freeze until firm.

6 Whisk the egg whites in a greasefree bowl until they are stiff. Gradually whisk in the sugar, a tablespoonful at a time, whisking well after each addition, until the mixture has become stiff and glossy.

7 Using a rounded knife, spread a thick layer of the meringue onto each ice cream, making sure the meringue meets the cookies and seals in the ice cream. Swirl the surface decoratively. Return the covered ice creams to the freezer.

8 About 15 minutes before serving, preheat the oven to 450°F. Bake the Alaskas for about 2 minutes, until the meringue is pale golden. Serve immediately.

Coconut and Passion Fruit Baked Alaska

A really classic ice cream extravaganza, baked Alaska lends itself to many variations on the basic theme. This version comprises a passion-fruit-steeped coconut cake, topped with tropical fruit ice cream and smothered in a delicious coconut-flavored meringue.

SERVES EIGHT

INGREDIENTS

For the cake

½ cup UNSALTED BUTTER, softened

generous ½ cup SUGAR

2 EGGS

1 cup SELF-RISING FLOUR

½ teaspoon BAKING POWDER

1 teaspoon ALMOND EXTRACT

½ cup DRY, SHREDDED COCONUT

1 tablespoon MILK

To finish

4 cups PASSION FRUIT, MANGO or TROPICAL FRUIT ICE CREAM

¼ cup KIRSCH

3 PASSION FRUIT

3 EGG WHITES

generous ½ cup SUGAR

½ cup FRESHLY GRATED COCONUT

1 Preheat the oven to 350°F. Grease and line a 7-inch round cake pan. Put all the cake ingredients in a bowl and whisk until smooth. Spoon into the prepared pan, level the surface and bake for 35 minutes, until the cake is just firm. Let cool on a wire rack.

2 Dampen a 5-cup pudding mold and line it with plastic wrap. Remove the ice cream from the freezer for 15 minutes to soften slightly.

3 Pack the ice cream into the lined bowl and return it to the freezer for 1 hour. Place the cake on a small baking sheet or ovenproof plate and drizzle the surface with kirsch. Remove the pulp from the fruit and scoop onto the cake.

4 Dip the bowl containing the ice cream into very hot water for about 2 seconds to loosen the shaped ice cream. Invert it onto the cake. Peel off the plastic wrap and put the cake and ice cream in the freezer.

5 To make the meringue, whisk the egg whites in a clean bowl until stiff. Gradually add the sugar, a tablespoon at a time, whisking well after each addition, until the meringue is thick and glossy. Fold in the coconut.

6 Using a rounded knife, spread the meringue over the ice cream and cake to cover both completely. Return to the freezer.

7 About 15 minutes before serving, preheat the oven to 425°F. Bake for 4–5 minutes, watching closely, until the peaks are golden. Serve immediately.

Ice Cream Croissants with Chocolate Sauce

MAKES FOUR

INGREDIENTS

3 ounces SEMI-SWEET
CHOCOLATE, broken into pieces

1 tablespoon UNSALTED BUTTER

2 tablespoons LIGHT CORN SYRUP

4 CROISSANTS

6 tablespoons GOOD QUALITY
READY-MADE VANILLA
PUDDING

4 large scoops of VANILLA
ICE CREAM

CONFECTIONERS' SUGAR,
for dusting

1 Preheat the oven to 350°F.
Put the chocolate in a small,
heavy saucepan. Add the butter
and syrup and heat very gently
until smooth, stirring the
mixture frequently.

2 Split the croissants in half
horizontally and place the bottoms
on a baking sheet. Spoon the
custard onto the bottoms, cover
with the lids and bake for
5 minutes, until warmed through.

3 Remove the lids and place a
scoop of ice cream in each
croissant. Spoon half the sauce
onto the ice cream and press the
lids down gently. Bake the
croissants for 1 more minute.

4 Dust the filled croissants with
confectioners' sugar, spoon on the
remaining chocolate sauce and
serve immediately.

*A deliciously easy croissant "sandwich"
with a filling of vanilla custard, ice cream and
chocolate sauce.*

Baked Bananas with Ice Cream

*Baked bananas make perfect partners for delicious vanilla ice cream topped with a toasted
hazelnut sauce. A quick and easy dessert that looks as good as it tastes.*

SERVES FOUR

INGREDIENTS

4 LARGE BANANAS

1 tablespoon LEMON JUICE

4 large scoops of VANILLA
ICE CREAM

For the sauce

2 tablespoons UNSALTED
BUTTER

½ cup HAZELNUTS, toasted and
roughly chopped

3 tablespoons LIGHT CORN SYRUP

2 tablespoons LEMON JUICE

1 Preheat the oven to 350°F. Place
the unpeeled bananas on a baking
sheet and brush them with the
lemon juice. Bake for about
20 minutes, until the skins
turn black and the flesh gives
a little when the bananas are
gently squeezed.

COOK'S TIP *Cook the bananas over the
dying coals of a grill, if desired. Put
them on the rack as soon as you have
removed all the main course items.*

2 Meanwhile, make the sauce.
Melt the butter in a small
saucepan. Add the hazelnuts and
cook gently for 1 minute. Add the
syrup and lemon juice and heat,
stirring, for 1 more minute.

3 To serve, slit each banana open
with a knife and open out the
skins. Transfer to serving plates
and serve with scoops of ice
cream. Pour on the sauce.

Toasted Marzipan Parcels with Plums

Ice cream, encased in lightly toasted marzipan, is an irresistible dessert for anyone who likes the flavor of almonds. Lightly poached apricots, cherries, apples or pears can be used instead of the plums.

SERVES FOUR

INGREDIENTS

14 ounces MARZIPAN

CONFECTIONERS' SUGAR, for dusting

1 cup ALMOND, GINGER or VANILLA ICE CREAM

For the plum compote

3 RED PLUMS, about 9 ounces

2 tablespoons SUGAR

5 tablespoons WATER

1 Roll out the marzipan on a surface lightly dusted with confectioners' sugar into an 18 x 9-inch rectangle. Cut out eight rounds using a plain 4½-inch cookie cutter.

2 Place a spoonful of the ice cream in the center of one of the circles. Bring the marzipan up over the ice cream and press the edges together to completely encase.

3 Crimp the edges with your fingers. Transfer to a small baking sheet and freeze. Fill and shape the remaining parcels in the same way and freeze overnight.

4 Make the plum compote. Cut the plums in half, remove the pits, then cut each half into two wedges. Heat the sugar and water in a heavy saucepan, stirring occasionally, until the sugar has completely dissolved.

5 Add the plums and cook very gently for 5 minutes or until they have softened but retain their shape. Test with the tip of a sharp knife—the flesh of the plums should be just tender.

6 Preheat the broiler to high. Place the marzipan parcels on the broiler rack and cook for 1–2 minutes, watching closely, until the crimped edge of the marzipan is lightly browned. Transfer the parcels to serving plates and serve with the warm plum compote.

COOK'S TIP *Don't let the parcels become too brown under the broiler or the ice cream will quickly seep out. Use a firm-textured ice cream and make sure the parcels are frozen solid before broiling them.*

Hot Ice Cream Fritters

Deep-fried ice cream may seem to be a contradiction in terms, but once you've made these crisp fritters, you'll be converted! The secret is to encase the ice cream thoroughly in two layers of sweet cookie crumbs. This will turn crisp and golden during frying, and the ice cream inside will only melt slightly.

SERVES FOUR

INGREDIENTS

3 cups FIRM VANILLA
ICE CREAM

4 ounces AMARETTI or
RATAFIA COOKIES

2 cups FRESH BROWN
BREAD CRUMBS

1 EGG

3 tablespoons ALL-PURPOSE FLOUR

OIL, for deep frying

For the caramel sauce

generous ½ cup SUGAR

⅔ cup WATER

⅔ cup HEAVY CREAM

1 Line a baking sheet with waxed paper and put it in the freezer for 15 minutes, at the same time removing the ice cream from the freezer to soften slightly. Scoop about 12 balls of ice cream, making them as round as possible and place them on the lined baking sheet. Freeze for at least 1 hour, until firm.

2 Meanwhile, put the amaretti or ratafia cookies in a strong plastic bag and crush them with a rolling pin. Transfer to a bowl and add the bread crumbs. Mix well, and then transfer half the mixture to a plate. Beat the egg in a shallow dish. Sprinkle the flour onto a second plate.

3 Using cool hands, and working very quickly, roll each ice cream ball in the flour, then dip in the beaten egg until coated. Roll the balls in the mixed crumbs until completely covered. Return the coated ice cream balls to the baking sheet and freeze for at least 1 more hour.

4 Repeat the process, using the remaining flour, egg and bread crumbs, so that each ball has an additional coating. Return the ice cream balls to the freezer for at least 4 hours, preferably overnight.

5 Make the sauce. Heat the sugar and water in a small, heavy saucepan, stirring occasionally, until the sugar has dissolved. Bring to a boil and boil the syrup for about 10 minutes without stirring until deep golden. Immediately immerse the bottom of the pan in a bowl of cold water to prevent the syrup from cooking any more.

6 Pour the cream into the syrup and return the pan to the heat. Stir until the sauce is smooth. Set aside while you fry the ice cream.

7 Pour oil into a heavy saucepan to a depth of 3 inches. Heat to 365°F or until a cube of bread added to the oil browns in 30 seconds. Add several of the ice cream balls and fry for about 1 minute, until the coating on each is golden. Drain on paper towels and quickly cook the remainder in the same way. Serve the fritters with the caramel sauce.

COOK'S TIP *If the ice cream scoops are irregularly shaped, mold into neat balls after coating in the first layer.*

Phyllo, Ice Cream and Mincemeat Parcels

MAKES TWELVE

Looking much like crispy fried crêpes, these golden parcels reveal hot mincemeat and melting vanilla ice cream when cut open. They can be assembled days in advance, ready for easy, last-minute frying.

INGREDIENTS

1 FIRM PEAR

1 cup MINCEMEAT

finely grated zest of 1 LEMON

12 sheets of PHYLLO PASTRY,
thawed if frozen

a little beaten EGG

1 cup VANILLA ICE CREAM

OIL, for deep-frying

SUGAR
for dusting

5 When you are ready to serve, pour oil into a heavy saucepan to a depth of 3 inches. Heat it to 365°F or until a cube of bread added to the oil browns in 30 seconds.

6 Fry several parcels at a time for 1–2 minutes, until pale golden, turning them over during cooking. Drain on paper towels while frying the remainder. Dust with sugar and serve immediately.

1 Peel, core and chop the pear. Put it in a small bowl and then stir in the mincemeat and lemon zest.

2 Lay one phyllo sheet on the work surface and cut it into two 8-inch squares. Brush one square lightly with beaten egg, then cover with the second square.

3 Lay 2 teaspoons mincemeat on the phyllo, placing it 1-inch away from one edge and spreading it slightly to cover a 3-inch area. Lay 2 teaspoons of the ice cream on the mincemeat. Brush all around the edges of the phyllo with beaten egg.

4 Fold over the two opposite sides of the pastry to cover the filling. Roll up the strip, starting from the filled end. Transfer to a baking sheet and freeze. Make 11 more rolls in the same way.

COOK'S TIP *Phyllo pastry sheets vary considerably in size. Don't worry if you can't get two 8-inch squares from each slice. It won't matter if the squares are slightly smaller or even rectangular as long as they can be rolled to enclose the filling.*

Walnut and Vanilla Ice Palmiers

These walnut pastries can be served freshly baked, but for convenience, make them ahead and reheat them in a medium oven for 5 minutes.

MAKES SIX

INGREDIENTS

¼ cup WALNUT PIECES

12 ounces PUFF PASTRY,
thawed if frozen

beaten EGG, to glaze

3 tablespoons SUGAR

scant 1 cup VANILLA ICE CREAM

1 Preheat the oven to 400°F. Lightly grease a large baking sheet with butter. Chop the walnuts finely. On a lightly floured surface roll the pastry to a thin 12 x 8-inch rectangle.

2 Trim the edges of the pastry, then brush with the egg. Sprinkle on all but 3 tablespoons of the walnuts and 2 tablespoons of the sugar. Run the rolling pin over the walnuts to press them into the pastry.

3 Roll up the pastry from one short side to the center, then roll up the other side until the two rolls meet. Brush the points where the rolls meet with a little beaten egg. Using a sharp knife, cut the pastry into slices ½ inch thick.

4 Lay the slices on the work surface and flatten them with a rolling pin. Transfer to the baking sheet. Brush with more of the beaten egg and sprinkle with the reserved walnuts and sugar.

5 Bake for about 15 minutes, until pale golden. Serve warm, in pairs, sandwiched with ice cream.

Peach, Blackberry and Ice Cream Gratin

A wonderfully easy dessert in which the flavors of the peaches, blackberries, ice cream and brown sugar mingle together as they cook. Use large, ripe peaches with enough space for the filling.

2 Brush the cut surfaces with lemon juice and transfer to a shallow flameproof dish. Broil for 2 minutes. Remove from heat, but leave the broiler on to maintain the temperature.

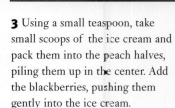

3 Using a small teaspoon, take small scoops of the ice cream and pack them into the peach halves, piling them up in the center. Add the blackberries, pushing them gently into the ice cream.

4 Sprinkle the filled peaches with the brown sugar and replace under the hot broiler for 1–2 minutes, until the sugar has dissolved and the ice cream is beginning to melt. Serve immediately.

SERVES FOUR

INGREDIENTS

4 LARGE PEACHES

1 tablespoon LEMON JUICE

½ cup FIRM VANILLA ICE CREAM

1 cup SMALL BLACKBERRIES

3 tablespoons LIGHT BROWN SUGAR

1 Preheat the broiler. Cut the peaches in half and remove the pits. Cut a thin slice off the rounded side of each peach so that they sit flat on the surface.

VARIATION *Other berries, such as fresh blueberries, can be used instead of blackberries, if you prefer.*
Don't take the ice cream out of the freezer until just before you are ready to fill the peaches, and then work quickly. The ice cream must still be solid or it will melt too quickly when the dessert is under the hot broiler.

Apple Ice Cream with Cinnamon Bread

Cooking the apples with butter, lemon and spice accentuates their flavor and makes a great ice cream. It is good with apple pie and other pastries, but even better with crisp fried sugared bread.

SERVES SIX

INGREDIENTS

1½ pounds APPLES

¼ cup UNSALTED BUTTER

½ teaspoon ALLSPICE

finely grated zest and juice of 1 LEMON

scant ½ cup CREAM CHEESE

2 EGG WHITES, beaten

⅔ cup HEAVY CREAM

MINT SPRIGS, to decorate

For the cinnamon bread

6 thick slices of WHITE BREAD

1 EGG, beaten

1 EGG YOLK

½ teaspoon VANILLA EXTRACT

⅔ cup LIGHT CREAM

5 tablespoons SUGAR

½ teaspoon GROUND CINNAMON

2 tablespoons UNSALTED BUTTER

3 tablespoons OIL

1 Peel, core and slice the apples. Melt the butter in a saucepan. Add the apple slices, allspice and lemon zest. Cover and cook very gently for 10 minutes, until the apple slices are soft. Let cool.

2 Transfer the apples and juices to a food processor, then add the lemon juice and cream cheese. Blend until smooth. In separate bowls, whisk the egg whites until stiff and the cream until it forms soft peaks.

3 Scrape the purée into a bowl. Fold in the cream, then the egg whites. Spoon into a plastic container and freeze overnight.

4 Make the cinnamon bread about 20 minutes before serving. Cut the crusts off the bread slices, then cut each slice diagonally in half. Beat together the egg, egg yolk, vanilla, cream and 1 tablespoon of the sugar.

5 Arrange the bread triangles in a single layer on a large, shallow plate or tray. Pour the cream mixture onto the bread triangles and let sit for about 10 minutes, until the mixture has been thoroughly absorbed.

6 Mix the remaining sugar with the cinnamon on a plate. Melt the butter in the oil in a large frying pan. When it is hot, add half the bread and fry until golden underneath. Turn the slices with a spatula and fry the other side.

7 Drain the slices lightly on paper towels, then coat them on both sides in the cinnamon sugar and keep them hot. Cook the remaining slices in the same way. Serve immediately, topped with scoops of the apple ice cream. Decorate with the mint sprigs.

Ice Cream with Hot Cherry Sauce

Hot cherry sauce makes a classic yet really simple accompaniment to ice cream for serving on any occasion. Use only good-quality chocolate and vanilla.

SERVES FOUR

INGREDIENTS

15-ounce can PITTED BLACK CHERRIES

2 teaspoons CORNSTARCH

finely grated zest of 1 LEMON, plus 2 teaspoons JUICE

1 tablespoon SUGAR

½ teaspoon GROUND CINNAMON

2 tablespoons BRANDY or KIRSCH (optional)

1⅓ cups DARK CHOCOLATE ICE CREAM

1⅓ cups VANILLA ICE CREAM

HOT CHOCOLATE POWDER, for dusting

1 Drain the cherries, reserving the canning juices. Spoon the cornstarch into a small saucepan and blend into a paste with a little of the reserved juice.

2 Stir in the remaining canning juice with the lemon zest and juice, sugar and cinnamon. Bring to a boil, stirring, until smooth and glossy.

3 Add the cherries, with the brandy or kirsch, if using. Stir gently, then cook for 1 minute. Scoop the ice cream into shallow dishes. Spoon on the sauce, dust with hot chocolate powder and serve.

Syrupy Brioche Slices with Vanilla Ice Cream

Keep a few individual brioche buns in the freezer to make this fabulous five-minute dessert. For a slightly tarter taste, use lemon instead of orange zest.

SERVES FOUR

INGREDIENTS

BUTTER, for greasing

finely grated zest and juice of 1 ORANGE

¼ cup SUGAR

6 tablespoons WATER

¼ teaspoon GROUND CINNAMON

4 BRIOCHE BUNS

1 tablespoon CONFECTIONERS' SUGAR

1⅓ cups VANILLA ICE CREAM

1 Lightly grease a gratin dish and set aside. Put the orange zest and juice, sugar, water and cinnamon in a heavy saucepan. Heat gently, stirring, until the sugar has dissolved, then boil for 2 minutes without stirring.

2 Remove the syrup from heat and pour it into a shallow heatproof dish. Preheat the broiler. Cut each brioche vertically into three thick slices. Dip one side of each slice in the hot syrup and arrange in the gratin dish, syrupy sides down. Reserve the remaining syrup. Broil the brioche until lightly toasted.

3 Turn over and dust with confectioners' sugar. Broil for 2–3 more minutes, until they begin to caramelize around the edges.

4 Transfer to serving plates and top with scoops of ice cream. Spoon on the remaining syrup and serve immediately.

Blueberry and Vanilla Crumble Torte

In this heavenly dessert, vanilla ice cream is packed into a buttery crust and baked until

the ice cream starts to melt. Remember that you need to start making

this the day before you intend to serve it.

SERVES EIGHT

INGREDIENTS

2 cups ALL-PURPOSE FLOUR

1 teaspoon BAKING POWDER

¼ cup UNSALTED BUTTER, diced

¼ cup SUGAR

1 EGG

¼ cup GROUND ALMONDS

2 teaspoons VANILLA EXTRACT

1 teaspoon ALLSPICE

2¼ cups VANILLA ICE CREAM

1½ cups BLUEBERRIES

CONFECTIONERS' SUGAR, for dusting

1 Preheat the oven to 350°F. Put the flour and baking powder in a food processor. Add the butter and process briefly to mix. Add the sugar and process briefly again until the mixture is crumbly. Remove about 1½ cups of the crumble mixture and set aside.

2 Add the egg, ground almonds, vanilla and allspice to the remaining crumble mixture and blend into a paste.

3 Scrape the paste into an 8-inch springform pan. Press it firmly on to the bottom and halfway up the sides to make an even crust. Line the pastry shell with waxed paper and fill with baking beans.

4 Sprinkle the crumble mixture onto a baking sheet. Bake the crumble for 20 minutes and the crust for about 30 minutes, until pale golden. Remove the paper and beans from the crust and bake it for 5 more minutes. Let both the crumble and the crust cool.

5 Pack the ice cream into the almond pastry crust and level the surface. Sprinkle on the blueberries and then the baked crumble mixture. Freeze overnight.

6 About 25 minutes before serving, preheat the oven to 350°F. Bake the torte for 10–15 minutes, until the ice cream has started to soften. Dust with confectioners' sugar and serve in wedges.

COOK'S TIP *The crumble mixture can be made without a food processor if you do not have one. Simply rub the butter into the flour and baking powder, then stir in the sugar. To make the paste, simply stir the additional ingredients into the remaining crumble mixture.*

Orange Crêpes with Mascarpone Cream

Baking these delicate crêpes does not actually make them hot when served. Quite simply, the sorbet and mascarpone start to melt together in their crisp pancake shells to make a delicious dessert that is neither too rich nor too-sweet.

SERVES EIGHT

INGREDIENTS

For the crêpes

1 cup ALL-PURPOSE FLOUR

1¼ cups MILK

1 EGG, plus 1 EGG YOLK

finely grated zest of 1 ORANGE

2 tablespoons SUGAR

OIL, for frying

To finish

generous 1 cup MASCARPONE CHEESE

1 tablespoon CONFECTIONERS' SUGAR

6 tablespoons LIGHT CREAM

3 tablespoons COINTREAU or ORANGE JUICE

2¼ cups ORANGE SORBET

CONFECTIONERS' SUGAR, for dusting

1 Make the crêpes. Put the flour, milk, egg, egg yolk, orange zest and sugar in a food processor and blend until smooth. Pour the batter into a pitcher and let stand for 30 minutes.

2 Heat a little of the oil in a medium frying pan or crêpe pan until very hot. Drain off the excess. Pour a little of the batter into the pan, tilting the pan so that the batter coats the bottom thinly. Pour any excess back into the pitcher.

3 Cook the crêpe until the underside is golden, then flip it over with a spatula and cook the other side. Slide the crêpe onto a plate and cook seven more crêpes, lightly oiling the pan each time and stacking the cooked ones.

4 Preheat the oven to 400°F. In a bowl, beat the mascarpone with the confectioners' sugar, cream and liqueur or orange juice until smooth. Spread the mixture on the crêpes, taking it almost to the edges.

5 Using a teaspoon, scoop shavings of sorbet and arrange them to one side of each topped crêpe. Fold the crêpes in half and dust with confectioners' sugar. Fold again into quarters and dust with more confectioners' sugar. Lay the crêpes in a large shallow baking dish and bake for 2 minutes, until the sorbet starts to melt. Serve immediately.

elegant iced desserts

Presentation plays just as important a role with ice creams as it does with any other dessert. Whether scooped into glasses and bathed in a sweet glossy sauce, or cleverly contained in a chocolate shell, there is a dessert here to suit the mood of any occasion.

White Chocolate Castles

These impressive chocolate shells serve a wide variety of uses. They can be frozen with mousse or other creamy fillings in them or, as in this recipe, filled with scoops of ice cream and succulent fresh blueberries.

SERVES SIX

INGREDIENTS

8 ounces WHITE CHOCOLATE, broken into pieces

1 cup DOUBLE WHITE CHOCOLATE ice cream

1 cup CLASSIC DARK CHOCOLATE ice cream

1 cup BLUEBERRIES

UNSWEETENED COCOA POWDER or CONFECTIONERS' SUGAR for dusting

1 Put the white chocolate in a heatproof bowl, set it over a pan of gently simmering water and set aside until melted. Line a baking sheet with waxed paper. Cut out six 12 x 5-inch strips of waxed paper, then fold each in half lengthwise.

2 Stand a 3-inch pastry cutter on the baking sheet. Roll one strip of paper into a circle and fit inside the cutter with the folded edge on the bottom paper. Stick the edges together with tape.

3 Remove the cutter and shape more paper collars in the same way, leaving the pastry cutter in place around the final collar.

4 Spoon a little of the melted chocolate into the bottom of the collar supported by the cutter. Using a teaspoon, spread the chocolate on the bottom and up the sides of the collar, making the top edge uneven. Carefully lift up the cutter.

5 Make five more chocolate shells in the same way, using the cutter for extra support each time. Place the shells in a cool place or in the refrigerator to set.

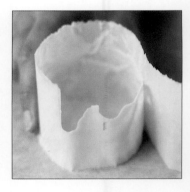

6 Carefully peel off the paper from the sides of the chocolate shells, then lift the shells off the bottom. Transfer to serving plates.

7 Using a large melon baller or teaspoon, scoop the white and dark chocolate ice creams into the shells and decorate with the fruit. Dust with cocoa powder or confectioners' sugar and serve immediately.

COOK'S TIP *To store the chocolate shells for up to three days, put them in an airtight container and keep in a cool place.*

Sorbet in an Ice Bowl

Nothing sets off a freshly scooped sorbet quite so effectively as an ice bowl inlaid with fresh flowers and leaves.

Ice bowls are easy to make, inexpensive and stunning enough to grace any special

celebration, from a lunch party to a country wedding.

4 Place some kitchen weights or food cans in the central bowl to stop it from rising, then fill the space between the bowls to the rim with more water. Freeze overnight until firm.

5 Release the inner bowl by pouring boiling water into it almost to the top. Quickly pour out the water and lift out the inner bowl. Repeat the process if the bowl won't come free instantly.

6 To remove the outer bowl, dip it quickly in a large bowl of very hot water until the ice bowl loosens. Return the ice bowl to the freezer.

7 Shortly before serving, scoop the sorbet into the bowl. Return to the freezer until ready to serve.

SERVES EIGHT TO TEN

INGREDIENTS

ICE CUBES

COLD WATER

selection of FRESH EDIBLE FLOWERS AND LEAVES

18–20 scoops of SORBET, to serve

1 Place some ice cubes in the bottom of a 15-cup clear plastic or glass freezerproof bowl. Tuck some flowers and leaves around the ice. Position a smaller bowl so that it rests on the ice cubes, leaving an even space between the two bowls.

2 Pour cold water into the space between the bowls until the water level starts to come up the sides. Freeze for 2–3 hours, until frozen.

3 Tuck more flowers and leaves between the two bowls, mixing the flowers and leaves so that they look attractive through the sides of the larger bowl.

COOK'S TIP *Use any edible flowers to decorate the bowl, matching the colors to those of the sorbet. Rose petals or small rose buds look lovely, as do any herb flowers, primulas, primroses, pot marigolds, violets, nasturtiums and pansies. Don't place them too closely or the light won't show through. If the inner bowl does not sit perfectly pack crumpled aluminum foil between the top edges of the bowls while freezing the ice in the base. When unmolding the bowl, the ice may crack, but it won't fall apart.*

Gooseberry and Elderflower Sorbet

A classic combination that makes for a really refreshing sorbet.

Make it in summer, as a stunning finale for an alfresco meal, or

save it for serving after a hearty winter's stew.

SERVES SIX

INGREDIENTS

⅔ cup SUGAR

¼ cup WATER

10 ELDERFLOWER HEADS

4 cups GOOSEBERRIES

scant 1 cup APPLE JUICE

dash of GREEN FOOD
COLORING (optional)

a little beaten EGG WHITE
and SUPERFINE SUGAR,
to decorate

1 Put 2 tablespoons of the sugar in a saucepan with 2 tablespoons of the water. Set aside. Mix the remaining sugar and water in a separate, heavy saucepan. Heat gently, stirring occasionally, until the sugar has dissolved. Bring to a boil and boil for 1 minute, without stirring, to make a syrup.

2 Remove from heat and add the elderflower heads, pressing them into the syrup with a wooden spoon. Let infuse for about 1 hour.

3 Strain the elderflower syrup through a sieve placed over a bowl. Set the syrup aside. Add the gooseberries to the pan containing the reserved sugar and water. Cover and cook very gently for about 5 minutes, until the gooseberries have softened.

4 Transfer to a food processor and add the apple juice. Process until smooth, then press through a sieve into a bowl. Let cool. Stir in the elderflower syrup and green food coloring. Chill until very cold.

5 BY HAND: Pour the mixture into a shallow container and freeze until thick, preferably overnight.

USING AN ICE CREAM MAKER: Churn the mixture until it holds its shape. Transfer to a freezerproof container and freeze for several hours or overnight.

6 To decorate the glasses, put a little egg white in a shallow bowl and a thin layer of superfine sugar on a flat plate. Dip the rim of each glass in the egg white, then the sugar to coat evenly. Let dry. Scoop the sorbet carefully into the glasses, decorate with elderflowers and serve.

Cranberry Sorbet in Lace Crêpes

Pretty lace crêpes make a really stunning presentation for sorbets and ice creams. The sweet yet tangy cranberry sorbet can be made using fresh or frozen cranberries, and the result is an impressive dinner party dessert at any time of the year.

SERVES SIX

INGREDIENTS

5 cups CRANBERRIES

1 cup SUGAR

1¼ cups ORANGE JUICE

¼ cup COINTREAU or other ORANGE-FLAVORED LIQUEUR

CONFECTIONERS' SUGAR, for dusting

extra CRANBERRIES and LIGHTLY WHIPPED CREAM, to serve

For the crêpes

½ cup ALL-PURPOSE FLOUR

½ teaspoon GROUND GINGER

1 EGG

1 tablespoon SUGAR

½ cup MILK

a little OIL, for frying

1 Put the cranberries, sugar and orange juice in a saucepan and heat gently until the sugar has dissolved. Cover and cook gently for 5–8 more minutes, until the cranberries are very tender. Let cool.

2 Transfer the mixture to a food processor and process until smooth. Press the purée through a sieve placed over a bowl to extract as much juice as possible. Stir the liqueur into the juice, then chill until very cold.

3 BY HAND: Pour the mixture into a shallow container and freeze for 3–4 hours, beating it twice as it thickens. Freeze again overnight.

USING AN ICE CREAM MAKER: Churn the mixture until the sorbet holds its shape. Scrape into a container and freeze overnight.

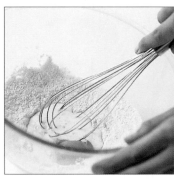

4 Make the crêpes. Sift the flour and ginger into a bowl. Add the egg, sugar and a little of the milk. Gradually whisk in the remaining milk to make a smooth batter. Heat a little oil in a small frying pan or crêpe pan. Pour off the excess oil and remove the pan from heat.

5 Using a teaspoon, drizzle a little of the batter on the bottom of the hot pan, using a scribbling action to give a lacy effect. (The crêpe should be about 5½ inches in diameter.) Return the pan to the heat and cook the mixture gently until the lacy crêpe is golden on the underside.

6 Carefully turn it over, and cook for 1 more minute. Slide onto a plate and let cool. Make five more crêpes in the same way, lightly oiling the pan each time.

7 To serve, lay a crêpe on a serving plate, underside facing up. Arrange several small scoops of the sorbet on one side of the pancake. Fold over and dust generously with confectioners' sugar. Sprinkle with extra cranberries. Serve with whipped cream.

COOK'S TIP *When drizzling the batter into the frying pan, make sure all the lacy edges are connected, otherwise the pancakes will fall apart when you try to turn them.*

Vanilla Brûlées

Freeze these little desserts in ramekins. Just before serving, sprinkle them with sugar and pop them under the broiler to caramelize the topping.

SERVES SIX

INGREDIENTS

1 VANILLA BEAN

2½ cups WHOLE MILK

¼ cup FLAKED RICE

finely grated zest of 2 LEMONS

¼ cup SUGAR

1¼ cups WHIPPING CREAM

sugared STRAWBERRIES, to serve

1 Split the vanilla bean lengthwise with a knife and put it in a saucepan. Pour in the milk and add the rice. Simmer for 8–10 minutes, until the rice is turning pulpy.

2 Remove the vanilla bean and scrape out the seeds. Return them to the pan and stir in the lemon zest and 6 tablespoons of the sugar. Let cool.

3 Stir in the cream and churn the mixture in an ice cream maker. Divide among six ½-cup ramekins or heatproof dishes, and freeze for at least 3 hours or until firm. Preheat a broiler. Sprinkle each dish with a thick layer of the remaining sugar.

4 Cook under the preheated broiler for about 5 minutes, until the sugar has caramelized. Serve with the sugared strawberries.

COOK'S TIP *If you don't have a vanilla bean, use 1 teaspoon vanilla extract instead.*

Miniature Chocolates

For summer entertaining, these little chocolates are a fun alternative to the more familiar after-dinner chocolates.

MAKES ABOUT 25

INGREDIENTS

3 cups CLASSIC VANILLA, CLASSIC DARK CHOCOLATE or CLASSIC COFFEE ICE CREAM

7 ounces SEMI-SWEET CHOCOLATE, broken into pieces

1 ounce MILK CHOCOLATE, broken into pieces

¼ cup chopped HAZELNUTS, lightly toasted

1 Put a large baking sheet in the freezer for 10 minutes. Using a melon baller, scoop balls of the ice cream and place these on the baking sheet. Freeze for at least 1 hour, until firm.

2 Line a second baking sheet with nonstick baking parchment and place in the freezer for 15 minutes. Melt the semi-sweet chocolate in a heatproof bowl set over a pan of gently simmering water. Melt the milk chocolate in a separate bowl.

3 Using a rounded knife, transfer the ice cream scoops to the paper-lined sheet. Spoon a little plain chocolate on one scoop so that most of it is coated.

4 Sprinkle chopped nuts on immediately, before the chocolate sets. Coat half the remaining scoops in the same way, sprinkling nuts on each one before the chocolate sets. Spoon the remaining semi-sweet chocolate over all the remaining scoops.

5 Using a teaspoon, drizzle the milk chocolate onto the chocolates that which are not topped with nuts. Freeze again until ready to serve.

COOK'S TIP *If the melted milk chocolate is very runny set it aside for a few minutes to thicken up slightly before spooning it onto the ice cream scoops. The milk chocolate can be piped on the chocolates, using a piping bag fitted with a writing nozzle.*

Chocolate Teardrops with Cherry Sauce

These sensational chocolate shells are surprisingly easy to make. Once filled, they freeze well, making them the perfect choice for a special occasion dessert.

SERVES SIX

INGREDIENTS

3½ ounces SEMI-SWEET CHOCOLATE, broken into pieces

4 ounces AMARETTI COOKIES

1¼ cups WHIPPING CREAM

½ teaspoon ALMOND EXTRACT

2 tablespoons CONFECTIONERS' SUGAR

6 pairs of FRESH CHERRIES, to decorate

For the sauce

½ teaspoon CORNSTARCH

5 tablespoons WATER

2 cups FRESH CHERRIES, pitted and halved

3 tablespoons SUGAR

2 teaspoons LEMON JUICE

3 tablespoons GIN

1 Cut out six acrylic plastic strips, each measuring 10½ x 1¼ inches. Put the chocolate in a heatproof bowl over a pan of simmering water. Set aside until melted, then remove from heat and let sit for 5 minutes. Line a baking sheet with waxed paper.

2 Coat the underside of an acrylic plastic strip in the chocolate, leaving ½ inch at each end. Try to keep the other side uncoated.

3 Bring the ends of the strip together so that the coated side is on the inside. Hold the ends with a paper clip, then put on the baking sheet to set. Make five more shapes in the same way. Chill until set.

4 Put the amaretti cookies in a plastic bag and crush them with a rolling pin. Pour the cream into a bowl, add the almond extract and confectioners' sugar and whip until thick but still soft. Fold in the cookies.

5 Spoon the mixture carefully into the chocolate shells, making sure the chocolate shape is completely filled with ice cream up to the rim.

6 Tap the baking sheet gently on the work surface so the filling becomes level. Freeze the filled chocolate shells for at least 3 hours or overnight.

7 Make the sauce. Put the cornstarch in a small saucepan and stir in a little of the water to make a paste. Stir in the remaining water, with the cherries, sugar and lemon juice. Bring just to a boil, stirring until thickened. Remove from heat and let cool. Stir in the gin.

8 To serve, remove the paper clips from the chocolate shapes, then carefully peel off the plastic. Transfer the shapes to individual dessert plates. Spoon a little sauce onto each plate and decorate with the pairs of cherries.

Chocolate Millefeuille

Although this stunning dessert takes a little time to prepare, the good news is that it can be assembled days in advance, ready to impress dinner guests. Simply transfer it to the refrigerator about 30 minutes before serving so that it becomes easier to slice.

SERVES EIGHT

INGREDIENTS

4 EGG YOLKS

2 teaspoons CORNSTARCH

1¼ cups MILK

¼ cup MAPLE SYRUP

1 cup CRÈME FRAÎCHE

1 cup PECANS, chopped

To finish

7 ounces SEMI-SWEET CHOCOLATE

1¼ cups HEAVY CREAM

3 tablespoons CONFECTIONERS' SUGAR

2 tablespoons BRANDY (optional)

lightly toasted PECANS

1 Whisk the egg yolks in a bowl with the cornstarch and a little of the milk until smooth. Pour the remaining milk into a pan, bring to a boil, then pour into the yolk mixture, stirring.

2 Return the mixture to the pan and stir in the maple syrup. Cook gently, stirring until thickened and smooth. Do not boil. Pour into a bowl and cover closely with waxed paper to prevent a skin from forming. Let cool.

3 BY HAND: Stir the crème fraîche into the cold custard and pour into a shallow container. Freeze for 3–4 hours, beating twice as it thickens, add the chopped pecans and freeze again overnight.

USING AN ICE CREAM MAKER: Churn until thick and creamy, then add the chopped pecans. Scrape into a freezerproof container and freeze overnight.

4 Break 5 ounces of the chocolate into pieces and melt in a bowl over a pan of simmering water. On waxed paper draw four rectangles, each measuring 7½ x 4½ inches. Spoon a quarter of the melted chocolate onto each rectangle and spread to the edges. Let set.

5 Pare thin curls from the remaining chocolate using a potato peeler. Then whip the cream with the confectioners' sugar and brandy if using, until it forms soft peaks. Carefully peel off the paper from a chocolate rectangle and place it on a flat freezerproof serving plate. Spread a third of the whipped cream on the chocolate, taking it almost to the edges.

6 Using a teaspoon, shape small scoops of the ice cream and lay these on the cream. Cover with a second chocolate rectangle. Repeat the layering, finishing with chocolate. Sprinkle on the toasted pecans and chocolate curls. Freeze overnight until firm. If freezing for longer, cover it loosely with aluminum foil once it is frozen solid.

7 Transfer the frozen millefeuille to the refrigerator 30 minutes before serving to soften slightly. Serve in slices.

COOK'S TIP *It is a good idea to assemble the millefeuille on the upside-down lid of a rectangular freezer container. The cover can then be fitted and the dessert frozen. Carefully slide the dessert onto a rectangular plate to serve.*

Hazelnut Cones with Vanilla Ice Cream and Hazelnut Caramel Sauce

Unlike bought ice cream cones, these hazelnut cookie cones not only fulfill a function but taste delicious too!

They keep well in an airtight container for several days, but should they start to soften, pop

them into a medium oven for a minute or two.

SERVES EIGHT

INGREDIENTS

scant 1 cup GROUND HAZELNUTS

½ cup ALL-PURPOSE FLOUR

¼ cup SUGAR

2 EGGS, lightly beaten

1 teaspoon VANILLA EXTRACT

1 tablespoon MILK

For the sauce

6 tablespoons SUGAR

¼ cup WATER

½ cup HAZELNUTS, lightly toasted and roughly chopped

1 tablespoon LEMON JUICE

2 tablespoons UNSALTED BUTTER

about 2¼ cups VANILLA ICE CREAM

1 Preheat the oven to 350°F. Line a baking sheet with nonstick baking parchment. Mix the ground hazelnuts, flour and sugar in a bowl. Add the eggs, vanilla and milk and mix to a smooth paste.

2 Scoop up a shallow tablespoonful of the mixture and spoon it onto one end of the baking sheet. Add a second spoonful at the opposite end. Using a rounded knife, spread each spoonful to a circle about 5 inches in diameter, making sure the paste is spread to an even thickness. Bake the cookies for about 5 minutes, until they start to turn pale gold around the edges.

3 Working quickly, lift a cookie off the paper and turn it over. Wrap it around a cream horn mold to make a cone shape. Repeat with the other cookie. As soon as the cookies become brittle, gently ease the cones away from the molds. Repeat with the remaining mixture to make eight cones in all.

4 Make the sauce. Heat the sugar and water in a small, heavy saucepan until the sugar has dissolved. Bring to a boil and boil rapidly, without stirring, until the caramel is a deep golden color. Immediately immerse the bottom of the pan in cold water to prevent the caramel from additional cooking. Protecting your hand with an oven mitt, add 4 tablespoons water, standing back in case the syrup splutters.

5 Add the hazelnuts, lemon juice and butter to the pan and cook gently until the sauce is smooth and glossy. Pour it into a small pitcher.

6 Scoop the vanilla ice cream into the hazelnut cones. Pour on a little sauce and serve immediately.

COOK'S TIP *Getting the cookies to the right thickness is quite tricky, so treat the first batch as a trial run. If the mixture is spread too thickly, the cookies will be rather soft; if too thin, they will crack when molded around the molds.*

Chocolate Ice Cream with Lime Sabayon

Sabayon sauce has a light, foamy texture that perfectly complements the rich, smooth flavor of ice cream.

This tangy lime version is delicious with chocolate ice cream but can also be served

with tropical fruit, berries or vanilla ice cream.

SERVES FOUR

INGREDIENTS

2 EGG YOLKS

5 tablespoons SUGAR

finely grated zest and juice of
2 LIMES

¼ cup WHITE WINE or
APPLE JUICE

3 tablespoons LIGHT CREAM

2¼ cups CHOCOLATE CHIP or
DARK CHOCOLATE ICE CREAM

pared strips of LIME ZEST,
to decorate

1 Put the egg yolks and sugar in a heatproof bowl and beat until combined. Beat in the lime zest and juice, then the white wine or apple juice.

2 Whisk the mixture over a pan of gently simmering water until the sabayon is smooth and thick, and the mixture leaves a trail when the whisk is lifted from the bowl. Lightly whisk in the cream. Remove the bowl from the pan and cover with a lid or plate.

3 Working quickly, scoop the ice cream into four glasses. Spoon the sabayon sauce onto the ice cream, decorate with the strips of lime zest and serve immediately.

Ice Cream with Sweet Pine Nut Sauce

SERVES FOUR

INGREDIENTS

5 tablespoons PINE NUTS

2 tablespoons UNSALTED BUTTER

2 tablespoons HONEY

2 tablespoons LIGHT
BROWN SUGAR

grated zest and juice of 1 LEMON

1 cup LEMON SORBET

1 cup VANILLA ICE CREAM

The delicious combination of lightly toasted pine nuts,

tangy lemon and butter makes an easy sauce, perfect

for enlivening vanilla ice cream and lemon sorbet.

1 Toast the pine nuts lightly, then chop them roughly. Melt the butter in a small, heavy saucepan with the honey and sugar. Remove from heat and stir in the lemon zest and juice.

2 Stir in the chopped pine nuts. Pour the sauce into a small pitcher. Let cool until ready to serve.

3 To serve, alternate small scoops of the lemon sorbet and the vanilla ice cream in four tall serving glasses. Generously spoon the pine nut sauce onto the ices and serve immediately.

COOK'S TIP *The sauce will be very thin while it is still warm, but it becomes thicker as it cools. Best served before it is quite cold.*

Frozen Coffee Cups

Small, sturdy coffee cups make attractive containers for this richly flavored ice cream. Alternatively use ramekins or other small freezerproof dishes.

SERVES SIX TO EIGHT

INGREDIENTS

⅔ cup WATER

5 tablespoons GROUND ESPRESSO COFFEE

1 teaspoon CORNSTARCH

4 EGG YOLKS

5 tablespoons LIGHT BROWN SUGAR

1¼ cups WHIPPING CREAM

2 tablespoons TIA MARIA or KAHLÚA LIQUEUR

lightly whipped CREAM and HOT CHOCOLATE POWDER, to decorate

1 Pour the water into a small saucepan and stir in the coffee powder. Bring to a boil, remove from heat and let infuse for 15 minutes.

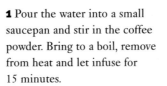

2 Strain through a muslin-lined sieve held over a bowl.

3 Spoon the cornstarch into a small, heavy saucepan. Stir in a little of the hot coffee, then add the remaining coffee with the egg yolks and sugar. Cook over low heat, stirring until thickened. Do not boil or the mixture may curdle. Scrape into a bowl, cover closely with waxed paper and let cool.

4 Whip the cream with the liqueur and cooled coffee mixture until it forms soft peaks.

5 Spoon the mixture into the coffee cups, tapping them gently to level the surface. Freeze for at least 3 hours.

6 Transfer the coffee cups to the refrigerator about 30 minutes before serving. Top with swirls of lightly whipped cream and dust with hot chocolate powder.

COOK'S TIP *The number of people this will serve depends on the size of the cups. If they are very small, this amount will serve at least eight.*

Chocolate Ice Cream in Florentine Baskets

A similar mixture to that used when making florentines is perfect for shaping fluted baskets for holding scoops of ice cream. For convenience, make the baskets a couple of days in advance, but dip the edges in chocolate on the day you serve them.

SERVES EIGHT

INGREDIENTS

½ cup UNSALTED BUTTER, plus extra for greasing

¼ cup SUGAR

6 tablespoons LIGHT CORN SYRUP

scant 1 cup ALL-PURPOSE FLOUR

½ cup SLICED ALMONDS

¼ cup CANDIED CHERRIES, finely chopped

3 tablespoons RAISINS, chopped

1 tablespoon finely chopped CANDIED GINGER

3½ ounces SEMI-SWEET CHOCOLATE, broken into pieces

about 3 cups DARK CHOCOLATE ICE CREAM

1 Preheat the oven to 375°F. Line two large baking sheets with lightly greased nonstick baking parchment. In a small, heavy saucepan, heat the butter until it has melted and add the sugar and corn syrup. Off the heat, stir in the flour, almonds, raisins, cherries and ginger.

2 Place a shallow tablespoonful of the mixture at either end of one baking sheet, then spread each spoonful into a 5 inch round, using the back of the spoon.

3 Bake for about 5 minutes, until each round has spread even more and looks lacy and deep golden. Meanwhile, spread more circles on the second baking sheet ready to put in the oven. Have ready several metal dariole molds for shaping the baskets.

4 Leave the cookies on the baking sheet for about 2 minutes to firm up slightly. Working quickly, lift one cookie on a spatula and lay it over an upturned dariole mold. Gently shape the cookie into flutes around the sides of the mold. Shape the other cookie around a mold in the same way.

5 Leave the cookies in place for about 2 minutes, until cool, then carefully lift the baskets off the dariole molds. Cook and shape the remaining cookie mixture in the same way until you have eight baskets in total.

6 Melt the chocolate in a heatproof bowl over a pan of gently simmering water. Carefully dip the edges of the baskets in the melted chocolate and place on individual dessert plates. Scoop the chocolate ice cream into the baskets to serve.

COOK'S TIP *If the cookies feel as though they are going to fall apart when you lift them from the baking sheet, let them firm up slightly. If they become brittle before you've had a chance to shape them, pop them back in the oven for a few moments to soften.*

Black Currant and Meringue Trifles

These desserts are made using crushed meringues, cream and sorbet. Before you start, remove the sorbet from the freezer for 20 minutes to soften slightly.

SERVES SIX

INGREDIENTS

1½ cups BLACK CURRANT SORBET

3 bought MERINGUES

several sprigs of FRESH MINT, plus extra MINT SPRIGS, to decorate

2 tablespoons CONFECTIONERS' SUGAR

4 teaspoons LEMON JUICE

1¼ cups DOUBLE or WHIPPING CREAM

6 tablespoons STRAINED, PLAIN YOGURT

2 Add the confectioners' sugar, lemon juice and cream. Whip until the mixture just holds its shape. Stir in the yogurt, then fold in the crushed meringues.

3 Spoon a little of the cream mixture into small, deep dishes or glasses. Add layers of sorbet and cream mixture, ending with cream mixture. Decorate with mint sprigs.

COOK'S TIP *The amount this will serve will depend on the size of the dishes used. If you opt for large bowl-shaped glasses, the mixture will probably serve four.*

1 Chop the mint finely and put it into a bowl. Roughly break the meringues into small pieces.

Fig, Port and Clementine Sundaes

SERVES SIX

INGREDIENTS

6 CLEMENTINES

2 tablespoons HONEY

1 CINNAMON STICK, halved

1 tablespoon LIGHT BROWN SUGAR

¼ cup PORT

6 FRESH FIGS

approx 2¼ cups ORANGE SORBET

The flavors of figs, cinnamon, clementines and port conjure up images of winter and hearty meals.

3 Slice the figs thinly and add to the clementines and syrup, tossing the ingredients together gently. Let sit for 10 minutes, then discard the cinnamon stick.

4 Arrange half the fig and clementine slices around the sides of six serving glasses. Half-fill the glasses with scoops of sorbet. Arrange the remaining fruit slices around the sides of the glasses, then pile more sorbet into the center. Pour on the port syrup and serve.

1 Finely grate the zest from two clementines and put it in a small, heavy pan. Using a small, sharp knife, cut the peel off all the clementines, then slice the flesh thinly. Add the honey, cinnamon, sugar and port to the clementine zest. Heat gently until the sugar has dissolved, to make a syrup.

2 Put the clementine slices in a heatproof bowl and pour in the syrup. Cool completely, then chill.

Raspberry and Almond Trifle

This delicious combination of almondy cake, sherried fruit, ice cream and mascarpone topping is sheer indulgence for trifle lovers. The cake and topping can be made a day in advance, and the assembled trifle will sit happily in the refrigerator for an hour before serving.

SERVES EIGHT TO TEN

INGREDIENTS

For the cake

½ cup UNSALTED BUTTER, softened

½ cup LIGHT BROWN SUGAR

2 EGGS

⅔ cup SELF-RISING FLOUR

½ teaspoon BAKING POWDER

1 cup GROUND ALMONDS

1 teaspoon ALMOND EXTRACT

1 tablespoon MILK

To finish

scant 2 cups RASPBERRIES

½ cup SLICED ALMONDS, toasted

6 tablespoons FRESH ORANGE JUICE

scant 1 cup MEDIUM SHERRY

2½ cups MASCARPONE CHEESE

⅔ cup STRAINED, PLAIN YOGURT

2 tablespoons CONFECTIONERS' SUGAR

about 1 cup VANILLA ICE CREAM

about 1 cup RASPBERRY ICE CREAM or SORBET

1 Preheat the oven to 350°F. Grease and line an 8-inch round cake pan. Put the butter, sugar, eggs, flour, baking powder, almonds and almond extract in a large bowl and beat with an electric beater for 2 minutes, until creamy. Stir in the milk.

2 Spoon the mixture into the prepared pan, level the surface and bake the cake for about 30 minutes or until it is just firm in the center. Transfer the cake to a wire rack and let cool.

3 Cut the cake into pieces and place these in the bottom of a 7½-cup glass serving dish. Sprinkle on half the raspberries and almonds. Mix the orange juice with 6 tablespoons of the sherry.

4 Spoon on the orange and sherry mixture. Beat the mascarpone in a bowl with the yogurt, confectioners' sugar and remaining sherry. Put the trifle dish and the mascarpone in the refrigerator until you are ready to assemble the trifle.

5 To serve, scoop the ice cream and sorbet into the trifle dish. Reserve a few of the remaining raspberries and almonds for the decoration, then sprinkle the rest on the ice cream. Spoon on the mascarpone mixture and sprinkle on the reserved raspberries and almonds. Chill the trifle for up to 1 hour before serving.

COOK'S TIP *The trifle will set better if all the ingredients are thoroughly chilled in the refrigerator before assembling. Chill again before serving.*

VARIATION *There are many variations on this recipe that work equally well. Try any other berries or tropical fruits and complementary ice creams or sorbets.*

Pear and Gingerbread Sundaes

The best sundaes do not consist solely of ice cream and sauce, but are a feast of flavors that melt

into each other, much like a trifle. Poach the pears and chill them well in advance,

so that the dessert can be assembled in minutes.

SERVES FOUR

INGREDIENTS

⅓ cup LIGHT
BROWN SUGAR

6 tablespoons WATER

2 tablespoons LEMON JUICE

⅓ cup GOLDEN RAISINS
or RAISINS

¼ teaspoon GROUND ALLSPICE

4 SMALL PEARS

5 ounces MOIST GINGERBREAD or
GINGER CAKE

1 cup CLASSIC VANILLA
ICE CREAM

1 Heat the sugar and water in a heavy saucepan until the sugar has dissolved. Add the lemon juice, golden raisins or raisins and spice. Peel, quarter and core the pears and add them to the pan.

2 Cover and simmer very gently for 5–10 minutes, until just tender. Cool the pears in the syrup. Lift them out of the syrup and put them in a bowl. Pour the syrup into a pitcher. Chill both.

3 Cut the gingerbread or ginger cake into four pieces and arrange in four serving glasses. Divide the pears among the glasses, then pile ice cream in the center of each portion. Pour a little of the syrup onto each sundae and serve.

VARIATION *This quick and easy dessert can be made just as successfully with tart apples.*

Coconut Ice Cream with Mango Sauce

Halved coconut shells make impressive serving containers for this rich and delicious

ice cream. You'll need to crack open three coconuts to get six serving cups,

plus enough trimmings to use in the ice cream.

SERVES SIX

INGREDIENTS

4 EGG YOLKS

½ cup SUGAR

1 tablespoon CORNSTARCH

1 teaspoon ALMOND EXTRACT

2½ cups MILK

1½ cups FRESHLY GRATED COCONUT

1¼ cups WHIPPING CREAM

For the sauce

1 LARGE RIPE MANGO

2 tablespoons SUGAR

1 tablespoon LEMON JUICE

¼ cup FRESH ORANGE JUICE

1 Beat the egg yolks, sugar, cornstarch, almond extract and a little of the milk until combined. Transfer the coconut to a food processor and process with 1¼ cups of the remaining milk until fairly smooth.

2 Pour the fresh coconut milk into a heavy saucepan and stir in the rest of the milk. Bring the milk almost to a boil.

3 Gradually pour the milk onto the egg yolks, whisking constantly. Return the mixture to the pan and cook very gently, stirring, until thickened. Pour the custard into a bowl, cover it with a circle of waxed paper and let cool.

4 BY HAND: Whip the cream and fold into the custard. Transfer to a freezer container and freeze for 3–4 hours, beating twice as it thickens. Freeze again overnight.

USING AN ICE CREAM MAKER: Stir in the cream and churn until it holds its shape. Spoon into a freezer container and freeze for several hours or overnight.

5 To make the sauce, slice the mango flesh off the pit and put it in a food processor. Add the sugar, lemon juice and orange juice and process until smooth. Pour into a small pitcher and chill.

6 To serve, scoop the prepared ice cream into the halved coconut shells, or into tall serving glasses. Add the mango sauce and serve immediately.

ice creams

with fruit

Whether served as an accompaniment or churned into ice cream or sorbet, an abundance of tangy fruit gives a light, fresh taste. For an invigorating summer cooler or finale to a rich meal, fruit ices are a vibrant marriage of color and flavor.

Passion Fruit Mousse

Passion fruit has a rich, tangy flavor that works wonderfully well in a creamy mousse. The raised paper collar is one of the tricks of the trade—peel it off and the texture and sophisticated shape of the mousse are revealed.

3 Sprinkle the gelatin on the water in a small, heatproof bowl and let soak for 5 minutes or until spongy. Whisk the egg yolks and sugar in a bowl until the mixture is pale and creamy.

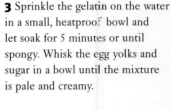

4 Stand the bowl of gelatin in a pan containing a little gently simmering water and let sit until dissolved. Beat the passion fruit juice and lemon juice into the whisked mixture, then add the liquid. Mix well. Let stand until thickened but not set. Whisk the egg whites until stiff. Whip the cream until it forms soft peaks.

SERVES SIX

INGREDIENTS

9 ripe PASSION FRUIT

2 teaspoons POWDERED GELATIN

3 tablespoons WATER

3 EGGS, separated

6 tablespoons SUGAR

2 tablespoons LEMON JUICE

1 cup HEAVY or WHIPPING CREAM

1 Cut out six 12 x 3-inch strips of nonstick baking parchment. Wrap each strip around a ⅔-cup ramekin, holding it in place with a paper clip. Secure with string under the rim of each paper collar.

2 Cut the passion fruit in half and use a teaspoon to scoop the pulp into a sieve set over a bowl. Press the pulp in the sieve with the back of a large spoon to extract as much juice as possible.

5 Using a large metal spoon, fold the cream into the yolk mixture. Stir in a quarter of the egg whites to loosen the mixture, then fold in the remainder. Spoon into the prepared dishes so that the mixture comes well above the rim of each dish. Freeze the mousses for at least 4 hours.

6 About 30 minutes before you intend to serve them, gently peel off the paper collars from the mousses and transfer them to the refrigerator to soften slightly.

COOK'S TIP *Before filling the ramekins, stand them on a small baking sheet. That way, you can transfer them all to the freezer all at once.*

Summer Pudding

SERVES SIX TO EIGHT

INGREDIENTS

2 tablespoons SUGAR

¼ cup WATER

5 tablespoons
STRAWBERRY JAM

¼ cup CRÈME DE
CASSIS

2 cups SMALL STRAWBERRIES,
thinly sliced

9 ounces GOOD QUALITY
MADEIRA CAKE

1 cup BERRY SORBET

2¼ cups STRAWBERRY
or RASPBERRY
ICE CREAM

This is a frozen version of the classic and ever-popular berry-filled dessert. Made using good-quality fruit sorbet and strawberry or raspberry ice cream, the result is just as delicious and looks very impressive.

1 Line a 6¼-cup pudding mold with plastic wrap. Heat the sugar and water in a small, heavy saucepan until the sugar has dissolved.

2 Meanwhile, press 2 tablespoons of the strawberry jam through a sieve into a small bowl. Stir in 1 tablespoon of the syrup and brush the mixture up the sides of the lined mold. Press the remaining jam through the sieve into the saucepan of syrup and stir in the crème de cassis until smooth.

3 Press the strawberry slices in a single layer on the bottom and sides of the mold, fitting them as tightly together as possible. Chill. Cut the cake into ½-inch slices.

4 Dip the cake slices in the remaining syrup and arrange in a single layer on the strawberries, cutting the cake to fit and trimming off the excess around the edges. Freeze for 30 minutes.

5 Remove the sorbet from the freezer to soften for about 15 minutes. Using a large metal spoon, pack the sorbet into the mold—it will fill it about three-quarters full—and level the surface. Return the mold to the freezer for 30 minutes. Remove the ice cream from the freezer for about 15 minutes to soften.

6 Pack the ice cream onto the sorbet, filling the mold. Level the surface and freeze for at least 4 hours or overnight.

7 To serve, dip the bowl in very hot water for 2 seconds, then invert the pudding onto a serving plate. Peel off the plastic wrap and serve the pudding in wedges.

COOK'S TIP *Any berry sorbet can be used. Raspberry sorbet has a wonderfully intense color; black currant or red currant sorbet would also be excellent choices.*

Peach Mousse Cakes

These light and airy frozen mousses, sandwiched between layers of cake, can be made ahead for a dinner party

dessert or thawed and served for a special tea. You will need a couple of

sheets of flexible acrylic plastic for shaping the molds.

MAKES EIGHT

INGREDIENTS

For the cake

3 EGGS

6 tablespoons SUGAR

⅔ cup ALL-PURPOSE FLOUR

CONFECTIONERS' SUGAR, for dusting

For the mousse

2 teaspoons POWDERED GELATIN

3 tablespoons WATER

6 RIPE PEACHES

finely grated zest of 1 ORANGE

6 tablespoons SUGAR

2 EGG WHITES

⅔ cup HEAVY CREAM

3 tablespoons COINTREAU or other ORANGE-FLAVORED LIQUEUR

1 Preheat the oven to 350°F. Grease a 13 x 9-inch jelly roll pan and line with waxed paper. Grease the paper. Put the eggs and sugar in a heatproof bowl, place over a pan of gently simmering water and whisk until the mixture forms a trail when the whisk is lifted from the bowl. Remove from heat and whisk for 2 minutes, until cool.

2 Sift the flour into the bowl and fold in, using a large metal spoon. Scrape into the prepared pan, gently spreading the mixture into the corners. Bake for about 15 minutes, until just firm. Let cool. Cut out eight 10 x 2-inch strips of acrylic plastic.

3 Using a 3-inch cookie cutter, cut out eight circles from the cake. Carefully slice each round horizontally in half. Roll a piece of acrylic plastic into a round and fit it around one of the pieces of cake so that the cake fits snugly in its acrylic plastic collar.

4 Secure the acrylic plastic with tape. Make sure the cut-side of the cake is facing up. Make seven more cake-based shells in the same way and place them on a small tray.

5 Make the mousse. Sprinkle the gelatin on the water in a small heatproof bowl. Let sit for about 5 minutes or until spongy. Peel the peaches, if desired, then cut them in half, remove the pits and chop the flesh roughly. Put it in a food processor, add the orange zest and process to a purée.

6 Put about a quarter of the purée in a small pan with the sugar and soaked gelatin; heat until both sugar and gelatin have dissolved. Beat the mixture into the remaining purée. Let sit until thickened but not set.

7 Whisk the egg whites in a clean, greasefree bowl until stiff. Whip the cream with the liqueur until soft peaks start to form. Using a large metal spoon, carefully fold the cream into the purée, followed by the egg whites.

8 Divide the mousse mixture evenly among the cake-filled shells and gently level the tops.

9 Position the remaining cake rounds on the filling, making sure the uncut sides of the cakes are facing up. Press down gently. Freeze for at least 3 hours.

10 To serve, dust the tops of the cakes with confectioners' sugar, then gently peel off the acrylic plastic.

COOK'S TIP *There are two main types of peaches: "freestone" and "clingstone." As the name suggests, the stone of the "freestone" type separates more easily from the flesh and is therefore better for this dish.*

Lemon Sorbet Cups with Berries

In this stunning dessert, lemon sorbet is molded into cup shapes to make pretty containers for a selection of berries. Other combinations, such as mango sorbet with tropical fruits, or orange sorbet with blueberries, also work well.

SERVES SIX

INGREDIENTS

2¼ cups LEMON SORBET

2 cups SMALL STRAWBERRIES

scant 1 cup RASPBERRIES

¾ cup RED CURRANTS, BLACK CURRANTS or WHITE CURRANTS

1 tablespoon SUGAR

3 tablespoons COINTREAU or other ORANGE-FLAVORED LIQUEUR

1 Put six ⅔-cup metal molds in the freezer for 15 minutes to chill. At the same time, remove the sorbet from the freezer to soften slightly.

3 Cut the strawberries in half and place in a bowl with the raspberries and red, black or white currants. Add the sugar and liqueur and toss the ingredients together lightly. Cover and chill for at least 2 hours.

4 Once the sorbet in the molds has frozen completely, loosen the edges with a knife, then dip in a bowl of very hot water for 2 seconds. Invert the sorbet cups on a small tray, using a fork to twist and loosen the cups if necessary.

5 If you need to, dip the molds very briefly in the hot water again. Turn the cups over so they are ready to fill and return to the freezer until required.

6 To serve, place the cups on serving plates and fill with the fruits, spooning over any juices.

COOK'S TIP *When lining a metal mold with the lemon sorbet it is a good idea to wrap your hand in a dish towel. This not only prevents your fingers from sticking to the metal, but also stops the heat from your hands from warming the mold.*

2 Using a teaspoon, pack the sorbet into the molds, building up a layer about ½ inch thick around the bottom and sides, and leaving a deep cavity in the center. Hold each mold in a dish towel as you work (see Cook's Tip). Return each mold to the freezer when it is lined.

Spiced Sorbet Pears

Pears poached in wine make an elegant dessert at any time of year.

In this recipe the pears are hollowed out and filled

with a wine-and-pear flavored sorbet.

5 Cut a deep 1-inch slice off the top of each pear and reserve. Use an apple corer to remove the cores.

6 Using a teaspoon, scoop out the center of each pear, leaving a thick shell. Put the scooped-out flesh in a food processor or blender and the hollowed pears and their lids in the freezer. Strain the poaching juices. Set 5 tablespoons aside for serving and add the rest to the food processor. Blend until smooth.

7 BY HAND: Pour the mixture into a container and freeze for 3–4 hours, beating twice as it thickens.

USING AN ICE CREAM MAKER:
Churn the mixture in an ice cream maker until it holds its shape.

Using a teaspoon, pack the sorbet into the frozen pears, piling it up high. Position the lids and return to the freezer overnight.

8 Remove the pears from the freezer and let them stand at room temperature for about 30 minutes before serving. The pears should have softened but the sorbet will remain frozen. Transfer to serving plates and spoon a little of the reserved syrup around each one.

SERVES SIX

INGREDIENTS

2½ cups RED WINE

2 CINNAMON STICKS, halved

generous ½ cup SUGAR

6 PLUMP PEARS

1 Put the wine, cinnamon sticks and sugar in a heavy pan that is big enough for the pears. Heat gently to dissolve the sugar.

2 Peel the pears, leaving the stems attached. Stand them upright in the syrup in the saucepan, taking care not to pack them too tightly.

3 Cover and simmer very gently for 10–20 minutes, until just tender, turning so they color evenly. (The cooking time varies depending on the softness of the pears.)

4 Lift out the pears with a slotted spoon and set them aside to cool. Boil the juices briefly until reduced to 1½ cups. Set aside and let cool.

Marinated Fruits with Sorbet Sauce

Mixed briefly in the food processor with fruit juice and liqueur, sorbet makes a wonderful sauce for spooning over fruit. A refreshing treat on a hot summer's afternoon.

SERVES FOUR

INGREDIENTS

12 LYCHEES, peeled

1 MANGO, peeled

1 PAPAYA, peeled

1 KIWI FRUIT, peeled

juice of 1 LIME

1 tablespoon SUGAR

¼ cup VODKA

1¼ cups MANGO or other TROPICAL FRUIT SORBET

2 tablespoons MANGO or ORANGE JUICE

1 Halve the lychees and remove the pits. Pit and slice the mango. Halve the papaya, remove the seeds and thinly slice or chop the flesh. Slice the kiwi fruit.

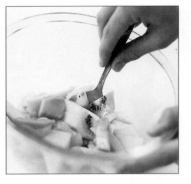

2 Put the fruits in a bowl. Add the lime juice, sugar and 1 tablespoon of the vodka and toss together lightly with a spoon. Cover and chill for at least 1 hour.

3 Stir the fruits together lightly and divide among four tall, narrow glasses. Chill until ready to serve.

4 Scoop the sorbet into a food processor, add the mango or orange juice and remaining vodka and blend very briefly until smooth and foamy. Immediately pour onto the fruits and serve.

COOK'S TIP *Although the sorbet mixture has to be blended at the last minute, you can arrange the fruits in the glasses well in advance.*

Mascarpone and Raspberry Ripple

Mascarpone makes a perfectly smooth, refreshing base for ice cream, particularly when mixed with a tangy lemon syrup and streaked with raspberry purée.

SERVES EIGHT

INGREDIENTS

1¼ cups SUGAR

scant 2 cups WATER

finely grated zest and juice of 1 LEMON

2 cups RASPBERRIES, plus extra, to decorate

2½ cups MASCARPONE CHEESE

1 Put 1 cup of the sugar in a heavy saucepan. Pour in the water and heat gently until the sugar dissolves. Bring to a boil, add the lemon zest and juice and boil for 3 minutes, without stirring, to make a syrup. Let cool.

2 Crush the raspberries lightly with a fork until broken up but not completely puréed, then stir in the remaining sugar.

3 Beat the mascarpone in a large bowl until smooth, gradually adding the lemon syrup.

4 BY HAND: Pour the mascarpone mixture into a freezer container and freeze for 3-4 hours, beating twice as it thickens.

USING AN ICE CREAM MAKER: Churn the mixture until thick, then transfer to a freezer container.

5 Spoon the crushed raspberries onto the ice cream. Using a metal spoon, fold them into the ice cream until rippled, making sure you reach the corners. Freeze for several hours or overnight until firm.

6 To serve, scoop the ice cream into glasses and decorate with the extra raspberries.

Frozen Melon with Pimm's

Freezing sorbet in hollowed out fruit, which is then cut into wedges, is an excellent idea. The novel presentation and refreshing flavor make this dessert irresistible on a hot summer's afternoon. The idea works particularly well with melon wedges laced with chilled Pimm's.

SERVES SIX

INGREDIENTS

¼ cup SUGAR

2 tablespoons HONEY

1 tablespoon LEMON JUICE

¼ cup WATER

1 medium CANTALOUPE or CHARENTAIS MELON, about 2¼ pounds

CRUSHED ICE, CUCUMBER SLICES and BORAGE LEAVES, to decorate

PIMM'S NO. 1, to serve

1 Put the sugar, honey, lemon juice and water in a small heavy saucepan and heat gently until the sugar dissolves. Bring to a boil and boil for 1 minute, without stirring, to make a syrup. Let cool.

2 Cut the melon in half and discard the seeds. Carefully scoop out the flesh and place into a food processor, taking care to keep the shells intact.

3 Blend the melon flesh until smooth. Then transfer to a bowl, stir in the cooled syrup and chill in the refrigerator until very cold. Invert the melon shells and let them drain on paper towels, then transfer to the freezer while making the sorbet.

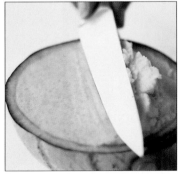

4 BY HAND: Pour the mixture into a container and freeze for 3-4 hours, beating twice with a fork, a whisk or in a food processor, to break up the ice crystals.

USING AN ICE CREAM MAKER: Churn the melon mixture in an ice cream maker until the sorbet holds its shape.

5 Pack the sorbet into the melon shells and level the surface with a knife. Then use a teaspoon to scoop out the center of each filled melon shell to simulate the seed cavity. Freeze overnight until firm.

6 To serve, use a large knife to cut each half into three wedges. Serve on a bed of ice on a large platter or individual serving plates, and decorate with the cucumber slices and borage. Drizzle on Pimm's to serve.

COOK'S TIP *If the melon sorbet is too firm to cut when taken out of the freezer, let it soften in the refrigerator slightly. Take care when slicing the frozen melon shell into wedges. A serrated kitchen knife is easiest to work with.*

Frozen Clementines

These pretty, sorbet-filled fruits store well in the freezer, and are perfect for an impromptu summer party, a picnic or simply a refreshing treat on a hot summer's afternoon.

MAKES 12

INGREDIENTS

16 LARGE CLEMENTINES

scant 1 cup SUGAR

7 tablespoons WATER

juice of 2 LEMONS

a little FRESH ORANGE JUICE (if necessary)

FRESH MINT or LEMON BALM LEAVES, to decorate

1 Slice the tops off 12 of the clementines to make lids. Set aside on a baking sheet. Loosen the clementine flesh with a sharp knife then carefully scoop it out into a bowl, keeping the shells intact. Scrape out as much of the membrane from the shells as possible. Add the shells to the lids and put them in the freezer.

2 Put the sugar and water in a heavy saucepan and heat gently, stirring until the sugar dissolves. Boil for 3 minutes without stirring, then let the syrup cool. Stir in the lemon juice.

3 Finely grate the zest from the remaining clementines. Squeeze the fruits and add the juice and zest to the syrup.

4 Process the clementine flesh in a food processor or blender, then press it through a sieve placed over a bowl to extract as much juice as possible. Add this to the syrup. You need about 3¾ cups of liquid. Add fresh orange juice if necessary.

5 BY HAND: Pour the mixture into a shallow container and freeze for 3-4 hours, beating twice as the sorbet thickens.

USING AN ICE CREAM MAKER: Churn the mixture until it holds its shape.

Pack the sorbet into the clementine shells, mounding them up slightly in the center. Position the lids and return to the freezer for several hours or overnight.

6 Transfer the clementines to the refrigerator about 30 minutes before serving, to soften. Serve on individual plates and decorate.

Peach and Almond Granita

Infused almonds make a richly flavored "milk" that forms the basis of this light, tangy dessert, which would be an ideal choice to follow a rich main course.

SERVES SIX

INGREDIENTS

1 cup GROUND ALMONDS

3¾ cups WATER

¼ cup SUGAR

1 teaspoon ALMOND EXTRACT

juice of 2 LEMONS

6 PEACHES

DISARONNO AMARETTO
LIQUEUR, to serve (optional)

1 Put the ground almonds in a saucepan and pour in 2½ cups of the water. Bring just to a boil, then lower the heat and simmer gently for 2 minutes. Remove from heat and let stand for 30 minutes.

2 Strain the mixture through a fine sieve placed over a bowl, and press lightly, with the back of a spoon, to extract as much liquid as possible. Pour the liquid into a clean, heavy saucepan.

3 Add the sugar and almond extract to the pan, with half the lemon juice and the remaining water. Heat gently until the sugar dissolves, then bring to a boil. Lower the heat and simmer gently for 3 minutes without stirring, taking care that the almond syrup does not boil over. Let cool completely.

4 Cut the peaches in half and remove the pits. Using a small knife, scoop out about half the flesh to enlarge the cavities. Put the flesh in a food processor. Brush the exposed flesh with the remaining lemon juice and chill the peaches until needed.

5 Add the almond syrup to the peach flesh and process until smooth. Pour into a shallow freezer container and freeze until ice crystals have formed around the edges. Stir with a fork, then freeze again until more crystals have formed around the edges. Repeat until the mixture has the consistency of crushed ice.

6 Lightly break up the granita with a fork to loosen the mixture. Spoon into the peach halves and serve two on each plate. Drizzle a little Amaretto liqueur on top, if desired.

COOK'S TIP *The scooped peach shells will keep overnight in the refrigerator if you brush them with lemon juice and wrap them in plastic wrap. If you want to make the granita even earlier, simply use the flesh of two peaches and serve the granita in tall glasses, instead of peach shells.*

Strawberry Semi-freddo

Serve this quick strawberry and ricotta dessert semi-frozen to enjoy the flavor at its best. The contrasting texture of crisp dessert cookies makes them the perfect accompaniment.

SERVES FOUR TO SIX

INGREDIENTS

generous 2 cups STRAWBERRIES

scant ½ cup STRAWBERRY JAM

generous 1 cup RICOTTA CHEESE

scant 1 cup STRAINED,
PLAIN YOGURT

1 teaspoon VANILLA EXTRACT

3 tablespoons SUGAR

EXTRA STRAWBERRIES and MINT
or LEMON BALM, to decorate

1 Put the strawberries in a bowl and mash them with a fork until broken into small pieces but not completely puréed. Stir in the strawberry jam. Drain off any whey from the ricotta.

2 Put the ricotta in a bowl and stir in the yogurt, vanilla and sugar. Using a teaspoon, gently fold the mashed strawberries into the ricotta mixture until rippled.

3 Spoon into individual freezer-proof dishes and freeze for at least 2 hours, until almost solid. Alternatively, freeze until completely solid, then transfer the ice cream to the refrigerator for about 45 minutes to soften before serving. Serve in small bowls with extra strawberries and decorated with mint or lemon balm.

COOK'S TIP *Don't mash the strawberries too much or they'll become too liquid. Freeze in a large freezer container if you don't have suitable small dishes. Transfer to the refrigerator to thaw slightly, then scoop into glasses.*

Sorbets on Sticks

*Almost any firm-textured sorbet can be frozen in ice popsicle molds, making a convenient and "fun"
presentation. For summer entertaining, a splash of alcohol in the sorbet gives added appeal for adults,
but this can easily be omitted if an alcohol-free version is preferred.*

MAKES ABOUT 24
depending on the size
of the molds

INGREDIENTS

**For the pineapple and
kirsch popsicles**

1 medium PINEAPPLE,
about 2½ pounds

½ cup SUGAR

1¼ cups WATER

2 tablespoons LIME JUICE

¼ cup KIRSCH

**For the pink grapefruit
and Campari popsicles**

3 PINK GRAPEFRUIT

½ cup SUGAR

⅔ cup WATER

5 tablespoons CAMPARI

a little GRAPEFRUIT or
ORANGE JUICE (optional)

VARIATION *Yellow-fleshed grapefruit
can be used instead of ruby grapefruit.*

1 For the pineapple popsicles, slice
the pineapple top and bottom, then
cut off the skin. Cut the pineapple
in half lengthwise and cut out the
core. Roughly chop the flesh and
blend it in a food processor until
smooth. Press the pulp through a
sieve placed over a bowl to extract
as much juice as possible.

2 Heat the sugar and water in a
heavy saucepan until the sugar
dissolves. Bring to a boil and boil
for 3 minutes, without stirring, to
make a syrup. Remove from heat
and let cool. Stir in the lime juice
and kirsch.

3 Stir the pineapple juice into the
syrup, then chill until very cold.
BY HAND: Pour the mixture into a
container and and freeze for 3–4
hours, beating twice as it thickens.

USING AN ICE CREAM MAKER: Churn
the sorbet until the mixture just
holds its own shape but is not firm.

4 Spoon into 12 popsicle molds.
Press a wooden popsicle stick into
the center of each sorbet. Freeze
overnight until firm.

5 To make the pink grapefruit and
Campari popsicles, cut the skin off
the grapefruit using a sharp knife.
Slice the flesh, discarding any seeds,
and blend in a food processor until
smooth, then press through a sieve
placed over a bowl to extract as
much juice as possible.

6 Measure the juice. You will need
a scant 2 cups for the sorbet. If
there is not enough, add a little
grapefruit or orange juice.

7 Heat the sugar and water in a
heavy saucepan until the sugar has
dissolved. Bring to a boil and boil
for 3 minutes, without stirring, to
make a syrup. Let cool completely,
then stir in the grapefruit juice and
Campari. Chill until very cold.

8 BY HAND: Pour the mixture into a
container and freeze for 3–4 hours,
beating twice as it thickens.

USING AN ICE CREAM MAKER: Churn
the mixture in an ice cream maker
until the sorbet just holds its
shape but is not firm. Spoon into
12 popsicle molds, position the
sticks as in Step 4, and freeze
overnight until firm.

9 To serve the popsicles, dip
the molds in very hot water for
1–2 seconds, then carefully pull
each popsicle from the mold.

COOK'S TIP *Don't let the fact that you
don't have popsicle molds deter you
from making this delicious dessert.
Use wooden popsicle sticks and small
plastic cups or even ice cube trays for
miniature popsicles.*

VARIATION *Other variations that are
just as delicious include orange sorbet
with a dash of Cointreau, or lemon
sorbet with gin. But don't be tempted to
add too much alcohol, or the sorbet will
not freeze.*

herb, spice & flower frozen desserts

For those with adventurous taste in ice cream, here is an intriguing repertoire of less predictable flavors such as Turkish delight, lavender and even chile. The ice creams in the following collection are quick and easy to make, and will have everyone trying to guess the intrinsic flavors.

Rosemary Ice Cream

Fresh rosemary has a lovely fragrance that works as well in sweet dishes as it does in savory.

Serve this ice cream as an accompaniment to berry or plum compote, or on its own,

with amaretti cookies.

SERVES SIX

INGREDIENTS

1¼ cups MILK

4 large FRESH ROSEMARY SPRIGS

3 EGG YOLKS

6 tablespoons SUGAR

2 teaspoons CORNSTARCH

1⅔ cups CRÈME FRAÎCHE

1 tablespoon BROWN SUGAR

FRESH ROSEMARY SPRIGS and HERB FLOWERS, to decorate

COOKIES, to serve

1 Put the milk and rosemary sprigs in a heavy saucepan. Bring almost to a boil, remove from heat and let infuse for about 20 minutes. Place the egg yolks in a bowl and whisk in the sugar and the cornstarch.

2 Return the pan to the heat and bring almost to a boil. Gradually pour in the yolk mixture and stir it in well. Return to the pan and cook over very low heat, stirring constantly, until it thickens. Do not let it boil or it may curdle.

3 Strain the custard through a sieve into a bowl. Cover the surface closely with waxed paper and let cool. Chill the custard until it is very cold, then stir in the crème fraîche.

4 BY HAND: Pour the mixture into a container and freeze for 3–4 hours, beating twice as it thickens. Return to the freezer until ready to serve.

USING AN ICE CREAM MAKER: Churn the mixture until it is thick, then scrape it into a freezerproof container. Freeze until ready to serve.

5 Transfer the ice cream to the refrigerator 30 minutes before serving to soften slightly. Scoop into dessert dishes, sprinkle lightly with brown sugar and decorate with fresh rosemary sprigs and herb flowers. Serve with cookies.

COOK'S TIP *For a very attractive effect use herb flowers that complement the color of your dessert dishes.*

Lavender and Honey Ice Cream

Lavender and honey forge a memorable partnership in this old-fashioned and elegant ice cream.

Serve scooped into glasses or set in little molds and top with lightly whipped cream.

Pretty lavender flowers add the finishing touch.

SERVES SIX TO EIGHT

INGREDIENTS

6 tablespoons HONEY

4 EGG YOLKS

2 teaspoons CORNSTARCH

8 LAVENDER SPRIGS,
plus extra, to decorate

scant 2 cups MILK

scant 2 cups WHIPPING CREAM

COOKIES, to serve

1 Put the honey, egg yolk, and cornstarch in a bowl. Separate the lavender flowers and add them plus a little milk. Whisk lightly. In a heavy saucepan bring the remaining milk to a boil. Add to the egg yolk mixture, stirring well.

2 Return the mixture to the pan and cook very gently, stirring until the mixture thickens. Pour the custard into a bowl, cover the surface closely with a circle of waxed paper and let cool, then chill until very cold.

3 BY HAND: Whip the cream and fold into the custard. Pour into a container and freeze for 3–4 hours, beating twice as it thickens. Return to the freezer until ready to serve.

USING AN ICE CREAM MAKER: Stir the cream into the custard, then churn the mixture until it holds its shape. Transfer to a freezerproof container and freeze until ready to serve.

4 Transfer the ice cream to the refrigerator 30 minutes before serving, so that it softens slightly. Scoop the ice cream into small dishes, decorate with lavender flowers and serve with cookies.

Bay Leaf and Macaroon Ice Cream

Bay leaves give a warm but delicate flavor to ice cream and combine particularly well with almond flavors.

Serve with fresh apricots, plums, peaches or berries.

SERVES SIX

INGREDIENTS

1¼ cups MILK

4 FRESH BAY LEAVES

4 EGG YOLKS

6 tablespoons SUGAR

2 teaspoons CORNSTARCH

5 ounces MACAROONS

1¼ cups WHIPPING CREAM

1 Put the milk in a saucepan, add the fresh bay leaves and bring slowly to a boil. Remove from heat and set aside for 30 minutes to infuse. Whisk the egg yolks in a bowl with the sugar and cornstarch.

2 Strain the milk into the egg yolk mixture and stir well. Return to the saucepan and cook over low heat, stirring constantly, until the custard thickens. Do not let it boil or it may curdle. Transfer the custard to a bowl, cover the surface closely with waxed paper and let cool completely. Chill until very cold.

3 Place the cookies in a plastic bag and crush them using a rolling pin.

BY HAND: In a separate bowl, lightly whip the cream and fold into the custard, then stir in 2 ounces of the crushed cookies.

USING AN ICE CREAM MAKER: Add the cream and churn the mixture until thick, then scrape into a bowl. Add 2 ounces of crushed cookies.

4 Working quickly, spoon the ice cream onto a sheet of waxed paper, packing it into a log shape about 2½ inches thick and 10 inches long.

5 Bring the waxed paper up around the ice cream to pack it together tightly and give it a good shape. Support the ice cream log on a baking sheet and freeze for at least 3 hours or overnight.

6 Spread the remaining crushed cookies on a sheet of waxed paper. Unwrap the ice cream log and roll it quickly in the crumbs to coat. Return to the freezer until needed. Serve in slices.

COOK'S TIP *If the ice cream is too soft to successfully shape into a log, freeze it for a couple of hours first.*

Peppermint Swirl

This ice cream looks very sophisticated, with its delicate colors and marbled appearance. The refreshing taste of peppermint makes it ideal for serving after a rich main course.

SERVES SIX

INGREDIENTS

6 tablespoons SUGAR

¼ cup WATER

10 large FRESH PEPPERMINT SPRIGS

½ teaspoon PEPPERMINT EXTRACT

scant 2 cups HEAVY CREAM

a few drops of GREEN FOOD COLORING

scant 1 cup STRAINED, PLAIN YOGURT

1 Put the sugar, water and fresh peppermint in a small, heavy saucepan and heat gently, stirring occasionally, until the sugar has dissolved. Bring to a boil and cook without stirring for about 3 minutes to make a syrup.

2 Strain the syrup into a medium bowl and stir in the peppermint extract. Transfer 4 tablespoons of the mixture to a large bowl.

3 Remove from heat and let cool. Dampen a 1-pound loaf pan with a little water, then line it with plastic wrap.

4 Add 3 tablespoons of the cream and a few drops of food coloring to the medium bowl and stir until smooth. Add the remaining cream to the mixture in the large bowl, then stir in the yogurt. Whisk the mixture until it starts to hold its shape.

5 Place alternate spoonfuls of the two mixtures in the prepared pan. When the pan is full, swirl the two mixtures together, using a teaspoon. Cover and freeze for at least 4 hours or overnight.

6 To serve, dip the pan in very hot water for 1–2 seconds, then invert the frozen swirl onto a serving plate. Serve in slices.

Basil and Orange Granita

More often associated with savory dishes, basil has a sweet, aromatic flavor that complements tangy oranges beautifully. This classic combination makes a perfect refresher between courses.

SERVES SIX

INGREDIENTS

5 LARGE ORANGES

scant 1 cup SUGAR

scant 2 cups WATER

ORANGE JUICE (if necessary)

½ cup FRESH BASIL LEAVES

TINY FRESH BASIL LEAVES, to decorate

1 Pare the zest thinly from three oranges and place in a saucepan. Add the sugar and water. Heat gently until the sugar has dissolved. Cool, pour into a bowl and chill.

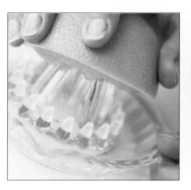

2 Squeeze the juice from all the oranges and pour it into a large measuring cup. You should have about 2¼ cups. Add fresh orange juice, if necessary, until you have enough.

3 Pour the juice into a food processor or blender and add the basil leaves. Process the mixture in short bursts until the basil has been chopped into small pieces.

4 Using a slotted spoon, remove the orange zest from the chilled syrup. Stir in the orange juice and basil mixture, then pour into a large plastic or other freezerproof container. Cover and freeze for about 2 hours or until the mixture around the edges is mushy. Break up the ice crystals with a fork and stir well.

5 Freeze for 30 more minutes, until once again frozen around the edges. Mash with a fork and return to the freezer. Repeat the process until the ice forms fine crystals.

6 To serve, spoon the granita into tall glasses and decorate with the tiny basil leaves.

Star Anise and Grapefruit Granita

With its aniseed flavor, star anise makes an interesting addition to many fruit desserts, and its dramatic appearance makes it the ideal decoration. This refreshing granita will stand out, as it is both tangy and sweet.

SERVES SIX

INGREDIENTS

1 cup SUGAR

scant 2 cups WATER

6 WHOLE STAR ANISE

4 GRAPEFRUIT

1 Put the sugar and water in a saucepan and heat gently, stirring occasionally, until the sugar has completely dissolved. Stir in the star anise and heat the syrup gently for 2 minutes, without stirring. Remove from heat and let cool.

2 Take a slice off the top and bottom of each grapefruit, then slice off the skin and pith. Chop the flesh roughly and put it in a food processor. Process until almost smooth, then press the pulp through a sieve into a bowl.

3 Strain the syrup into the bowl, reserving the star anise. Mix well, then pour the mixture into a shallow freezerproof container. Cover and freeze for about 2 hours, until the mixture starts to freeze and form ice crystals around the edges of the container.

4 Using a fork, break up the ice crystals, then return the mixture to the freezer. Freeze for 30 more minutes more, mash with a fork again, then return to the freezer. Repeat the process until the mixture forms fine ice crystals.

5 To serve, spoon the granita into glasses and decorate with the reserved star anise.

COOK'S TIP *Buy whole star anise at a gourmet shop or market that sells spices loose or packaged in clear cellophane. When the spice is packed in boxes, it is often broken into sections and the quality and flavor has deteriorated.*

Lemon and Cardamom Ice Cream

The classic partnership of lemon and cardamom gives this rich ice cream a lovely "clean" tang. It is a perfect choice for serving after a spicy main course.

SERVES SIX

INGREDIENTS

1 tablespoon CARDAMOM PODS

4 EGG YOLKS

generous ½ cup SUGAR

2 teaspoons CORNSTARCH

grated zest and juice of 3 LEMONS

1¼ cups MILK

1¼ cups WHIPPING CREAM

FRESH LEMON BALM SPRIGS and CONFECTIONERS' SUGAR, to decorate

1 Put the cardamom pods in a mortar and crush them with a pestle to release the seeds. Pick out and discard the shells, then grind the seeds to break them up slightly.

2 Put the egg yolks, sugar, cornstarch, lemon zest and juice in a bowl. Add the cardamom seeds and whisk well.

3 Bring the milk to a boil in a heavy saucepan, then pour it over the egg yolk mixture, stirring well. Return the mixture to the pan and cook over very low heat, stirring constantly, until the custard thickens.

4 Pour the custard into a bowl, cover the surface closely with a circle of waxed paper and let cool. Chill until very cold.

5 BY HAND: Whip the cream lightly and fold into the custard. Pour into a container and freeze for 3–4 hours, beating twice as it thickens. Return to the freezer until needed.

USING AN ICE CREAM MAKER: Whisk the cream lightly into custard and churn the mixture until it holds its shape. Transfer to a container and freeze until needed.

6 Transfer the ice cream to the refrigerator 30 minutes before serving. Scoop into glasses and decorate with lemon balm and sugar.

COOK'S TIP *Lemon balm is an easy herb to grow. The leaves are best picked before the flowering period, when they are at their most fragrant.*

Saffron, Apricot and Almond Ice Cream

SERVES SIX TO EIGHT

This vibrant ice cream has a slightly Middle-Eastern flavor. Although saffron is expensive, its intense color and distinctive flavor are well worth it, and you only need a small amount.

INGREDIENTS

⅔ cup DRIED APRICOTS

¼ cup COINTREAU or other
ORANGE-FLAVORED LIQUEUR

½ teaspoon SAFFRON THREADS,
lightly crushed

1 tablespoon BOILING WATER

3 EGG YOLKS

6 tablespoons SUGAR

2 teaspoons CORNSTARCH

1¼ cups MILK

1¼ cups LIGHT CREAM

¾ cup UNBLANCHED ALMONDS,
lightly toasted

AMARETTI COOKIES,
to serve (optional)

1 Chop the apricots into small pieces and put them in a bowl. Add the liqueur and let sit for about 1 hour or until absorbed. Put the saffron in a cup with the boiling water and let stand while you make the custard.

2 Whisk the egg yolks, sugar and cornstarch with a little of the milk in a bowl. Pour the milk into a pan, bring it almost to a boil, then pour it into the yolk mixture, stirring. Return the mixture to the pan and cook it over very low heat, stirring until the custard thickens. Do not let it boil or it may curdle.

3 Stir in the saffron, with its liquid, then cover the surface of the custard with waxed paper and let it cool. Chill until it is very cold.

4 BY HAND: Whip the cream and fold into the custard. Add the apricots and nuts and pour the mixture into a container. Freeze for 3–4 hours, beating twice as it thickens, and return to the freezer.

USING AN ICE CREAM MAKER: Stir in the cream and churn until thick. Add the apricots and nuts and churn for 5 more minutes, until well mixed. Spoon into a plastic or other freezerproof container and freeze overnight.

5 Transfer the ice cream to the refrigerator 30 minutes before serving, to soften. Scoop into glasses and serve with amaretti cookies.

COOK'S TIP *This ice cream looks most attractive served in small glasses or little glass cups with handles.*

Ginger and Kiwi Sorbet

Freshly grated ginger root gives a lively, aromatic flavor to sorbets and ice creams. Here, it is combined with kiwi fruit to make a refreshing sorbet.

SERVES SIX

INGREDIENTS

2 ounces FRESH GINGER ROOT

½ cup SUGAR

1¼ cups WATER

5 KIWI FRUIT

FRESH MINT SPRIGS or CHOPPED KIWI FRUIT, to decorate

1 Peel the ginger and grate it finely. Put the sugar and water in a saucepan and heat gently until the sugar has dissolved. Add the ginger and cook for 1 minute, then let cool. Strain into a bowl and chill until very cold.

2 Peel the kiwi fruit and blend until smooth. Add the purée to the chilled syrup and mix well.

3 BY HAND: Pour the mixture into a container and freeze for 3–4 hours, beating twice as it thickens. Return to the freezer until ready to serve.

USING AN ICE CREAM MAKER: Churn the mixture until it thickens. Transfer to a plastic or other freezerproof container and freeze until ready to serve.

4 Spoon into glasses, decorate with mint sprigs or chopped kiwi fruit, and serve.

Chili Sorbet

Served during or after dinner this unusual but refreshing sorbet is sure to become a talking point.

SERVES SIX

INGREDIENTS

1 FRESH RED CHILE

finely grated zest and juice of 2 LEMONS

finely grated zest and juice of 2 LIMES

1 cup SUGAR

3 cups WATER

PARED LEMON or LIME ZEST, to decorate

1 Cut the chile in half, removing all the seeds and any pith with a small sharp knife, and then chop the flesh very finely.

2 Put the chile, lemon and lime zest, sugar and water in a heavy saucepan. Heat gently and stir while the sugar dissolves. Bring to a boil, then simmer for 2 minutes without stirring. Let cool.

3 Add lemon and lime juice to the chili syrup and chill until very cold.

4 BY HAND: Pour the mixture into a container and freeze for 3–4 hours, beating twice as it thickens. Return to the freezer until ready to serve.

USING AN ICE CREAM MAKER: Churn the mixture until it holds its shape. Scrape into a container and freeze until ready to serve. Spoon into glasses and decorate with the thinly pared lemon or lime zest.

COOK'S TIP *Use a medium-hot chile rather than any of the fiery varieties. For an added kick, drizzle on tequila or vodka before serving. To avoid getting chile juice on your skin, wash your hands after dealing with them.*

Turkish Delight Sorbet

Anyone who likes Turkish delight will adore the taste and aroma of this intriguing dessert. Because of its sweetness, it is best served in small portions and is delicious with after-dinner coffee.

4 Spoon the sorbet into the cups and tap them lightly on the surface to compact the mixture. Cover with the overlapping plastic wrap and freeze for at least 3 hours or overnight.

5 Make a paper piping bag. Put the chocolate in a heatproof bowl and melt it over a pan of gently simmering water.

6 Meanwhile, remove the sorbets from the freezer, let them stand at room temperature for 5 minutes, then pull them out of the cups. Transfer to serving plates and peel off the plastic wrap. Spoon the melted chocolate into the piping bag, snip off the tip and scribble a design on the sorbet and the plate. Sprinkle on the almonds and serve.

SERVES EIGHT

INGREDIENTS

9 ounces ROSEWATER-FLAVORED TURKISH DELIGHT

2 tablespoons SUGAR

3 cups WATER

2 tablespoons LEMON JUICE

2 ounces WHITE CHOCOLATE, broken into pieces

roughly chopped JORDAN ALMONDS, to decorate

1 Cut the cubes of Turkish delight into small pieces. Put half the pieces in a heavy saucepan with the sugar. Pour in half the water. Heat gently until the Turkish delight has dissolved.

2 Cool, then stir in the lemon juice with the remaining water and Turkish delight. Chill well.

3 BY HAND: Pour the mixture into a container and freeze for 3–4 hours, beating twice as it thickens. Return to the freezer until ready to serve.

USING AN ICE CREAM MAKER: Churn the mixture until it holds its shape.

While the sorbet is freezing, dampen eight very small plastic cups or glasses, then line them with plastic wrap.

COOK'S TIP *You will probably find it easiest to use scissors to cut the cubes of Turkish delight into smaller pieces, rather than a knife.*

Mulled Wine Sorbet

This dramatic-looking sorbet provides a brief and welcome respite from the general overindulgence that takes place during the festive season, or any other celebration. It is spicy and flavorful, with quite a powerful kick to revive you from any seasonal sluggishness!

SERVES SIX

INGREDIENTS

1 bottle RED WINE

2 CLEMENTINES or
1 LARGE ORANGE

16 WHOLE CLOVES

2 CINNAMON STICKS, HALVED

1 APPLE, roughly chopped

1 teaspoon ALLSPICE

scant ½ cup LIGHT BROWN
SUGAR

⅔ cup WATER

scant 1 cup FRESHLY SQUEEZED
ORANGE JUICE

3 tablespoons BRANDY

strips of pared ORANGE ZEST,
to decorate

1 Pour the bottle of wine into a saucepan. Stud the clementines or orange with the cloves, then cut them in half. Add to the wine, with the cinnamon sticks, apple, allspice, sugar and water. Heat gently, stirring occasionally, until the sugar has dissolved.

2 Cover the pan and cook the mixture gently for 15 minutes. Remove from heat and let cool.

3 Strain the mixture into a large bowl, then stir in the orange juice and brandy. Chill until very cold.

4 BY HAND: Pour the mixture into a container and freeze for 3–4 hours, beating twice as it thickens. Return to the freezer until ready to serve.

USING AN ICE CREAM MAKER: Churn the mixture until it thickens. Transfer to a plastic or other freezerproof container and freeze until ready to serve.

5 To serve, spoon or scoop into small glasses and decorate with the strips of pared orange zest.

Rose Geranium Marquise

Rose geranium leaves give this ice cream a delicate, scented flavor. If you can't find savoiardi cookies, ordinary ladyfingers can be used instead. As they tend to be smaller, you may need to adjust the size of the marquise accordingly.

SERVES EIGHT

INGREDIENTS

generous 1 cup SUGAR

1⅓ cups WATER

24 FRESH ROSE
GERANIUM LEAVES

3 tablespoons LEMON JUICE

generous 1 cup MASCARPONE
CHEESE

1¼ cups HEAVY or
WHIPPING CREAM

7 ounces SAVOIARDI or
LADYFINGERS

scant 1 cup ALMONDS,
finely chopped and toasted

GERANIUM FLOWERS
and CONFECTIONERS' SUGAR,
to decorate

1 Put the sugar and water in a heavy saucepan and heat gently, stirring occasionally, until the sugar has dissolved. Add the geranium leaves and cook gently for 2 minutes. Let cool.

2 Strain the geranium syrup into a measuring cup and add the lemon juice. Put the mascarpone in a bowl and beat it until softened. Gradually beat in ⅔ cup of the syrup mixture. Whip the cream until it forms peaks, then fold it into the mascarpone mixture. At this stage the mixture should hold its shape. If necessary, whip the mixture a little more.

3 Spoon a little of the mixture onto a flat, freezerproof serving plate and spread it out to form an 8½ x 4½-inch rectangle. Pour the remaining syrup into a shallow bowl. Arrange a third of the cookies on the rectangle, having first dipped them in the syrup until they are very moist but not actually disintegrating.

4 Spread another thin layer of the cream mixture on the cookies. Set aside 1 tablespoon of the nuts for the topping. Sprinkle half the remainder on the cream. Make another two layers of syrup-steeped cookies, sandwiching them with more cream and the remaining nuts, but leaving enough cream mixture to coat the dessert completely.

5 Spread the remaining cream mixture on the top and sides of the cake until it is evenly coated. Sprinkle with the reserved nuts. Freeze the marquise for at least 4 hours or overnight.

6 Transfer the marquise to the refrigerator for 30 minutes before serving, so that it softens slightly. Scatter with geranium flowers, dust with confectioners' sugar, and serve in slices.

COOK'S TIP *Lemon geranium leaves can also be used for this recipe, but other varieties of geranium are not suitable.*

Elderflower and Lime Frozen Yogurt

These fragrant flowerheads have a wonderful flavor, but they are only in season for a very short time.
Fortunately, good quality bought or homemade elderflower cordial is readily available and combines beautifully
with limes to make a very refreshing frozen dessert.

SERVES SIX

INGREDIENTS

4 EGG YOLKS

¼ cup SUGAR

2 teaspoons CORNSTARCH

1¼ cups MILK

finely grated zest and juice of
2 LIMES

⅔ cup ELDERFLOWER CORDIAL

scant 1 cup STRAINED, PLAIN
YOGURT

⅔ cup HEAVY CREAM

GRATED LIME,
to decorate

2 Pour the custard into a bowl and add the lime zest and juice. Pour in the elderflower cordial and mix lightly. Cover the surface of the mixture closely with waxed paper. Let cool, then chill until very cold.

3 BY HAND: Whip the yogurt and cream and fold into the custard Pour the mixture into a container and freeze for 3–4 hours, beating twice as it thickens. Scoop into individual dishes and return to the freezer until ready to serve.

USING AN ICE CREAM MAKER: Stir the yogurt and cream into the chilled mixture and churn until it thickens. Transfer the yogurt into individual dishes or a plastic container and freeze until needed.

4 Transfer the frozen yogurt to the refrigerator 30 minutes before serving. Decorate with the grated lime zest and serve.

COOK'S TIP *Yogurt gives this a slightly tangier flavor than cream, but use all cream if you prefer.*

1 Whisk the egg yolks in a bowl with the sugar, cornstarch and a little of the milk. Pour the remaining milk into a heavy saucepan, bring it to a boil, then pour it into the yolk mixture, whisking constantly. Return the mixture to the saucepan and cook over very low heat, stirring constantly, until the custard thickens. Do not let it boil or it may curdle.

Pomegranate and Orange Flower Water Ice Cream

Take advantage of the availability of fresh pomegranates when in season to make this wonderfully colored dessert. The color will range from pastel pink to vibrant cerise, depending on the type of pomegranates used but whatever shade you achieve, the finished result will be very impressive.

SERVES SIX

INGREDIENTS

2 teaspoons CORNSTARCH

1¼ cups MILK

2 tablespoons SUGAR

2 LARGE POMEGRANATES

2 tablespoons ORANGE FLOWER WATER

5 tablespoons GRENADINE

1¼ cups WHIPPING CREAM

extra POMEGRANATE SEEDS and ORANGE FLOWER WATER, to serve

1 Put the cornstarch in a saucepan and blend into a paste with a little of the milk. Stir in the remaining milk and the sugar and cook, stirring constantly, until the mixture thickens. Pour it into a bowl, cover the surface closely with waxed paper and let it cool.

5 Transfer the creams to the refrigerator 30 minutes before serving, to let them soften. Top each of them with pomegranate seeds tossed in the extra orange flower water.

VARIATION *To accentuate the Middle-Eastern flavor of this dessert, the seeds from 12 cardamom pods can be added with the orange flower water.*

2 Cut the pomegranates in half and squeeze out the juice, using a lemon squeezer. Add the juice to the cornstarch mixture, with the orange flower water, grenadine and cream. Stir lightly to mix.

3 **BY HAND:** Stir to mix, then pour into a container and freeze for 3–4 hours, beating twice as it thickens.

USING AN ICE CREAM MAKER: Churn the mixture until it is thick enough to hold its shape.

4 Spoon the ice cream into one large, or six individual freezerproof serving dishes and freeze for at least 2 hours, or overnight.

ozen drinks

Keep a supply of classic ice creams and sorbets for making a wide range of exciting drinks. Blend with a splash of liqueur for a cooler drink with a kick, scoop into glasses and add soda, or mix with fruit for a wonderful drink and dessert in one.

Frozen Margaritas

This smooth sorbet drink has all the punch of Mexico's renowned cocktail! Serve it in tall, slim glasses with a capacity of about 1 cup.

SERVES TWO

INGREDIENTS

7 teaspoons FRESHLY SQUEEZED LIME JUICE

a little SUGAR, for frosting

4 LIME and 4 LEMON SLICES

½ cup TEQUILA

2 tablespoons COINTREAU

6–8 small scoops of ORANGE or LIME SORBET

⅔ cup CHILLED LEMONADE

sprigs of LEMON BALM, to decorate

1 Brush the rims of two tall glasses with 1 teaspoon of the lime juice. Spread out the sugar on a plate. Dip the rims of the glasses in the sugar to give a frosted edge.

2 Carefully add two lime and two lemon slices to each glass, standing them on end, so they will be fully visible through the glass.

3 Mix the tequila, Cointreau and remaining lime juice in a bowl. Scoop the sorbet into the glasses.

4 Spoon an equal amount of the tequila mixture into each glass. Add lemonade and serve immediately, decorated with lemon balm.

VARIATION *For a "shorter" version of this drink, use cocktail glasses and just one scoop of sorbet. The rims of the glasses can be frosted with salt instead of sugar, as for traditional Margaritas.*

Gin and Lemon Fizz

If gin and tonic is your drink, try this chilled alternative. The fruit and flower ice cubes make a lively decoration for any frozen drink.

SERVES TWO

INGREDIENTS

mixture of small EDIBLE BERRIES

pieces of thinly pared LEMON or ORANGE ZEST

tiny edible FLOWERS

4 scoops of LEMON SORBET

2 tablespoons GIN

about ½ cup CHILLED TONIC WATER

1 To make the decorated ice cubes, place each fruit, piece of zest or flower in a section of an ice cube tray. Carefully fill with water and freeze for several hours until the cubes are solid.

2 Divide the sorbet between two cocktail glasses or use small tumblers, with a capacity of about ⅔ cup.

3 Spoon in the gin and add a couple of the ornamental ice cubes to each glass. Add tonic water and serve immediately.

COOK'S TIP *When making the ice cubes, choose small herb flowers such as borage or mint, or edible flowers such as rose geraniums, primulas or rose buds.*

Lemonade on Ice

Homemade lemonade has a fresh, tangy flavor, unmatched by bought drinks.

The basic lemonade will keep well in the refrigerator for up to two weeks and is a

thirst-quenching drink at any time of day.

SERVES SIX

INGREDIENTS

6 LEMONS

1 cup SUGAR

7½ cups BOILING WATER

For each iced drink

4 scoops of LEMON SORBET

THIN LEMON and LIME SLICES

3 ICE CUBES,
crushed

MINT SPRIGS and halved LEMON
and LIME SLICES, to decorate

VARIATION *Use freshly squeezed lime juice instead of lemon juice or bruise some mint leaves and add them to the syrup for a subtle mint flavor. For pink lemonade, add a few drops of grenadine to each glass when serving.*

1 Start by making the lemonade. Wash the lemons and dry them thoroughly. Pare all the lemons thinly, avoiding the bitter white pith, and put the zest in a large heatproof bowl. Add the sugar. Squeeze the lemons and set the juice aside.

2 Pour the measured boiling water onto the lemon zests and sugar. Stir until the sugar dissolves. Let cool, then stir in the lemon juice. Strain the lemonade into a large pitcher and chill.

3 For each glass of lemonade, place four scoops of sorbet in a tall glass and tuck some lemon and lime slices down the sides. Add the crushed ice. Fill each glass up with about 1 cup of the lemonade. Decorate with mint and halved lemon and lime slices.

Cranberry, Cinnamon and Ginger Spritzer

Partially freezing fruit juice gives it a wonderfully slushy texture that is very refreshing. The combination of cranberry and apple juice contributes a tart, clean flavor that's not too sweet.

SERVES FOUR

INGREDIENTS

2½ cups CHILLED CRANBERRY JUICE

⅔ cup CLEAR APPLE JUICE

4 CINNAMON STICKS

about 1⅓ cups CHILLED GINGER ALE

a few FRESH or FROZEN CRANBERRIES, to decorate

1 Pour the cranberry juice into a shallow freezerproof container and freeze for about 2 hours or until a thick layer of ice crystals has formed around the edges.

2 Mash with a fork to break up the ice, then return the mixture to the freezer for another 2–3 hours, until almost solid.

3 Pour the apple juice into a small saucepan, add 2 cinnamon sticks and bring to just below the boiling point. Pour into a pitcher and let cool, then remove the cinnamon sticks and set them aside with the other cinnamon sticks. Chill the juice until it is very cold.

4 Spoon the cranberry ice into a food processor. Add the apple juice and blend very briefly until slushy.

5 Pile into cocktail glasses or flutes, add chilled ginger ale and decorate with the fresh or frozen cranberries. Stick a long cinnamon stick into each glass, to use as a swizzle stick.

VARIATION *As an alternative decoration, thread cranberries on four toothpicks and add one to each glass instead of a cinnamon stick.*

Berry and Ginger Cup

A colorful medley of berries steeped in vodka and served with an icy blend of sorbet and ginger ale. You will definitely need spoons for this one.

SERVES FOUR

INGREDIENTS

1 cup STRAWBERRIES, hulled

⅔ cup RASPBERRIES, hulled

½ cup BLUEBERRIES

1 tablespoon SUGAR

6 tablespoons VODKA

2½ cups GINGER ALE

4 large scoops of ORANGE SORBET

about 8 ICE CUBES

4 teaspoons GRENADINE

4 CAPE GOOSEBERRIES, to decorate

1 Cut the strawberries in half and put them in a bowl with the raspberries, blueberries and sugar. Pour in the vodka and toss lightly. Cover and chill for at least 30 minutes.

2 Put the ginger ale and sorbet in a blender or food processor and process until smooth. Pour into four bowl-shaped glasses and add a couple of ice cubes to each glass of sorbet mixture.

3 Spoon a teaspoon of grenadine onto the ice cubes in each glass, then spoon the vodka-steeped fruits on top of the sorbet mixture and ice cubes. Decorate each glass with a cape gooseberry and serve the drinks immediately.

VARIATION *Any combination of berries can be used for this frozen drink. Blackberries, for example, would also work well.*

Sparkling Peach Melba

This refreshing fruit drink is an excellent choice for summer celebrations. As with most fruit recipes, its success depends on using the ripest, tastiest peaches and raspberries available.

SERVES FOUR

INGREDIENTS

3 RIPE PEACHES

6 tablespoons ORANGE JUICE

½ cup RASPBERRIES

2 teaspoons CONFECTIONERS' SUGAR

about 2¼ cups RASPBERRY SORBET

about 1⅓ cups CHILLED SPARKLING WHITE WINE

FRESH MINT SPRIGS, to decorate

1 Put the peaches in a heatproof bowl and pour in boiling water to cover. Let sit for 60 seconds, then drain the peaches and peel off the skins.

2 Cut the fruit in half and remove the pits. Chop the peach halves roughly and purée them with the orange juice in a food processor or blender until smooth. Scrape the purée into a bowl.

3 Put the raspberries in the food processor or blender. Add the confectioners' sugar and process until smooth. Press the raspberry purée through a sieve into a bowl. Chill both purées for at least 1 hour.

4 Spoon the chilled peach purée into four tall glasses.

5 Add scoops of sorbet to come to the top of the glasses. Spoon the raspberry purée around the sorbet.

6 Fill each glass up with sparkling wine. Decorate with the mint sprigs and serve.

VARIATION *When fresh ripe peaches are unavailable, use canned peach halves in juice or light syrup.*

Frozen Mango Lassi

Based on a traditional Indian drink, this is excellent with spicy food, or as a welcome cooler at any time of day.

The frozen yogurt that is the basis of this drink is a useful recipe to add to your repertoire—

it is lighter and fresher than cream-based versions.

SERVES THREE TO FOUR

INGREDIENTS

For the frozen yogurt

¼ cup SUGAR

⅔ cup WATER

2 LEMONS

generous 2 cups STRAINED,
PLAIN YOGURT

For each drink

½ cup MANGO JUICE

2–3 ICE CUBES
(optional)

FRESH MINT SPRIGS and
WEDGES of MANGO,
to serve

1 To make the frozen yogurt, put the sugar and water in a saucepan and heat gently, stirring occasionally, until the sugar has dissolved. Pour the syrup into a pitcher. Let cool, then chill until very cold.

2 Grate the lemons and then squeeze them. Add the zest and juice to the chilled syrup and stir well to mix.

3 BY HAND: Pour the syrup mixture into a container and freeze until thickened. Beat in the yogurt and return to the freezer until thick enough to scoop.

USING AN ICE CREAM MAKER: Churn the mixture until it thickens. Stir in the yogurt and churn for 2 minutes more until well mixed. Transfer to a plastic or other freezerproof container and freeze.

4 To make each lassi, briefly blend the mango juice with three small scoops of the frozen yogurt in a food processor or blender until just smooth. Pour the mixture into a tall glass or tumbler and add the ice cubes, if using,

5 Top each drink with another scoop of the frozen yogurt and decorate. Serve immediately.

VARIATION *Add one small chopped banana when blending the ingredients together for a substantial summer smoothie.*

COOK'S TIP *Make sure you buy good-quality yogurt for this drink, as it adds a lovely, sharp tang.*

Tropical Fruit Sodas

For many children, scoops of vanilla ice cream, served in a froth of lemonade, would be a perfect treat. This more elaborate version will appeal to adults too.

SERVES FOUR

INGREDIENTS

2 teaspoons SUGAR

1 PAPAYA

1 SMALL RIPE MANGO

2 PASSION FRUIT

8 large scoops of CLASSIC VANILLA ICE CREAM

8 large scoops of CARAMEL or TOFFEE ICE CREAM

about 1⅓ cups CHILLED LEMONADE or SELTZER

1 Line a baking sheet with aluminum foil. Make four small mounds of sugar on the foil, using about ½ teaspoon each time and spacing them well apart. Place under a medium broiler for about 2 minutes, until the sugar mounds have turned to a pale golden caramel.

2 Immediately swirl each pool of caramel with the tip of a toothpick or skewer to give a slightly feathery finish. Let cool.

3 Cut the papaya in half. Scoop out and discard the seeds, then remove the skin and chop the flesh. Skin the mango, cut the flesh off the pit and chop it into bite-size chunks. Mix the papaya and mango in a bowl.

4 Cut each passion fruit in half and scoop the pulp into the bowl of fruit. Mix well, cover and chill until ready to serve.

5 Divide the chilled fruit mixture among four large tumblers, each with a capacity of about 1¼ cups.

6 Add one scoop of each type of ice cream to each glass. Peel the caramel decorations carefully off the foil and press gently into the ice cream. Fill up with lemonade or seltzer and serve.

VARIATIONS *Use a mixture of strawberries and raspberries or other more familiar fruits for children. For adults, a splash of vodka or kirsch can be added to the fruits.*

Snowball

For many of us, a "snowball" is a drink we indulge in once or twice at Christmas time. This frozen version,

enhanced with vanilla ice cream, lime and nutmeg, may provide the motivation

for drinking advocaat on other occasions too.

SERVES FOUR

INGREDIENTS

8 scoops of CLASSIC VANILLA
ICE CREAM

½ cup ADVOCAAT

¼ cup FRESHLY SQUEEZED
LIME JUICE

FRESHLY GRATED NUTMEG

about 1¼ cups CHILLED
LEMONADE

1 Put half the vanilla ice cream in a food processor or blender and add the advocaat and the lime juice, with plenty of freshly grated nutmeg. Process the mixture briefly until well combined.

2 Scoop the remaining ice cream into four medium tumblers. Spoon on the Advocaat mixture and fill up the glasses with lemonade. Sprinkle with more nutmeg and serve immediately.

COOK'S TIP *Freshly grated nutmeg has a warm, nutty aroma and flavor that works as well in creamy drinks as it does in sweet and savory dishes. A small nutmeg grater is a worthwhile investment if you don't have one.*

Strawberry Daiquiri

Based on the classic cocktail, this version is a wonderful drink that retains the essential ingredients

of rum and lime and combines them with fresh strawberries and strawberry ice cream

to create a thick frozen fruit purée.

SERVES FOUR

INGREDIENTS

2 cups STRAWBERRIES, hulled

1 teaspoon SUGAR

½ cup BACARDI RUM

2 tablespoons FRESHLY
SQUEEZED LIME JUICE

8 scoops of SIMPLE STRAWBERRY
ICE CREAM

about ⅔ cup CHILLED LEMONADE

extra STRAWBERRIES
and LIME SLICES,
to decorate

1 Blend the strawberries with the sugar in a food processor or blender, then press the purée through a sieve into a bowl. Return the strawberry purée to the blender with the rum, lime juice and half the strawberry ice cream. Blend until smooth.

2 Scoop the remaining strawberry ice cream into four cocktail glasses or small tumblers and pour in the blended mixture.

3 Fill up with lemonade, decorate with fresh strawberries and lime slices, and serve.

VARIATION *Orange-flavored liqueur or vodka could be used instead of the rum, if you prefer.*

COOK'S TIP *For the best results, use luxury ice cream, or preferably, homemade. This will avoid the risk of synthetic flavor and garish color.*

Coffee Frappé

This creamy, smooth creation, strictly for adults, makes a wonderful alternative to a dessert on a hot summer's evening. Use cappuccino cups or small glasses for serving and provide your guests with both straws and long-handled spoons.

SERVES FOUR

INGREDIENTS

8 scoops of COFFEE ICE CREAM

6 tablespoons KAHLÙA or TIA MARIA LIQUEUR

⅔ cup LIGHT CREAM

¼ teaspoon GROUND CINNAMON (optional)

CRUSHED ICE

CINNAMON, for sprinkling

2 Spoon the coffee cream onto the ice cream, then add the crushed ice. Sprinkle with cinnamon and serve immediately.

VARIATION *For a nonalcoholic version, substitute strong black coffee for the liqueur.*

1 Put half the coffee ice cream in a food processor or blender. Add the liqueur, then pour in the cream, with a little cinnamon, if desired. Scoop the remaining ice cream into four cups or glasses.

Warm Chocolate Float

Hot chocolate milk and scoops of chocolate and vanilla ice cream are combined here to make a meltingly delicious drink that will be a big success with children and adults alike.

SERVES TWO

INGREDIENTS

4 ounces SEMI-SWEET CHOCOLATE, broken into pieces

1 cup MILK

1 tablespoon SUGAR

4 large scoops of VANILLA ICE CREAM

4 large scoops of DARK CHOCOLATE ICE CREAM

a little lightly WHIPPED CREAM

GRATED CHOCOLATE or CHOCOLATE CURLS, to decorate

1 Put the chocolate in a saucepan and add the milk and sugar. Heat gently, stirring with a wooden spoon, until the chocolate has melted and the mixture is smooth.

2 Place two scoops of each type of ice cream alternately in two heatproof tumblers.

3 Pour on the hot chocolate milk. Top with lightly whipped cream and grated chocolate or chocolate curls.

VARIATION *Try substituting banana, coconut or toffee ice cream for the chocolate and vanilla.*

Picture credits

The publishers would like to thank the following companies for their kind permission to reproduce their photographs: p9 left and right, Charmet; p7 top right and center, p11 top, p12 right, left, and bottom, p14 right and bottom, p15 right, Hulton Getty; p7 top left, The Advertising Archives; p8 top and bottom, private collection, The Bridgeman Art Library; p10 left and right, p11 bottom, p13 top left, AKG Photographic Library.

All other photographs are by Gus Filgate and Craig Robertson.

Acknowledgments

The author and publishers would like to thank Magimix and Gaggia for their invaluable help. The recipe development and photography of this book would not have been possible without the kind loan of their ice cream machines.

The authors would like to extend their special thanks to Julie Beresford, Annabel Ford and Kate Jay for their enthusiasm and help throughout the busy days of photography and to their families for trying every ice cream that has appeared in this book.

Suppliers

Worldwide, ice cream makers are generally available from electrical suppliers and also from department stores. Ice cream molds and other equipment aare usually available from specialty kitchenware shops and also by mail order.

UNITED KINGDOM

ICE CREAM MACHINES

Homeware Brand Ltd
Crown House
Milecross Road
Halifax, West Yorkshire
HX1 4HN
Tel: 01422 330295 for your nearest Gaggia ice cream machine stockist.

Magimix (U.K.) Ltd
19 Bridge Street
Godalming
Surrey
GU7 1HY
Tel: 01483 427411 for your nearest Magimix ice cream machine stockist.

WOODEN CONE MOLDS

Randal and Juli Marr
Magdalene House Designs
Magdalene House
Langthorne, Bedale,
North Yorkshire
DL8 1PQ
Tel: 01677 424332

ICE CREAM MOLDS

Divertimenti
45–47 Wigmore Street
London W1H 9LE
Tel: 020 7935 0689 for details, goods available by mail order.

UNITED STATES

PLASTIC KULFI MOLDS

Popat Store
158 Ealing Road
Wembley, Middlesex
HAO 4PH
Tel: 020 8903 6397

GENERAL EQUIPMENT

including plastic ice bowl kits, ice cream machines, scoops and containers.

Lakeland Ltd
Alexandra Buildings
Windermere, Cumbria
LA23 1BQ
Tel: 01539 488100 for details of your nearest shop or to obtain a mail-order catalog.

New York Cake & Baking Distributor
56 West 22nd Street
New York, NY 10010
Tel: (800) 94-CAKE-9
Fax: (212) 675-7099

Chef's Catalog
P.O. Box 620048
Dallas, TX 75262
Tel: (800) 338-3232
Fax: (800) 967-3291
www.chefscatalog.com

A Cook's Wares
211 37th Street
Beaver Falls, PA 15010
Tel: (800) 915-9788
Fax: (800) 916-2886
www.cookswares.com

Sur La Table
1765 6th Avenue South
Seattle, WA 98134
Tel: (800) 243-0852
www.surlatable.com

Bridge Kitchenware
214 East 52nd Street
New York, NY 10022
Tel: (212) 688-4220
Fax: (212) 758-5387
www.bridgekitchenware.com

Broadway Panhandler
477 Broome Street
New York, NY 10013
Tel: (212) 966-3434
www.broadwaypanhandler.com

Bowery Kitchen Supply
460 West 16th Street
New York, NY 10011
Tel: (212) 376-4982
www.bowerykitchen.com

Online Site for Ice Cream Makers, Supplies and Info
MakeIceCream.com
6J Gill Street
Woburn, MA 01801
Tel: (781) 933-4113
www.makeicecream.com

AUSTRALIA

all David Jones and Myer Stores
Stockist of Breville and Phillips Ice cream machines

SYDNEY
Accoutrement
Tel: (02) 9969 101/9418 2992
Stockist of Gaggia and Girmi ice cream machines
Anti-freeze ice cream scoops
Natisco ice cream scoops

Bay Tree
Tel: (02) 9328 101
Stockist of Gaggia Gelatiera ice cream machines
French molds
Ice cream scoops

Peter's of Kensington
Tel: (02) 9662 1099

MELBOURNE
London & American Supply Stores
Tel: (03) 9329 7181
Stockist of Simo ice cream machines.

Minimax
Tel: (03) 9826 0022
Stockist of Girmi ice cream machines.

Scullerymade
The largest range of molds in Australia and distributed nationally (does not supply ice cream machines).
Tel: (03) 9509 4003 for your nearest stockist.

QUEENSLAND
Robins Kitchen
13 stores in Queensland.
Tel: (07) 3831 7717 for details of your nearest shop.
Stockist of Girmi ice cream machines
ice cream scoops
molds

Bibliography

Mrs Mary Eales Receipts (1718. Prospect Books, London, reproduced from the 1733 edition.)

Marshall, A.B. *The Book of Ices* (Marshall's, London, 1885)

Paul, Charlie. *American and other Iced Drinks* (Farrow and Jackson, London, 1909)

Herman Senn, C. *Luncheon and Dinner Sweets including the Art of Ice Making* (Ward Lock, 1919)

The History of Ice Cream (International Association of Ice Cream Manufacturers, Washington D.C., 1978)

Extracts from Petits Propos Culinaires 3rd November 1979
Stallings, W.S. Jr. *Ice Cream and Water Ices in 17th- and 18th-century England*
David, Elizabeth. (articles in the same journal)

The Great Ice Cream Book, edited by Edwards, R. and Croft, J. (Absolute Press, 1984)

Beamon, Sylvia P. and Roaf, Susan. *The Ice Houses of Britain* (Routledge, 1990)

Copi, Terri. *The Italian Factor: The Italian Community in Great Britain* (Mainstream, Edinburgh, 1991)

Buxham, Tim. *Icehouses* (Shire Publication, 1992, reprinted 1998)

David, Elizabeth. *Harvest of the Cold Months: The Social History of Ice and Ices* (Michael Joseph, 1994)

Weir, Robin and Liddell, Caroline. *Ices The Definitive Guide* (Grub Street, London, 1995, reprinted 1996, 1998)

Glossary

Bleeding The term used to describe the merging of flavors or syrups when making a layered frozen dessert. To prevent this, smooth each additional layer of ice cream or sorbet and freeze until firm before adding the next, so that the layers of the finished ice cream appear well defined.

Cassata This is the name given to an Italian ice cream-based dessert, which is made with three different ice creams, set in layers, in a round, bombe-shaped mold. The mold is sometimes lined with thinly sliced Madeira or Genoese sponge cake.

Dasher A plastic-coated paddle used in ice cream machines.

Float This popular drink is made with soda, fruit syrup and a scoop of vanilla ice cream.

Frappé Similar in texture to a granita, this frozen drink can be made with fruit purée, fruit syrup or liqueur and crushed ice or ice cream. One example is the classic green crème-de-menthe frappé.

Gelato This is the Italian word for ice cream. A true Italian ice cream is lighter, with less cream and sugar, than American, English and French ice creams.

Granita An Italian water-based frozen dessert that is beaten frequently during freezing to form grainy snow-like flakes of ice. Coffee granita is the classic version, but fruit flavors are also popular.

Knickerbocker glory This technicolor British sundae is made with scoops of vanilla ice cream and spoonfuls of different colored gelatin layered in tall sundae glasses, topped with whipped cream, strawberry sauce and candy, then decorated with a wafer cookie.

Ice Also known as "water ice" or "Italian ice" in some areas of the country, this is made like a sorbet but usually without the addition of eggs, although egg whites are sometimes added to improve the texture. Ices were very popular during the Georgian and Victorian eras and were often flavored with flowers, spices, fruits, wine and liqueurs.

Kulfi This rich Indian ice cream is made by slowly boiling milk for several hours before flavoring it with cardamom. It is traditionally frozen in small, conical-shaped molds.

Neapolitan ice cream First sold in ice cream parlors and tea rooms in the 1850s, this ice cream is made of three contrasting colors of ice cream. It is set in a rectangular mold and served sliced. The most famous combination is chocolate, strawberry and vanilla ice creams.

Parfait This rich, creamy traditional French ice cream dessert does not need to be beaten during freezing. It is made by whisking a hot sugar syrup into beaten egg yolks and, because the syrup is heated to the soft-ball stage, the finished ice cream has a wonderful texture even when served right from the freezer. Parfait is usually set in individual serving dishes or molds.

Popsicle A summertime favorite, patented in the United States in 1923 as the Epsicle, by Frank Epperson. The original Epsicle was flavored with lemon.

Saccharometer This glass measuring device is used to measure the sugar density of sorbets and ice creams. If there is too much sugar, the finished ice cream will be too soft; too little and the ice cream will have a hard, icy texture. It is used by professionals and enthusiastic amateurs, but it is not essential unless you intend to create your own recipes or variations.

Semi-freddo This is a semi-frozen Italian ice cream. The ice cream is mixed with crumbled cookies, sponge cake or chopped candied fruit and set in containers or molds. Semi-freddo is never beaten during freezing and is served when only just firm enough to scoop or slice.

Sherbet This is made in the same way as a sorbet, but with the addition of milk or cream. The term is most probably derived from the Arabic "Sharab," an early semi-frozen, sweet, milk-based drink.

Sorbet Classically made with sugar syrup and puréed fruit, this French concoction can also be made using wine or liqueurs. Sorbets are sometimes mixed with a little egg white to lighten the mixture.

Sorbetti This is the Italian word for sorbet.

Sundae This frozen dessert is traditionally served in rounded glass dishes filled with scoops of different flavored ice creams, then topped with fruit syrups or sauces, whipped cream and sprinkles with a cherry on top.

Syrup All water-based ice desserts are based on a simple sugar syrup, which is usually made with granulated sugar. When making a large batch of sorbet, prepare a large batch of syrup. It can be stored in the refrigerator in a covered container for 2–3 days or until needed.

Zester This useful, hand-held gadget is used to pare fine curls of zest from citrus fruits. It has four or five tiny metal holes that slice narrow strips of zest. Quick and easy to use, the citrus curls make a pretty finishing touch to even the most simple ice creams and sorbets.

Index